iOS Programming for .NET Developers
A Field Guide to the Other Side
By Josh Smith

Thank you for buying my book!

ISBN-10: 0985784512

ISBN-13: 978-0-9857845-1-5

The Author

Josh Smith is a mobile software artisan who sharpened his teeth for many years in the trenches of .NET programming. Four of those years were spent as a Microsoft MVP thanks to his technical and written contributions in the Client Application Development space. His passion for iOS programming and the future of mobile software compels him to do crazy things like write books in his free time.

Josh is a Senior Experience Developer with Cynergy, an agency that designs and develops excellent mobile software experiences. He is blessed with the opportunity to architect and develop complex mobile software solutions for Fortune 500 companies.

When he isn't being a computer geek Josh spends time playing the piano, riding his bicycle, studying whatever topic tickles his fancy, and enjoying quality time with his lovely wife Sarah and their dog Thor. Visit Josh online at iJoshSmith.com or get in touch with him over email at iOSArtisan@gmail.com

The Technical Reviewers

Jordan Nolan is the Founder and Principal of Buttercup Mobile (buttercupmobile.com), a Boston-based consulting firm focused on enterprise mobile software development. He is a seasoned software developer, architect, and manager with extensive experience designing and delivering software solutions for Fortune 500 companies. Before discovering the beauty of iOS Jordan worked extensively with .NET technologies such as WPF, Silverlight, and ASP.NET. If your company is looking for a mobile solution feel free to contact him at jordan.nolan@buttercupmobile.com

Josh Wagoner is a software developer with fourteen years of experience. He has been developing iOS applications since 2009. Before moving to iOS development he worked with numerous Microsoft technologies; including WPF, Silverlight, ASP.NET and COM. Currently he is a co-founder of Kairos (kairoslabs.com) and does freelance development consulting. Contact Josh to discuss iOS contract work at josh@theotherdingo.com

[Part I: Prepare for Landing]

The structure of this book parallels the process of colonizing another planet. The first few chapters prepare you for landing on the planet iOS, with a review of its ecosystem and the tools needed to survive. The second part shows how to speak with the locals in their native language of Objective-C, and relate their unusual ideas to your .NET worldview. Once you have acclimatized and gotten a lay of the land, the third and final part of the book explains how to start building your software civilization with their strange, yet elegant, technology.

In other words, this book teaches .NET developers how to understand and work with a radically different programming platform. First things first, let's review what iOS is all about and how to find your way around Apple's development environment.

Chapter 1: Greetings, Earthling!

We are witnessing the dawn of the mobile revolution. Mobile devices have been part of the computing landscape for quite some time, but only in the past two or three years have they become ubiquitous. Demand for mobile applications in the consumer space is exploding. Many people now expect companies to have a mobile presence. Similarly, there is large and rapidly growing demand for mobile software in the business world, which is where most professional software developers earn a living. The majority of professional software developers have little to no experience creating mobile applications. While the iron is in the fire, the wise developer prepares to strike.

Why learning iOS matters

It should come as no surprise to hear that Apple has had enormous success with their iOS operating system and the devices on which it runs. The iPhone redefined the term "smartphone." The iPad is the world's first successful tablet computer, and it created a market in which it is unrivaled. These computing devices, and the software running on them, have propelled Apple into a position of fabulous wealth and power.

The world has changed. Microsoft is no longer the supreme ruler in the realms of personal and business computing. There is a new contender in living rooms, coffeehouses, and office buildings around the world. People love their Apple devices and are obsessed with apps. Business executives are becoming aware of the unique advantages and capabilities that mobile devices offer. The world is willing and eager to pay for iOS apps.

If that isn't a good reason to learn iOS programming, what is?

Why you should read this book

After having spent many years doing only .NET development, this is the book I wished for when I started learning native iOS programming. There have been countless books published about every conceivable topic in iOS. Unfortunately, none of them were designed to help you get over the steep iOS learning curve by leveraging your existing knowledge of .NET development. I wanted a book that would help me map what I already knew to what I was learning. In essence, I wanted a tour guide who could also translate. If that is how you would like to learn iOS programming, this book is for you.

This book is not the one and only thing you should read to master iOS programming. It is a field guide kept in your pocket while exploring the foreign lands of Apple. Along the way I recommend books and online resources that dive deep into topics covered here at a high level.

The sample code is not available online

I firmly believe that typing code is a much better way to gain experience with a programming platform than pasting code copied from a sample project. This book contains many short code snippets, but is not accompanied by a source code download. To use this book's code snippets in an app, you will need to type them by hand.

Native vs. MonoTouch vs. Hybrid

The subject of this book is native iOS programming using Objective-C, Xcode, and Cocoa Touch. It is not about how to use MonoTouch, nor will I discuss making apps that are simple shells around Web pages imitating the look and feel of an iOS app. With that said, it is worthwhile to briefly review some of the options available for making apps that run on an iOS device.

• **Native** development means creating iOS apps using the platform, frameworks, and tools published and supported by Apple. This typically involves using the Xcode Integrated Development Environment (IDE) to edit and compile Objective-C source code that makes use of frameworks published by Apple and third parties. This is the only kind of iOS app guaranteed to have full access to all the publicly available features of the device's operating system. Objective-C code runs very fast and is supported by a lightweight runtime, somewhat analogous to the .NET Common Language Runtime.

- The major advantages of "going native" are that your code runs very fast and has full access to iOS platform features, the platform is well documented by Apple, and it is actively discussed and explained on many blogs and community sites like StackOverflow.

- The major disadvantage is the daunting task of learning a different programming language, platform, and IDE.

• **MonoTouch** is a product previously developed by Novell, but now developed by a small company named Xamarin. It provides an SDK for Mac OS X that lets you use .NET programming languages to create apps for iOS devices. MonoTouch is based on the Mono implementation of the .NET framework. The code in a MonoTouch app is compiled down to native ARM assembly code, rather than the Intermediate Language bytecode of normal .NET applications.

- The big appeals of MonoTouch are that it reduces the learning curve for a .NET developer getting into iOS programming, and some of your .NET code can be reused on other mobile platforms.

- The big drawback is that you depend on Xamarin to expose a stable subset of the iOS SDK that includes the platform features your apps need. You also need to hope that Xamarin does not stop supporting MonoTouch, or go out of business.

• **Hybrid** apps consist of a thin native shell around a UIWebView control, which renders HTML and executes JavaScript. A hybrid application is deployed as a set of Web pages made available by a native iOS host app that can be downloaded from the App Store. This approach is commonly implemented using products such as PhoneGap or Sencha Touch. These products involve an interop system that allows your JavaScript code and the mobile device to communicate with each other.

- The major benefits of taking the hybrid approach are that Web developers can leverage their HTML, CSS, and JavaScript skills, and these Web pages can, in theory, run on other mobile platforms (e.g. Android).

- The major downsides are that your app will have limited access to the host device platform, custom plugins that access unexposed device features must be written in native code (not JavaScript), the UI will not look and feel quite like a native iOS app, and some of these products are known to have significant breaking changes from release to release. It is Web programming, after all!

How iOS exposes platform features

In the previous section I mentioned that native applications are guaranteed to have complete access to all the publicly available features of iOS. Let's take a moment to see how the operating system partitions and exposes those features to an application.

Frameworks are the iOS equivalent of .NET assemblies. They are reusable code libraries that expose a set of related functionality through an application programming interface (API). When a new iOS project is created in Xcode, it links to a few of the most essential frameworks by default. If an application needs functionality in another framework, such as using EventKit to gain access to the user's calendar event data, add a link to it in Xcode and then your app can use its API.

Certain low-level or less commonly used features of the operating system are not exposed through a framework. Instead, these specialty features are made available through a *dynamic library*, which has the file extension of *dylib*. Most iOS apps don't directly use a dynamic library; except for *libsqlite3.dylib* which is often used to manage local SQLite databases.

Xcode vs. AppCode

In this book I show screenshots of and make references to Apple's IDE, named Xcode. There is another IDE, published by JetBrains, that some people prefer for writing Objective-C code, called AppCode. At the time of this writing, AppCode has richer support for refactoring, quick-fix, and unit testing than Xcode. This makes sense considering JetBrains is the company that built the ReSharper plug-in for Visual Studio, which adds many very popular refactoring and quick-fix features to that IDE.

On the other hand, AppCode lacks some fundamental features such as integration with Interface Builder (the topic of Chapter 8), integration with the Core Data model editor (reviewed in Chapter 10), and the ability to create an IPA file (which is submitted to the App Store). Working in AppCode typically involves having an instance of Xcode open as well. I mention this to make you aware that

Xcode is not the only IDE you can use for iOS development. By the time you read this it is quite possible that AppCode will have matured considerably so it is definitely worth investigating, if you are interested.

Setting up a development environment

You can be up and running with a fully functional iOS development environment in less than an hour. You will need a decent Apple computer, but nothing too fancy. If you're on a budget consider buying a Mac Mini, which is a relatively inexpensive desktop option that can be plugged into any monitor.

Upgrade to the latest version of the OS X operating system, then download and install Xcode using the Mac App Store. The App Store ships with the operating system and allows you to browse, buy, and install applications on your Mac.

iOS simulator vs. iOS device

iOS apps can be run and debugged without using an iOS device. Xcode's installer includes the iOS Simulator, which is a desktop application that simulates an iOS device. When running an app in the simulator Xcode will attach a debugger to it so that you can stop at breakpoints in your code, just like in Visual Studio. The simulator is quite good at what it does, and can help you hit the ground running when learning how to write iOS programs. Eventually, however, apps should be tested on a real iOS device. As discussed in the next section, you will need to join Apple's iOS Developer Program and follow their instructions to prepare a development environment for running apps on an iOS device. Once that chore is out of the way simply plug an iOS device into your Mac via a USB port and Xcode will detect it, allowing the app to be run on that device.

There are major differences between the iOS Simulator and a real iOS device. For example, the simulator runs on the CPU of your desktop or laptop, which is much more powerful than the processor in a mobile device. This causes the simulator to run apps faster than a real iOS device. Likewise, the simulator has a huge amount of RAM compared to what is available on, say, an iPhone. Running in the simulator will prevent an app from ever using up all of its memory, which is a serious concern when running on an iOS device.

The simulator does not support several major APIs available in iOS. For example, the camera APIs do not work and push notifications cannot be received. A real iOS device must be used to test and debug the parts of your application that leverage these features.

On the other hand, the simulator has many useful features for testing and debugging apps that are not available on a real iOS device. It can simulate low-memory conditions by sending an app warnings to reduce its memory footprint. It can slow down animations, making them easier to troubleshoot. Also, the iOS Simulator can simulate multiple iOS device types, including iPhones and iPads with and without a Retina (hi-def) display.

Join the iOS Developer Program

To run your apps on an iOS device, and submit them to the App Store, you must be a registered iOS developer. Sign up with Apple and pay a $99 yearly fee to be in the iOS Developer Program. Once part of the program you will also have full access to Apple's developer resources in the iOS Developer Center. The details of how to sign up are easy to find online, so I won't bother explaining it here.

Some people moan and groan about having to pay $99 per year to be able to run their apps on an iPhone or iPad. That is a silly way to think about it. Consider it an investment in your career. Plus, if you publish an app or two in the App Store, you might earn that money right back, and then some. I did!

Summary

The software development world has no choice but to adapt to what is now a full-scale mobile revolution. It's here, it's happening, and it's unstoppable. Apple's mobile platform is the dominant player and should not be ignored. This book was designed to help you leverage your existing .NET knowledge and skills in the exotic landscape of native iOS programming. It is easy to set up a development environment and immediately begin learning this valuable new skill set. So, why wait? Let's get started...

Chapter 2: From Windows to OS X

Writing software for Apple's mobile platform requires fluency with their desktop operating system, OS X. There are plenty of books and Web sites that provide all the details for learning how to master OS X, but much of that information is unnecessary to get started with developing iOS apps. This chapter provides an OS X newbie with tips and tricks for the most common and necessary things needed to be productive in OS X. If you are already fluent with a Mac, feel free to skip this chapter.

Right-clicking

Apple computers have always had a mouse with only one button, until the recent introduction of the Mighty Mouse. This is one of the first big changes for Windows users when trying out a Mac. If there's only one mouse button, how can you right-click?

- The old-school way is to hold the Control key while clicking the mouse.

- When using a trackpad, tap down with two fingers at the same time.

- If using the Mighty Mouse, go into *System Preferences*, select *Keyboard & Mouse*, and set it up to recognize the righthand side of the mouse as the "Secondary Button."

Desktop and the Dock

The OS X desktop is quite similar to the Windows desktop. It's seen after booting up a Mac and logging in. You can store files, create folders on it, and add aliases to it. An alias is like a shortcut to a file or folder in Windows. For example, create an alias by right-clicking on an app icon in the Applications folder, then click the *Make Alias* menu item, and then drag the new alias file to the desktop.

It is easy to access commonly used applications by keeping them in the Dock. The Dock is like the Taskbar in Windows; it's where icons for folders, the trash can, and running applications live. By default the Dock is displayed on the bottom of the desktop, as seen in **Figure 1**.

Figure 1 - Dock enables quick access to app icons and common folders

After right-clicking on a running app's icon in the Dock, you can tell OS X to always show that app in the Dock even if it isn't running, as seen in **Figure 2**. This makes it easier to open frequently used apps. It's exactly like the *Pin this program to the Taskbar* command in Windows.

Figure 2 - Telling OS X to always show Xcode's icon in the dock for easy access

If you are working on a small screen, and don't like to have the Dock sliding in and out of view to conserve space, consider moving it to the left or right side of the desktop. This will give you more vertical space to work with in Xcode. Do this by right-clicking on the dashed lines in the Dock, select *Dock Preferences...*, then choose either the *Left* or *Right* value for the *Position on screen* setting.

Menu bar

If you cannot find the main menu in Xcode, it's because OS X applications show their menu on the very top of the screen. The shared menu bar displays menu items from most recently used application.

One nice aspect of this standardized menu approach is that it's easy to find an application's Preferences screen. It's always under the application's first top level menu item, with the same name as the app, as seen in **Figure 3**. As a developer, you probably are keen on configuring programs exactly how you like them. This makes it easy to let your inner control freak go wild!

Figure 3 - Accessing the Xcode preferences screen via the menu bar

Closing a window vs. Quitting an app

Another difference between Windows and OS X has to do with how to quit an application. For most Windows applications if the main window is closed, the application's process is killed and removed from memory. This is not a standard convention in OS X.

For example, closing all Xcode windows will not quit the Xcode process. It will still be running in the background, and its menu items will continue to appear in the menu bar. Open an application's leftmost menu item and click the *Quit* menu item, or press Command+Q, to quit the process entirely. For some OS X programs, such as the Calculator utility, closing the app's window also quits the app. This behavior is determined by the application author, based on expected use cases of that particular application.

Keyboard shortcuts for common editing commands

As a Windows power user, you probably use the keyboard to perform common tasks several hundred times per day. Prepare to rewire your brain to use a new set of keyboard shortcuts, and experience some frustration during the process. The following table lists the most essential shortcuts.

Command	OS X	Windows
Cut	Cmd+X	Ctrl+X
Copy	Cmd+C	Ctrl+C
Paste	Cmd+V	Ctrl+V
Undo	Cmd+Z	Ctrl+Z
Redo	Shift+Cmd+Z	Ctrl+Y
SelectAll	Cmd+A	Ctrl+A
Find	Cmd+F	Ctrl+F
DeleteLeft	Delete	Backspace
DeleteRight	Ctrl+D	Delete
LineStart	Cmd+Left	Home
LineEnd	Cmd+Right	End
WordStart	Option+Left	Ctrl+Left
WordEnd	Option+Right	Ctrl+Right

Deleting a file

Move a file from the file system to the Trash by right-clicking on the file and selecting *Move to Trash* from the context menu. Using the keyboard, the Command +Delete shortcut has the same effect. The Trash serves the same purpose as the Recycle Bin in Windows.

Exploring the file system with Finder

OS X users view and modify the file system using the Finder program, whose icon is in the Dock, see **Figure 4**. Finder serves the same purpose as Windows Explorer.

Figure 4 - Finder's icon in the Dock

Searching with Spotlight

Quickly search for files, emails, calendar events, Web pages visited, or the entire Web for a search term using Spotlight. The menu bar's rightmost icon looks like a magnifying glass. Click on it to bring up Spotlight, and then start typing in your search term, as seen in **Figure 5**. Using the keyboard, type Command+Space to open Spotlight.

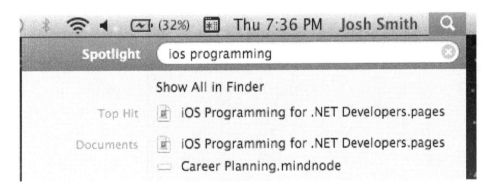

Figure 5 - Searching for something with Spotlight

A popular alternative to using Spotlight is the Alfred app. It offers a broad range of features that go beyond Spotlight. It's worth trying out, and it's free.

Viewing file properties

Metadata about a file on disk can be viewed by right-clicking on the file and choosing *Get Info* from the context menu. This is equivalent to clicking the *Properties* context menu item of a file on Windows. Using the keyboard, press Command+I to view information about the selected file.

Another handy tip is that a file can be previewed by selecting it and then pressing the spacebar. The preview window offers a button to open that file in the default application for the file's extension.

Taking a screenshot

When developing user interfaces it can often be useful to take a screenshot. There is no dedicated key on an Apple keyboard for taking a screenshot. Instead use one of the following keyboard shortcuts.

- Command+Shift+3 for a screenshot of the entire screen

- Command+Shift+4 then click and drag to capture an area of the screen

- Command+Shift+4 followed by Space to capture only a specific window

> Tip: Hold the Control key while taking a screenshot to have it save to the clipboard instead of a file on the desktop.

Terminal is your new command line

In Windows you run "cmd" to open a command prompt, but in OS X you open the Terminal app instead. Terminal provides a command-line interface to the UNIX shell on which OS X was built. The commands that Terminal accepts are different from those accepted by the Windows command prompt, so if you are a command-line jockey be sure to set aside some time to get acquainted with them.

TextEdit is your new Notepad

The Notepad program in Windows is great for working with simple plaintext. If you frequently use Notepad, be sure to check out the TextEdit app in the Applications folder. By default it creates a rich text file, which preserves the formatting of text pasted to it from the clipboard. To work with plaintext, toggle to a plaintext editor by pressing Command+Shift+T. To work with plaintext by default, open TextEdit's preferences window and select the *Plain text* option in the *Format* section.

If you prefer to use more advanced text editors, there are several very popular options available. Be sure to look into TextWrangler if you don't want to pay, or TextMate if you don't mind forking over some money for a quality tool.

Summary

Your productivity as a software developer is a function of your fluency with the tools on which you depend. It is important to study and practice using Apple's desktop operating system. It might take a while to get the hang of OS X, but once up to speed it's quite pleasant to use. This chapter reviewed some of the essential features you will need on a regular basis, and related them to equivalent features in Windows. I suggest searching the Web for more in-depth information about OS X, and get on your way to becoming an OS X power user.

Chapter 3: From Visual Studio to Xcode

As developers we tend to be passionate about the tools we use to write and debug code. Most .NET developers are accustomed to working in an Integrated Development Environment (IDE). The vast majority of us know and love, to varying degrees, Microsoft's Visual Studio (VS). When working on iOS software, however, you cannot use VS. In this chapter, I show how to use Apple's IDE called Xcode. At the time of this writing the current version of Xcode is 4.3.3.

I have met people who try out Xcode and immediately say how terrible it is. They point out all the ways that it is not like VS, or whatever IDE they know best. Those who take the time to learn Xcode typically end up liking it. It's certainly not perfect, but it is a powerful and flexible tool used to create many great applications.

This chapter is a high-level overview of how to use Xcode, pointing out parallels it has with VS. I present enough practical knowledge so that you can start using Xcode right away without feeling like you've suddenly found yourself on Mars. There are whole books devoted entirely to Xcode 4, and Apple has published great documentation on how to use their IDE. It's a big topic, worthy of serious study.

Workspaces, Projects, and Targets

Xcode 4 is organized in a hierarchical system somewhat similar to VS. The top level is called a *workspace*, which is analogous to a VS solution. A workspace represents a group of one or more *projects* and any other files you want to include. Just like in VS, a project is a collection of source files that can be compiled into an app. When creating a new project Xcode implicitly adds a workspace behind the scenes, in the same way that VS creates a solution for a standalone project.

When a project is created it has one *target* by default. A target is like a recipe for building source files in a project. It explains how Xcode should create a *product* for that project. For example, a new iPhone application project has a target that contains all the details needed to compile the project into an *application bundle* which can run on an iPhone.

When creating the project if you had checked the *Include Unit Tests* checkbox (see **Figure 1**) the new project would be born with two targets instead of one.

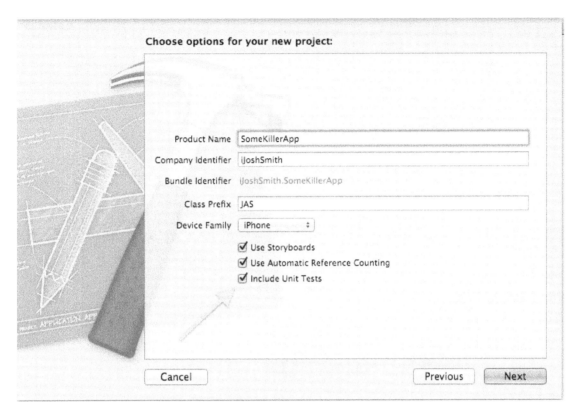

Figure 1 - Adding a unit test target to a new iPhone application project

The project's second target is used when running its unit tests. That target creates a product suitable to be run by Xcode's OCUnit testing framework (also known as SenTest), as seen in **Figure 2**.

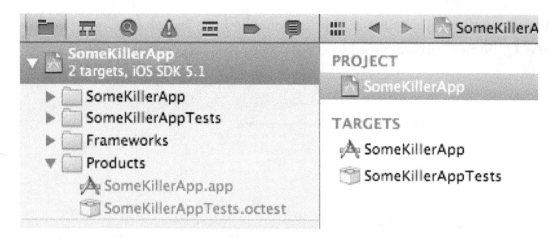

Figure 2 - One project with two targets and two products

Refer to Chapter 12 for more information about unit testing support in Xcode.

Project templates

When creating a new project there is a list of project templates to choose from, as seen in **Figure 3**. Each template contains enough boilerplate code to produce a project that will compile and run on the iOS device type(s) selected in the project creation wizard.

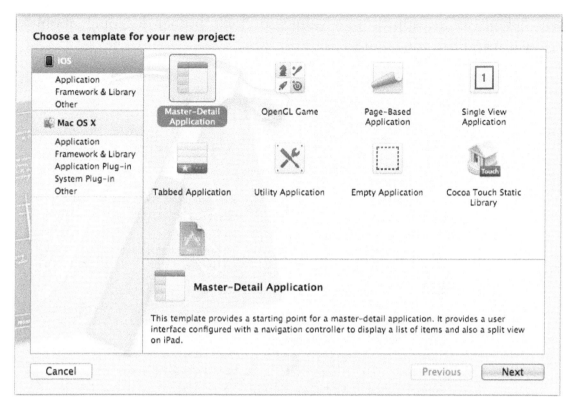

Figure 3 - Project templates included in Xcode for iOS applications

Just like in VS, custom project templates can be added to this list. That topic is outside the scope of this book, but there is plenty of information about it on the Web if you are interested.

The build system

The build system in Xcode 4 is quite sophisticated and flexible. There are several key concepts to be aware of, which should be researched in greater depth when working on a complex iOS project. For now, let's just get a sense of what is involved with managing how a project is configured and built. Think of these concepts as building on top of one another, each adding a higher level of abstraction.

A project, and each target within it, has a huge number of *build settings*. These settings are low-level options used by various compilers, the linker, and the packager, some of which are seen in **Figure 4**. For most projects these build settings default to an appropriate value, so don't bother learning about every esoteric setting (unless you want to).

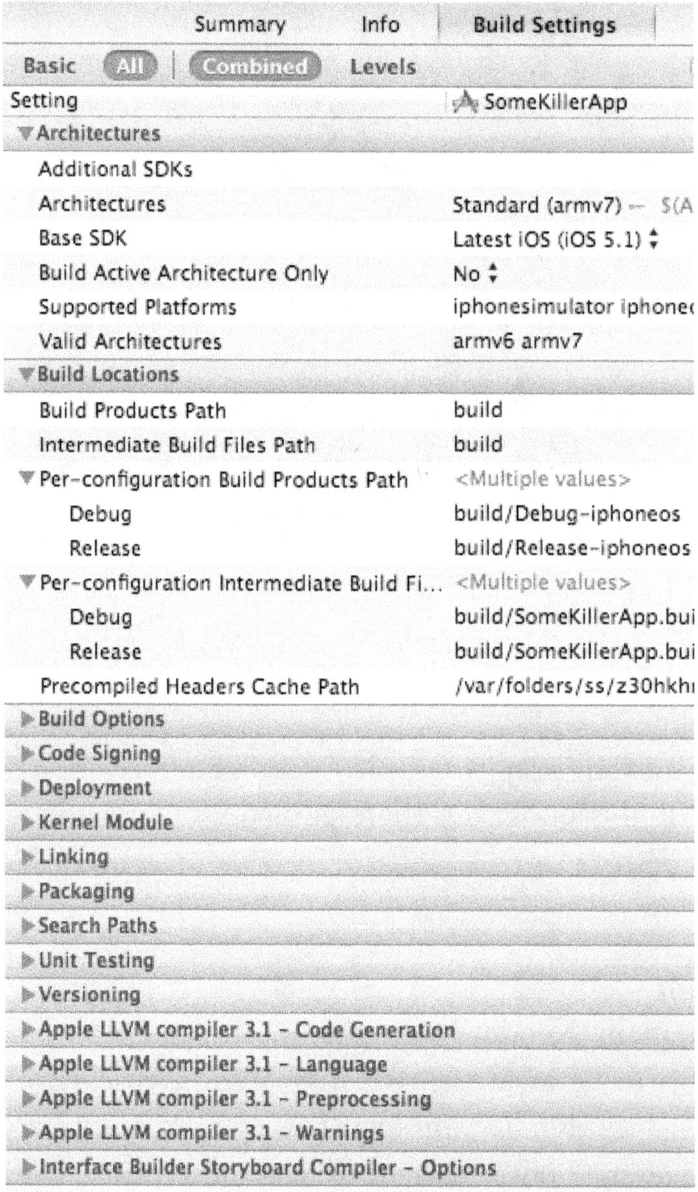

Figure 4 - A few build settings available for an iPhone app project

The next level up the build system hierarchy are *build options*. The build options include all information needed to make a target's product. This includes information such as which device orientations an app supports (portrait, landscape left, etc.), app icon files, app version information, and more. Build options also include the build settings. See **Figure 5** for a sampling of an iPhone application target's build options.

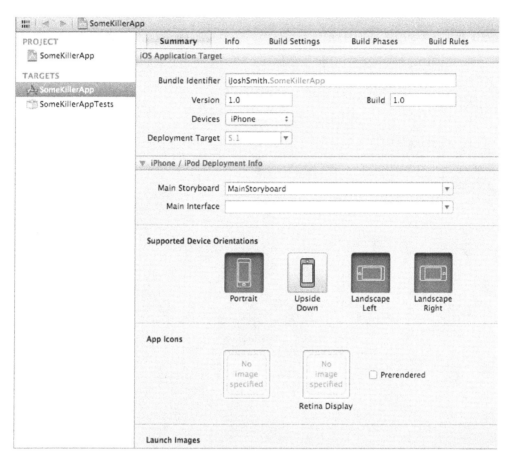

Figure 5 - Some of the build options available for an iPhone application

Several build options are stored in an application's PLIST file, which is a form of configuration file deployed as part of an app. PLIST stands for property list. The build options can be edited directly in a PLIST file from within Xcode.

Xcode and VS both have the concept of a *configuration* and provide each project with Debug and Release configurations by default. A configuration is a name given to a particular arrangement of build settings. For example, the Debug configuration will cause the compiler to include debugging symbols that enable breakpoints to be hit.

You can duplicate a configuration and edit the new configuration's settings (see **Figure 6**). This is part of the workflow one can follow to submit an app to the App Store. Another reason one might duplicate a configuration is to create a build of an app that calls data services on a staging server, instead of pointing to the production environment. When running under the Staging configuration your code could use the staging server's base URL for data services. Refer to Chapter 9 for an example of how this can be implemented.

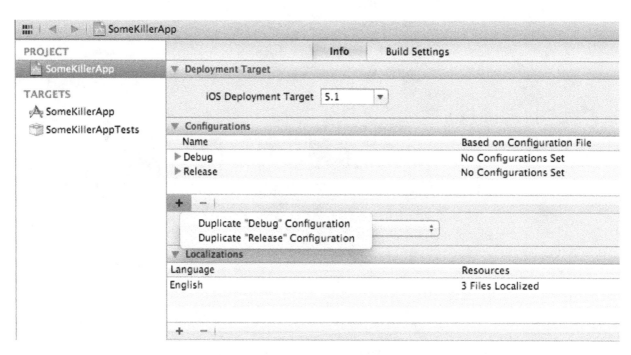

Figure 6 - Duplicating a configuration in Xcode

Once a configuration has been duplicated you can give it a name that reflects its purpose, as seen in **Figure 7**.

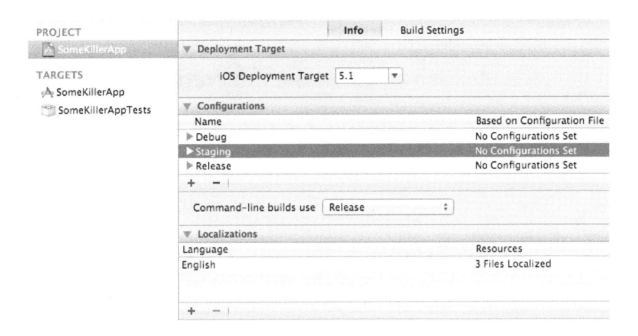

Figure 7 - The project now has a Staging configuration based on the Debug configuration

A *scheme* is the highest level in the build system hierarchy. It adds additional information around configuration settings and build options. You can have as many schemes as you want by adding them via the Manage Schemes window (see **Figure 8**), which is available in the Product menu. There can only be one active scheme at a time. By default a project has one scheme, and often that is sufficient.

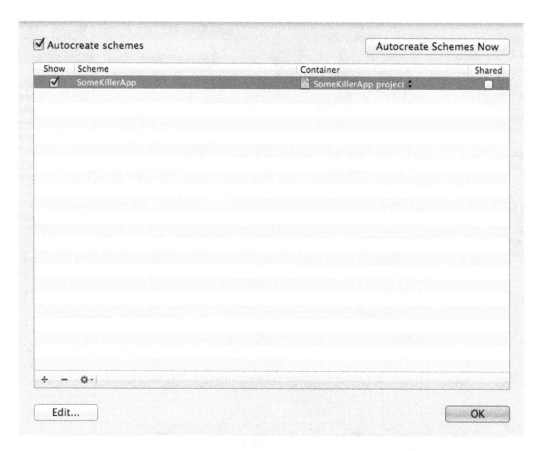

Figure 8 - You can add more schemes via the Manage Schemes window

A scheme contains information about each *build action* available for an application. Xcode includes several build actions, which are seen on the lefthand side of **Figure 9**. Each action defines a procedure for Xcode to follow when executed.

- The **Build** action builds an application.

- The **Run** action builds an application and runs it with a debugger attached.

- The **Test** action builds an application and then runs its unit tests.

- The **Profile** action builds an application and attaches it to an instance of Instruments, which is a profiler used for tracking down performance and memory problems.

- The **Analyze** action builds an application and then runs the Clang code analyzer on your source code files to look for potential problems.

• The **Archive** action builds and packages an application into an IPA archive file which is then added to the Archive list in Organizer (more on that later). You distribute the archive file when deploying an iOS app.

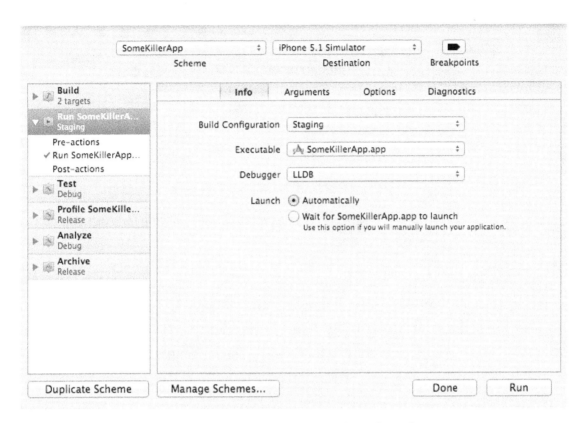

Figure 9 - Editing the Run action of a scheme

There are several ways to have Xcode execute one of the build actions. The simplest way to access commonly used actions is to click and hold on the Run button in the top left corner of the window, which summons the list of buttons seen in **Figure 10**.

Figure 10 - Accessing common build actions by click-and-holding the Run button

I have reviewed how Xcode organizes files into a logical hierarchy of workspaces, projects, and targets. Following that I gave a brief tour of the build system and how it, too, is a hierarchy that allows you to work with various levels of configuration granularity. That's great and all, but it won't do much good unless you know how to use Xcode to actually write software. Up next you will learn how to do just that.

The five major areas of the workspace window

While working in Xcode you end up spending most of your time in the application's workspace window, seen in **Figure 11**. That window can be divided into five major areas, each of which contains certain types of tools. Unlike VS these areas cannot be rearranged by dragging them around and docking them to other sides of the window.

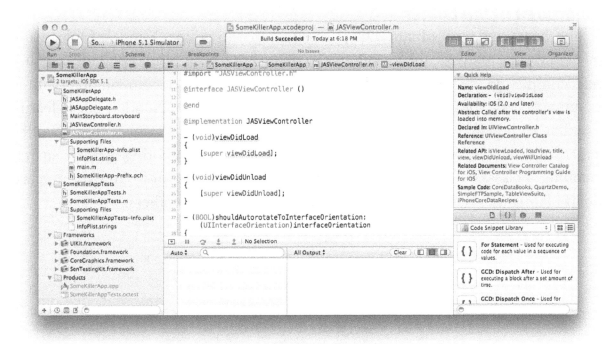

Figure 11 - Xcode has five major areas in the workspace window

The five major areas of the primary Xcode UI are summarized below:

• The **Toolbar** area on the top of the window contains an assortment of various features, including buttons that build and run an app, an activity viewer that shows the status of any task Xcode is currently performing, and an area on the right that shows and hides other areas of the workspace window.

• The **Editor** area in the center of the window is where you edit files in a project.

• The **Navigator** area on the left contains seven tools that are all (loosely) categorized as being related to navigation of your code base.

• The **Utilities** area on the right contains tools that provide information about the selected item in another area. It also contains the library pane, offering commonly used things such as code snippets and controls for an app's UI.

• The **Debug** area on the bottom contains the Variables View and Console, which are useful while debugging applications.

Editor area in the center

The heart and soul of an IDE is its source code editor. Xcode's Objective-C code editor has many of the productivity enhancers Visual Studio provides; such as code completion (see **Figure 12**), context sensitive API documentation, tabbed documents, code folding/collapsing, and symbol navigation. Xcode's Fix-It feature is similar to how VS points out problems in C# code while you type, and offers suggestions to fix them. Xcode also includes some basic refactoring features such as renaming a class, renaming a method, creating a superclass from an existing class, encapsulating an instance variable with accessors, and a few others.

```
- (void)viewDidLoad
{
    [super viewDidLoad];

    self.view.backgroundColor
}   UIColor * backgroundColor          ?
       BOOL becomeFirstResponder
       CGRect bounds
```

Figure 12 - Press Esc while editing to use code completion

The Editor area in Xcode is configurable via three toggle buttons in the workspace window's toolbar. The Standard Editor button is selected by default, as seen in **Figure 13**, which means that only one source file is shown at a time.

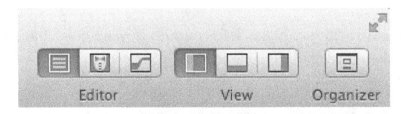

Figure 13 - The leftmost Editor option means only one source file is shown

The center Editor button in the toolbar has a rather strange icon that looks like a tuxedo with a bow tie. Clearly, we are not using Visual Studio any more! That button enables what Apple calls the *Assistant editor*. I think they should have called it the "Jeeves editor" but they never asked for my opinion. Regardless of the name, this enables viewing multiple files at the same time, as seen in **Figure 14**. The Assistant editor can automatically open related files, such as opening the header file for the implementation file currently being edited (I explain those file types in the next chapter). Also, in the chapter about Interface Builder I demonstrate how using the Assistant editor makes wiring up user interfaces a breeze.

Figure 14 - Viewing two files at the same time with the Assistant editor

The Editor area can also be put into a mode that allows for comparing different versions of a file from a source control system. Xcode supports Subversion (SVN) and Git, which can be configured in the Organizer window, presented later in this chapter. If your project is under source control, and Xcode is aware of the repository, use the Version editor to view the history of any file in the repository. **Figure 15** shows the Version editor in action.

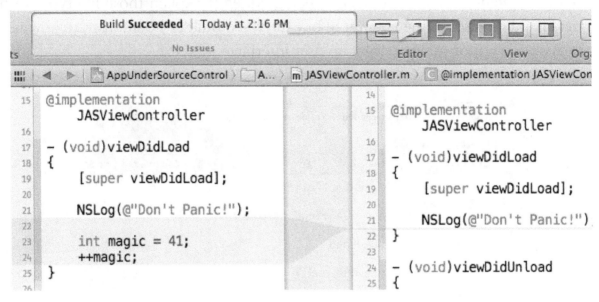

Figure 15 - Comparing two versions of the same file from a Git repository

Navigator area on the left

On the lefthand side of Xcode's workspace window is the Navigator area. It has a toolbar with seven icons. Each icon represents a tool that can be opened in the Navigator area. Refer to **Figure 16** for an annotated screenshot of this toolbar.

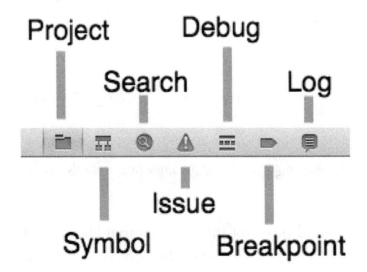

Figure 16 - The Navigator area toolbar has icons for seven navigators

It is easy to open each navigator using the keyboard. The first navigator's keyboard shortcut is Command+1, the second navigator's shortcut is Command +2, etc. Use the Command+0 shortcut to show and hide the entire Navigator area.

Let's take a quick look at each of the navigators, moving from left to right along the toolbar. At the bottom of each navigator is another toolbar with a few extra buttons and/or a search box. These additional features are not reviewed here, but they are worth checking out.

Project navigator, seen in **Figure 17**, is Xcode's version of the Solution Explorer window in VS. It contains a hierarchical view of the files in your workspace and project(s). Files are organized into *groups* which look like folders but do not necessarily correspond to directories in the file system, similar to VS solution folders.

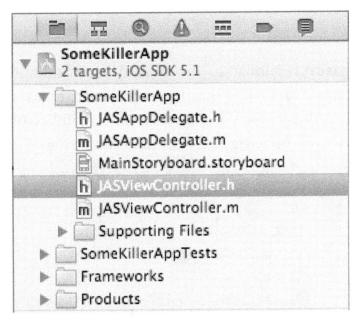

Figure 17 - Project navigator is like Solution Explorer in VS

What strikes VS users as odd is that, unlike Solution Explorer, Project navigator does not sort files and groups. They can easily be sorted, however, by clicking on a project in the navigator and then *Edit | Sort | By Name* or *By Type* from the menu bar.

Files can be opened from Project navigator in several ways:

• Single-click a file to open it in the Editor area.

• Double-click a file to open it in a new window.

• Option+click a file to open it in an Assistant editor.

• Option+Shift+click a file to choose where it should open using a popup window.

> Tip: Press Command+Shift+O to launch the Open Quickly window and then start typing the name of a file you want to open. It will list all files in the workspace that contain your search text. Use the Up and Down arrow keys to select file names in the list. Press Return to open the selected file.

Symbol navigator is similar to the Class View window in VS. As seen in **Figure 18** it provides a tree view that represents your types and their members (collectively referred to as *symbols*). If you click on a member of a class, such as a method, that member will be navigated to in the Editor area.

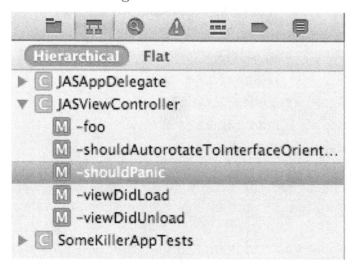

Figure 18 - Symbol navigator is similar to the Class View in VS

This navigator can also be used to view symbols defined by Apple's iOS frameworks, by adjusting a few toggle buttons in the bottom toolbar.

Search navigator, seen in **Figure 19**, finds and optionally replaces text in your projects' files. Click on the magnifying glass icon embedded in the search box to configure options such as whether searches are case sensitive or should use regular expressions. Selecting a search result causes the matching text to be navigated to in the Editor area, just like in VS.

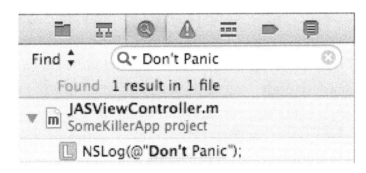

Figure 19 - Search navigator is useful for finding and replacing text

If you are going to use Search navigator to perform a Replace All operation, but don't want it to replace every occurrence of the target string, click the Preview button. It opens a window that allows you to select which occurrences of the string should not be replaced.

Issue navigator displays build errors and warnings, as seen in **Figure 20**. Clicking on a warning or error in the navigator causes the offending line of code to be opened in the Editor area, if applicable.

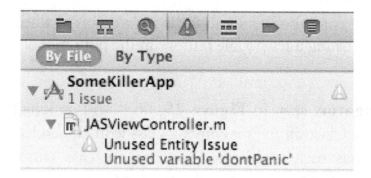

Figure 20 - Issue navigator displays build errors and warnings

Debug navigator serves the same purpose as the Call Stack window in VS. It lists all methods on the call stack (a.k.a. backtrace) for each thread in the process, as seen in **Figure 21**. Being able to easily view each thread's call stack is helpful when debugging multithreaded code, because you can see what code each thread is executing. Just like in VS, clicking on an item in a call stack causes the source code for that method to be opened in the Editor area, assuming the code is available. This navigator is only useful while an application is stopped at a breakpoint during a debugging session.

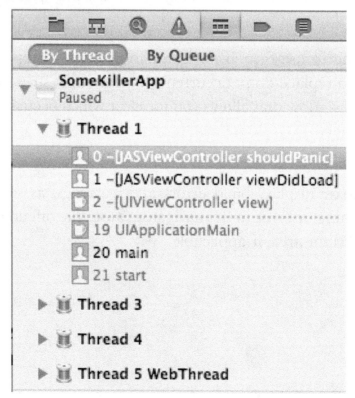

Figure 21 - Viewing the call stack of a thread while stopped at a breakpoint

Breakpoint navigator, as seen in **Figure 22**, displays all the breakpoints set in your code base, just like the Breakpoints window in VS. It allows multiple breakpoints to be disabled or deleted at the same time. Clicking on a breakpoint causes the Editor area to navigate to the line of code on which it was set. Refer to Chapter 11 for more information about using breakpoints in Xcode.

Figure 22 - Breakpoint navigator lists the breakpoints set in your code

Log navigator keeps track of all the tasks you perform in a project or workspace. As seen in **Figure 23** this navigator displays a list of builds, debugging sessions, source control commits, and more. Clicking on an item in the list causes the Editor area to display details about the task. This tool is arguably not a "navigator," but such is life.

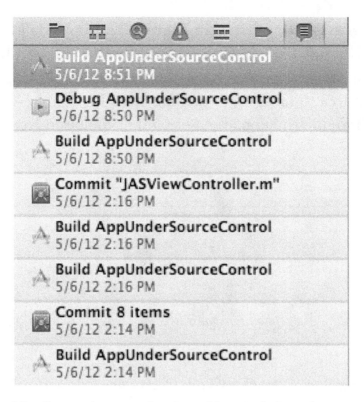

Figure 23 - Log navigator maintains a history of the tasks you perform

Utilities area on the right

On the righthand side of the workspace window is the Utilities area. This area is split into two panes. The top pane contains tools known as *inspectors* because they are used to inspect properties about things such as files, classes, and UI controls. The bottom pane contains tools known as *libraries* because they contain collections of reusable things such as code snippets and UI controls. Open the Utilities area by clicking the rightmost View button in the window's toolbar (see **Figure 24**), or press Command+Option+0 (zero).

Figure 24 - Open the Utilities area via the rightmost View button

Most of the time the top pane contains two inspectors. When building user interfaces in the Interface Builder tool there are more inspectors available. Refer to Chapter 8 for more information about those additional inspectors. Here I focus on the two inspectors that are always available.

File inspector, seen in **Figure 25**, displays information about the selected file in the currently focused navigator or editor. This includes things like text encoding of the file, which target(s) the file is a member of, and more. Most of the information can be edited.

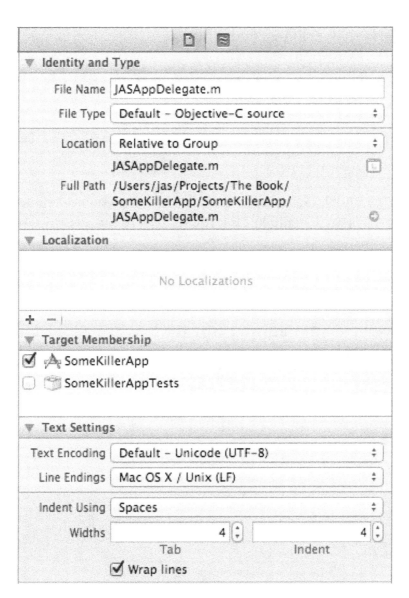

Figure 25 - File inspector displays editable metadata about a file

Quick Help inspector displays API documentation about the currently selected class, method, etc., in the Editor area or Navigator area, as seen in **Figure 26**. It will also display information about UI controls selected in Interface Builder.

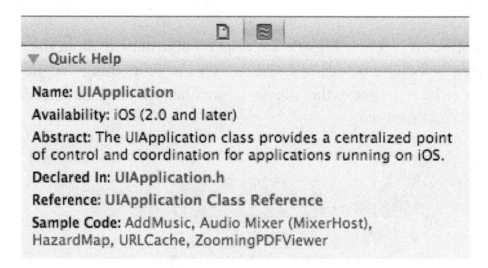

Figure 26 - Quick Help inspector shows API documentation and links to info

Tip: If the Quick Help inspector is closed while you are editing code, Option+click on a symbol in the Editor area to see a tooltip with the API documentation.

The bottom pane in the Utilities area contains library tools. For example, **Figure 27** shows the **Code Snippet library** that can be used to drag and drop reusable pieces of code into the Editor area. Code snippets can contain placeholders that are selected by pressing Tab and then replaced by typing in a meaningful value, just like in VS.

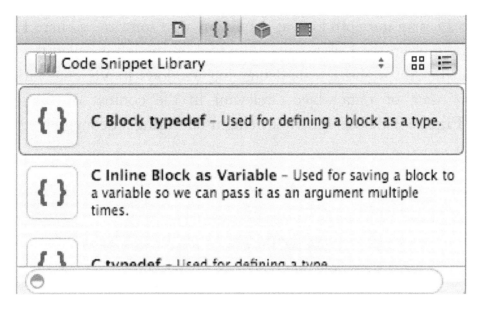

Figure 27 - Code Snippet library in the bottom pane of the Utilities area.

There are three other libraries in the bottom pane. The one used most often is the **Object library**, whose icon looks like a cube. That library is reviewed in Chapter 8, where I explain how to use Interface Builder. The other two libraries contain file templates and media files. I have never had a use for those two libraries. For the sake of completeness, I will mention that the **File Template library** provides an alternate way to add a new file to a project, and the **Media library** lists all the media resources (such as image files) added to a project.

Debug area on the bottom

On the bottom of the workspace window is the Debug area. This area contains tools used while debugging an application. Open the Debug area by clicking the middle View button in the window's toolbar (see **Figure 28**), or press Command +Shift+Y.

Figure 28 - Open the Debug area via the middle View button

Chapter 11 is an in-depth look at debugging iOS software, so here I only take a glance at the tools in the Debug area. The tool on the left is called the **Variables View**. Like the Autos and Locals debugging windows in VS, the Variables View displays the state of data objects relevant in the context of the code being debugged. **Figure 29** shows this view being used during a debugging session.

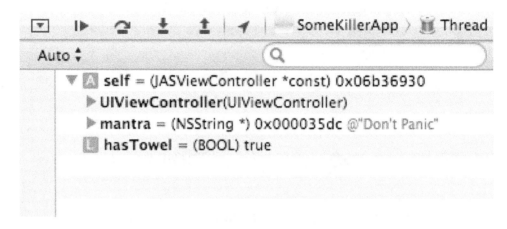

Figure 29 - Inspecting the state of data in the Variables View

The **Console** is displayed on the righthand side of the Debug area, as seen in **Figure 30**. It serves two purposes; displaying text logged by a running application and allowing you to interact with the debugger via textual commands. The Console and Variables View are discussed at length in Chapter 11.

```
All Output ▼                                    Clear  ▢ ▤ ▢
2012-05-07 18:16:35.904 SomeKillerApp[1113:f803] HELLO!
(lldb) po mantra
(NSString *) $3 = 0x000035dc Don't Panic
(lldb) expression
Enter expressions, then terminate with an empty line to evaluate:
mantra = @"He really knows where his towel is."

(NSString *) $4 = 0x06a9eb00
(lldb) po mantra
(NSString *) $5 = 0x06a9eb00 He really knows where his towel is.
(lldb)
```

Figure 30 - Console shows log statements and sends commands to the debugger

Organizer

Xcode has a dedicated window for handling administrative tasks, reading documentation, and other things related to developing an iOS application. That window is called Organizer and it can be opened by clicking the rightmost button in the workspace window's toolbar, as seen in **Figure 31**, or Command+Shift+2 when using the keyboard. Organizer shows information related to all of your workspaces, projects, devices, source code repositories, etc. Its content is not contextual with respect to the workspace window from which it was opened.

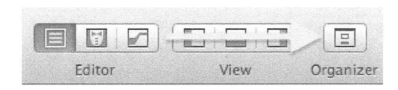

Figure 31 - Open the Organizer window by clicking this toolbar button

Organizer exposes its features via a set of buttons near the top of the window. Those buttons are shown in **Figure 32**.

Figure 32 - Organizer's five main features

The five main features of Organizer are summarized below.

• **Devices** - This is where you manage provisioning files, read device logs, view information stored on iOS devices connected to your Mac, and more.

• **Repositories** - This is where you manage and view source control repositories for your projects.

• **Projects** - Lists all the projects you have opened and shows snapshots that were taken, typically before a significant change or refactoring was made.

• **Archives** - This is where packaged, provisioned, and code-signed application archives can be found and submitted to the App Store.

• **Documentation** - This is where Apple's documentation about the iOS platform can be read.

Interface Builder

User interfaces can be created via drag-and-drop using the Interface Builder tool. Before Xcode 4 this was a standalone tool, but now it is fully integrated into the Xcode workspace window. I review Interface Builder at great length in Chapter 8.

Instruments

When an application has a memory leak, or a certain aspect of the app is running slowly, you should profile it with the Instruments tool. Attach Instruments to your app by using the Profile build action, as reviewed previously in this chapter. Instruments is examined in Chapter 11.

Source Control

One of the options involved with creating a project is deciding if Xcode should add the files to a new Git repository. This repository is local to your Mac, making it useful for only a limited number of situations. When working on code with others, Organizer's Repositories screen can be used to manage a remote repository, as discussed earlier.

I mentioned that Xcode supports SVN and Git. That's great if you happen to work at a company that uses either of them. Many .NET shops use Team Foundation Server (TFS) as their source control management (SCM) system. At the time of this writing there are no TFS plug-ins available for Xcode, because Xcode does not allow for third-party SCM plug-ins. I have read about some people using the Eclipse IDE to interact with a TFS server while developing in Xcode.

Another alternative is to set up an SvnBridge on your TFS server. This makes it possible to communicate with TFS from an SVN client. Setting that up on your server is outside the scope of this book, but if you fire up the Google machine and type in "svnbridge" it will find what you need.

SVN users should keep in mind that there are some great standalone SVN clients for the Mac. I use Cornerstone 2 to manage SVN repos and recommend it to anyone looking for a high-end SVN client. I prefer to use Cornerstone 2 instead of Xcode as an SVN client because it is easy to use, has more features, and is absolutely rock solid. Another popular SVN client is called Versions, which has the same reputation as Cornerstone 2 for high quality. Git users might want to try the SourceTree app, which is available in the Mac App Store for free.

Xcode shortcuts and gestures

Like any good developer tool, Xcode includes many keyboard shortcuts. It also includes some very useful trackpad gestures. What follows is a list, in no particular order, of shortcuts and gestures I use all the time. Xcode's Preferences window can be used to view and modify these key bindings.

Command	Shortcut/Gesture
ToggleNavigators	Cmd+0
ToggleUtilities	Cmd+Opt+0
ToggleDebugArea	Cmd+Shift+Y
Build	Cmd+B
Run	Cmd+R
Stop	Cmd+.
AutoComplete	Esc
Counterpart	Cmd+Ctrl+Up
OpenQuickly	Cmd+Shift+O
NextFile	Cmd+Ctrl+Right 2-FingerSwipeLeft

Command	Shortcut/Gesture
PrevFile	Cmd+Ctrl+Left
	2-FingerSwipeRight
GoToSymbol	Cmd+Click
SymbolHelp	Ctrl+Click
FoldCode	Cmd+Opt+Left
UnfoldCode	Cmd+Opt+Right
ToggleComment	Cmd+/
ToggleBreakpoint	Cmd+\
StepOver	fn+F6
StepInto	fn+F7
StepOut	fn+F8
Continue	Cmd+Ctrl+Y

Tip: Trackpad gestures are not always the same between all instances of Xcode, due to different versions of OS X and user preferences. Trackpad preferences can be adjusted in the System Preferences window, available via the leftmost item in the desktop's menu bar.

Summary

This chapter has been a whirlwind tour of the Xcode IDE. Many of Xcode's features are very similar to features in Visual Studio, just with a different name. For a veteran Visual Studio user, Xcode can be overwhelming at first because everything is different, at least in some small way. The good news is that you do not need to know and use the features of Xcode reviewed in this chapter all at once.

As you become more experienced with the IDE and start to wonder if there is a better way to do something, return to this chapter for some guidance. Consider picking up a book about Xcode to go deeper into the nitty gritty details. I own

<u>Xcode 4</u> by Richard Wentk, and consider it a trusted resource. Also, be sure to review Apple's <u>Xcode 4 User Guide</u>, it is really quite good.

[Part II: Ways of the World]

Learning a language, such as Italian or French, requires studying separate aspects of it in isolation. One must study grammar, vocabulary, and usage before combining them to form sentences and paragraphs that make sense to a native speaker.

In this part of the book I present how the Objective-C language can be used to make an iOS device bend to your will. The first step is to learn the "grammar" of Objective-C; it's syntax, parts of speech, etc. Chapters 4 and 5 explain the fundamentals of Objective-C and compare it to the C# language, with which so many .NET developers are fluent. Chapters 6 and 7 focus on the "vocabulary" of iOS development; namely, foundational classes and user interface controls used by almost all apps.

In the third and final part of the book, Chapters 9 and 10 contain lessons about "usage." They include code examples that combine Objective-C's grammar and vocabulary to solve realistic programming problems.

Chapter 4: From C# to Objective-C

The name "Objective-C" reveals two important facts about the language; it is an *object*-oriented superset of the *C* programming language. It is possible to write a program in Objective-C that does not use any classes, only C structures and functions. In practice, most Objective-C programs make heavy use of the language's object-oriented features, and include old-school C code when necessary.

.NET developers are familiar with a style of object-orientation strongly influenced by C++ and Java. Objective-C's style of object-orientation comes from a different lineage, strongly influenced by Smalltalk. The core concepts of classes, objects, instance methods, polymorphism, etc., are the same regardless of language. There are, however, enough differences in how the concepts are actualized by Objective-C to merit review.

All code examples in this chapter make use of Automatic Reference Counting (ARC), which prevents the code from being encumbered with memory management concerns. Memory management and ARC are the topic of the next chapter.

Header and implementation files

In Objective-C a class has, at a minimum, two source code files: a header file and an implementation file. A header file, which can be recognized by the file extension *.h*, is where methods and properties meant for use by other classes are declared. I refer to these members of a class as its *public interface* or *public API* interchangeably. The term "declare" in this context means, for example, providing the signature of a method but not its body, i.e. the code between braces. Header files show what a class can do, while implementation files make it happen. See **Figure 1** for an example of the header file of a class that represents a ninja.

```
// JASNinja.h
#import <Foundation/Foundation.h>

// This declares a class that derives
// from the NSObject class.
@interface JASNinja : NSObject
{
    @private
    // This is an ivar (instance variable).
    // It's known as a "field" in C#.
    // Ivars are @protected by default.
    NSArray *throwingStars;
}

// This is a method declaration.
// The method is defined in the .M file.
- (void)disappearIntoTheNight;

@end
```

Figure 1 - Header file for the JASNinja class

The JASNinja class declaration in **Figure 1** exists between the @interface and @end directives. The base class is declared to be NSObject, which is the iOS equivalent of System.Object in .NET programming. Technically a class is not required to derive from NSObject. In practice it is extremely common for classes to derive from NSObject because it offers fundamental APIs needed to manage memory, access type information, create hashes, and more.

Each JASNinja instance is given an array of deadly throwing stars as an *ivar*. That's the Objective-C name for an instance variable, or a "field" in C# lingo. By default a class's ivars are protected, which means only that class and its subclasses can access them. Use the @private directive to begin a list of ivars that should only be available to the class in which they are defined. If you are the type to throw caution to the wind, use the @public directive to make an object's ivars available for the rest of the world to abuse.

JASNinja's header file also contains the declaration of a method named **disappearIntoTheNight**. I review the syntax of methods in a later section of this chapter, so for now just take note that after the method signature is a semicolon, not a method body. The method body is defined in the class's implementation file.

An implementation file by convention has the same name as the associated header file, but with *.m* as the file extension. There does not appear to be a historical record of why the file extension is *.m* but I imagine it stands for "methods." This is the file in which definitions are written for the methods declared in a header file. An example of an implementation file is shown in **Figure 2**.

```objc
// JASNinja.m
#import "JASNinja.h"

@implementation JASNinja
{
    // Ivars can also now be declared
    // in the implementation file, which
    // is great for keeping them out of
    // the public-facing header file.
    BOOL isNearby;
}

- (void)disappearIntoTheNight
{
    isNearby = NO;
    [self evaporateLikeMist];
}

- (void)evaporateLikeMist
{
    NSLog(@"The ninja is gone!");
}

@end
```

Figure 2 - Implementation file for the JASNinja class

At the top of the implementation file is a `#import` directive which causes the class's header file to be made available to the compiler. Importing header files is discussed in a later section. For now think of it as being vaguely similar to the `using` directive for namespaces in C#.

The JASNinja class is defined between the `@implementation` and `@end` directives in **Figure 2**. Notice that ivars can be added between braces at the top of an implementation block. Allowing ivars to be kept out of header files is a relatively new addition to Objective-C. It promotes better encapsulation of a class's implementation details.

The **disappearIntoTheNight** method is defined in JASNinja's implementation file, as expected. The method makes use of another method named **evaporateLikeMist** that was not declared in the header file. This is similar to what a C# developer would think of as a private method. They are close, but not quite the same thing. The difference is that any other object can easily invoke an undeclared method in an implementation file, without needing to do anything tricky like .NET reflection. Xcode hides undeclared method names from the code editor when appropriate, and the compiler will complain if undeclared methods are not accessed the right way. Regardless, if someone is devious or desperate enough they can easily call any of an object's methods. Sometimes this dynamic programming style can be put to good use and simplify the way certain problems are solved. Like any tool, it can be used constructively or destructively. This can all be explained by the fact that Objective-C uses *message passing* instead of direct method calls. More on that later...

For C# developers the distinction between declaration and definition of a class's members is not a core concept. C# classes are both declared and defined in what is effectively an implementation file. C# includes access modifiers such as `public`, `protected`, and `private` to control which members of a class are directly accessible to various parts of a program. Objective-C does not support access modifiers for methods or properties. The public API of an Objective-C class is declared in its header file for all the world to see. The rest is tucked away in an implementation file; hidden from, but still accessible to, the outside world.

Namespace vs. Prefix

The previous section's sample code introduced a class named JASNinja. For a C# developer that might seem like a strange class name. A .NET developer would probably name the class Ninja. One might think that this book's author, Joshua Andrew Smith, must really like his initials to bother prefixing a class name with them. I assure you that's not the reason!

Objective-C does not have anything equivalent to .NET namespaces, which prevent type name collisions. In Objective-C, class name prefixes are used to avoid naming collisions. Apple reserves the right to use all the two-letter prefixes, such as NS and UI. They recommend application developers use a three-letter prefix for their type names, such as JAS. The convention is for class name prefixes to be all capital letters.

using vs. #import

Earlier I mentioned that `#import` is vaguely similar to the `using` directive in C#. That is quite a stretch since Objective-C does not have namespaces. Clearly these directives are very different.

C#'s `using` directive is typically used to avoid having fully qualified type names, such as System.Text.StringBuilder, in a code file. In theory, it is not necessary for a C# program to use that directive at all. In contrast, the Objective-C `#import` directive must be used to reference a class declared in a different file.

`#import` is a *preprocessor directive*. Before the Objective-C compiler processes a source code file each `#import` directive in the file is replaced by the content of the header file it imports. The compiler uses these imported header files to verify that symbols referenced in the current compilation unit are valid, such as class names and function signatures. This preprocessor directive is smart enough to avoid problems caused by cyclical references, where two header files import each other.

The #import directive can be used for system header files as well as your own header files, as seen in **Figure 3**. When a header file is specified between angle brackets (<>) it causes the preprocessor to search for the file in special system directories. Header files specified between double-quotes ("") are searched for in one or more directories, typically starting in the same directory as the file being processed. The exact search paths used to locate header files are build settings that can be configured in Xcode.

```
// Importing a system header file.
#import <UIKit/UIKit.h>

// Importing a local header file.
#import "JASNinja.h"

// A forward declaration avoids importing
// a header file into another header file.
// It avoids some problems and reduces the
// time it takes to compile.
@class JASNunchuck;
```

Figure 3 - Importing header files and making a forward declaration

Forward declarations

Figure 3 shows another directive commonly used in header files. The @class directive creates a *forward declaration* of a class. This is useful when a header file contains a reference to a class's name, but no other information about that class is required to keep the compiler happy. Most often this occurs when a class contains an ivar, property, method return type, or method parameter whose data type is a class. An example of this is shown in **Figure 4**.

```
// "Trust me, this class exists."
@class JASSword;

@interface JASNinja : NSObject
{
    // This ivar's type is mentioned
    // to the compiler by the @class
    // directive seen above. The
    // JASSword header file must be
    // #import'd into this class's
    // implementation file in order
    // to use members of JASSword.
    JASSword *sword;
}

@end
```

Figure 4 - The ivar is valid because JASSword is forward declared

The @class directive does not provide enough information to the compiler about the base class of the class declared in a header file. The base class's header file must be imported to avoid a build error. This is because the compiler needs to know information about the base class, such as what ivars it has, which is only available by importing its header file.

It is quite common to see forward declarations in header files, even though strictly not necessary in most situations. I use them whenever possible because they help clarify a class's dependencies, reduce the time it takes a project to compile (even a slight improvement adds up quickly), and avoid potential problems caused by circular file references.

Reference vs. Pointer

Every object in a program exists at a unique memory address. Most of the time C# code stores the location of an object as a variable in the form of a *reference*. In contrast, Objective-C stores the memory address as a variable in the form of a *pointer*. C# also supports pointers, but only in blocks of code explicitly marked as 'unsafe.' Objective-C only supports pointers.

In iOS software every pointer consumes four bytes of memory, according to the `sizeof()` operator. Those bytes store a number. That number happens to be a memory address of either zero (which is known as *nil*) or an address at which a data object *should* exist. Note that I did not say a data object *must* exist at the address stored in a non-nil pointer. This is the fundamental difference between pointers and references. Pointers are more flexible than references, but less safe.

Another way to think about the difference between references and pointers is to consider how they are used. In .NET programming there is a garbage collector (GC) that removes unreferenced objects from memory. The GC also moves objects around on the *heap* (the section of memory where objects are allocated) in order to create contiguous blocks of available memory, making subsequent allocations faster. The fact that objects are moving around on the heap is completely irrelevant to C# code that only uses references to access those objects. The .NET runtime takes care of adjusting references to ensure they point to relocated objects. A reference points to an object, regardless of where it currently happens to be in memory.

Pointers, on the other hand, point to a specific location in an application's memory address space. If an object is moved, pointers to the object's original memory address are not automatically updated with the new address. However, since the Objective-C runtime on iOS does not have a garbage collector, and objects do not move around in memory on their own, this is not as much of a problem as one might think. The additional burden imposed by pointers on application developers is partially mitigated by Automatic Reference Counting, which I review in Chapter 5. Also, what is lost in safety and convenience by not having references is compensated by the flexibility of using pointers.

Pointer syntax
The syntax used to create and manipulate pointers in Objective-C is exactly the same as in C. In this section I present the most commonly needed syntax and concepts for working with pointers in Objective-C. Most books about C

programming have an entire chapter on using pointers, including topics such as pointer arithmetic. To learn more, I suggest reading <u>The C Programming Language</u> by Kernighan and Ritchie. Those are the guys who invented C, and their book is a classic.

The code in **Figure 5** demonstrates the basics of using pointers.

```
// A pointer to an int.
int *pointerToInt = NULL;

// An int variable on the stack.
int someInt = 42;

// The pointer now stores
// the address of someInt.
pointerToInt = &someInt;

// Dereference the pointer and
// assign a new value to someInt.
*pointerToInt = 101;

// This prints: someInt = 101
NSLog(@"someInt = %d", someInt);
```

Figure 5 - Using a pointer to indirectly modify an integer

An asterisk (*) is used when creating and dereferencing a pointer. The first line of code in **Figure 5** uses an asterisk to create a variable whose data type is known as "pointer to an int." The fourth line of code uses an asterisk to *dereference* the pointer, which means to access the memory address stored by the pointer. Once dereferenced the number 101 is stored at that location in memory. As the last line of code shows, this indirectly assigns the value 101 to the 'someInt' variable. This is possible because the third line of code assigns the address of 'someInt' to the pointer. The memory address of a variable can be retrieved by putting an ampersand (&) to the left of the variable name.

The address of a pointer can itself be used as a pointer. It is a pointer that just happens to contain the memory address of another pointer. Do you get my point? If not, perhaps **Figure 6** will help clarify this important concept. If this code example looks very strange right now, I assure you it will all make sense by the end of this chapter. The important thing for now is how the 'error' variable is used.

```
// Attempt to save text to a file.
NSString *text = @"Some text to save...";
NSError *error = nil;
BOOL success =
[text writeToFile:someFilePath
        atomically:YES
          encoding:NSUTF8StringEncoding
              // NOTE: The 'error' parameter type is
              // (NSError **), which means it is
              // a pointer to a pointer to an NSError.
              // That is why I pass the address of (&)
              // the error pointer.
              error:&error];
// Log an error message if the operation failed.
if (success == NO && error != nil)
    NSLog(@"Houston, we have a problem: %@", error);
```

Figure 6 - Passing a pointer by ref to a method

The code in **Figure 6** demonstrates how to achieve the "pass by reference" semantics that C# offers via the `ref` keyword applied to method parameters. This is more generally known as an "out parameter." It allows a method to return multiple values. Passing the address of a pointer (known as a "pointer to a pointer") allows a method to change the memory address stored by the pointer used by the caller.

null vs. nil, Nil, NULL, and NSNull

In C# a reference can either point to an object or to null. If a program attempts to access a member of a null reference, such as calling a method, the runtime throws a NullReferenceException and the sky comes crashing down.

In Objective-C a pointer can point to any memory address, regardless of what happens to exist at that location in memory. There is a special address at which no object can exist. That memory address is 0. It goes by the names of *nil*, *Nil*, and *NULL*.

• A pointer to an Objective-C **object** should be set to **nil** when there is no object at which to point it. This is by far the most commonly used representation of null in object-oriented Objective-C programming.

• A pointer to an Objective-C **Class** variable should be set to **Nil** (with a capital N) when there is no Class at which to point it.

• A pointer to a **non-object type**, such as a pointer to an integer, should be set to **NULL** when there is nothing at which to point it.

• A nil pointer cannot be added to the commonly used **collections**, such as NSArray. A designated object that represents nil must be added instead. That artificial nil value is known as **NSNull**. Working with collections and NSNull is explained in detail by Chapter 6.

The reasoning behind the distinction between nil, Nil, and NULL is too esoteric to explain here. There are some good explanations on the Web if this interests you.

The C language does not draw a firm distinction between numeric and Boolean values. It treats the number zero as false, and all nonzero numbers as true. This behavior is commonly used when checking if a pointer is nil or not. It is not necessary to explicitly compare a pointer variable to nil, Nil, or NULL. If the pointer points at nil/Nil/NULL, its bytes store the number 0, which is considered to be false. For example, the following two expressions, which compare a pointer variable named 'ptr', are equivalent when used as the condition of an `if()` statement: `(ptr)` and `(ptr != nil)`.

this vs. self

The object for which an instance method executes can be accessed from within that method. It is made available via an implicit parameter that precedes any other parameters declared in the method signature. In C# the object is made available via a reference named *this*. In Objective-C the variable is a pointer named *self*.

The C# compiler prevents you from assigning a new value to the *this* reference. In Objective-C it is common practice to assign the *self* pointer, such as in the object initializer seen in **Figure 7**. I examine initializers later in this chapter, but for now think of them as being similar to constructors in C#.

```objc
- (id)init
{
    // Assign the return value
    // of the super class's init
    // method to the self pointer.
    self = [super init];

    // Objective-C convention is
    // to check if the self pointer
    // is still valid. It might be
    // nil if the super class stops
    // multiple instances of the
    // class from being created.
    if (self != nil)
    {
        // These are both valid ways
        // to assign an ivar.
        self->someIvar = 42;
        someIvar = 999;

        // Properties are accessed
        // via dot notation.
        self.someProperty = @"Dent";

        // The self pointer is used
        // when an object executes
        // its own instance methods.
        [self someMethod];
    }
    return self;
}
```

*Figure 7 - Using the *self* pointer in an object initializer*

There is a further twist in how the *self* pointer works, which can be rather confusing for a C# developer at first. In C# there are static methods, which do not receive the *this* reference because static methods are not executed for an instance of the class. In Objective-C there are class methods, which serve the same purpose as static methods in C#. However, a class method does in fact receive the *self* pointer. In a class method the self pointer points to the Class for which the method was invoked.

For example, **Figure 8** shows a class with a class method that creates and configures an object. The type of object created is determined by the class to which the **createInstance** message is passed. Note that it uses a variable of type Class, which serves a similar purpose to System.Type in the .NET Framework. It is an object that represents a data type available in the program.

```objc
#import "JASAbstractWidget.h"

@implementation JASAbstractWidget
{
    BOOL enjoysMayhem;
    int deathRays;
    NSString *evilLaugh;
}

+ (JASAbstractWidget *)createInstance
{
    JASAbstractWidget *instance = nil;

    // The self pointer points to a structure
    // containing information about the type of
    // widget to create. If the createInstance
    // method is called on a class that derives
    // from the JASAbstractWidget, the self pointer
    // references info about the derived class.
    Class derivedWidgetType = self;
    instance = [[derivedWidgetType alloc] init];
    instance->enjoysMayhem = YES;
    instance->deathRays = 999;
    instance->evilLaugh = @"Muahahaha!";

    return instance;
}

@end
```

Figure 8 - A factory method using the `self` *pointer*

Figure 9 demonstrates how this factory method can be used. Assume that a subclass of JASAbstractWidget exists, named JASConcreteWidget.

```
JASAbstractWidget *widget = nil;

// Use the createInstance method defined in
// the JASAbstractWidget base class. Since the
// createInstance message is passed to the derived
// JASConcreteWidget class, an instance of that
// derived type will be created and returned.
widget = [JASConcreteWidget createInstance];

// This prints out: Widget type is JASConcreteWidget
NSLog(@"Widget type is %@", [widget class]);
```

Figure 9 - Using the base class factory method to instantiate a derived class

Method calling vs. Message passing

One of the biggest conceptual differences between C# and Objective-C is how methods are invoked. Objective-C was designed from the ground up to support *dynamic dispatch*. Instead of calling a method on an Objective-C object, a *message* is *passed* to it. Passing a message is also commonly referred to as *sending* a message. The Objective-C runtime performs a highly optimized lookup procedure to determine which one of an object's methods to execute in response to a message. The determination of which method of an object to execute occurs at run-time, not at compile-time. C# recently gained support for this style of programming thanks to the `dynamic` keyword. The C# compiler emits an error if a method called on an object reference is not declared or inherited by the object's class, unless it is a `dynamic` reference.

This difference between the two platforms is more significant than it might initially seem. The first section of this chapter, titled "Header and implementation files," mentioned that any method of an Objective-C object can be invoked by any other object. There are no truly private methods. This is a result of how the Objective-C runtime passes messages to objects in order to invoke their methods. For example, refer to **Figure 10** to see a method in a class that is not meant to be used by the outside world.

```
#import "JASNinja.h"

@implementation JASNinja

// This method is not declared
// in the class's header file.
- (void)adjustUnderwear
{
    NSLog(@"Tighty whiteys adjusted.");
}

@end
```

Figure 10 - Nobody needs to know that a ninja gets wedgies

Figure 11 shows how to invoke that undeclared method without even getting a compiler warning.

```
JASNinja *ninja = [[JASNinja alloc] init];

// Sending the adjustUnderwear message to the
// ninja object causes this compiler error:
// "No visible @interface for 'JASNinja'
// declares the selector 'adjustUnderwear'."
//
//[ninja adjustUnderwear];

// The adjustUnderwear message can be sent to the
// ninja by telling it to perform a selector. This
// is how any method can be invoked on any object.
[ninja performSelector:@selector(adjustUnderwear)];
```

Figure 11 - Forcing a ninja to adjust his underwear, how rude!

Note the usage of the @selector() directive in **Figure 11**. A *selector* is an identifier used to indicate which method of an object should be invoked. The

'Message passing and method syntax' section of this chapter reviews selectors and how they fit into the bigger picture.

Message passing, and dynamic dispatch in general, enables Objective-C programs to be highly flexible in ways that are not intrinsically supported by statically dispatched languages. For example, an Objective-C object can add methods to its class at run-time. This technique underpins Apple's powerful Core Data framework, the topic of Chapter 10. The NSUndoManager creates an undo history for an application by recording messages passed to it, and later passes those messages back to objects, causing them to revert to a prior state. This flexibility in the platform is also leveraged by OS X software that bridges Objective-C with other languages, such as Python and Ruby.

Message to nil

Sending a message to a nil pointer does not result in an error. This reduces the amount of conditional logic in Objective-C code because it eliminates many of the null checks necessary in languages like C#. In general it's perfectly acceptable to use nil pointers. A message sent to nil evaluates to the default value of the method's return type (0, 0.0, NO, nil, etc.). In certain obscure situations, such as sending a message for a method that returns a C data structure, this can lead to undefined behavior. Consult Apple's documentation on the subject for all the details.

Message passing and method syntax

There are two kinds of methods: instance methods and class methods. Instance methods are invoked on a particular instance of a class, enabling the object to read and mutate its instance variables. Class methods are members of a class that are not executed on an instance of the class. In C# they are known as static methods, and their method definitions include the `static` keyword. As seen in **Figure 12**, Objective-C uses plus (+) and minus (-) signs to distinguish between a class method and an instance method, respectively.

```
@interface JASAbstractWidget : NSObject

// This is a class method.
+ (JASAbstractWidget *)createInstance;

// This is an instance method.
- (void)wreakHavocOnHumanity;

@end
```

Figure 12 - One class with two method declarations

To invoke a class method a message must be sent to a class. Invoking an instance method requires a message to be sent to the object for which the method should execute. Objective-C messaging syntax involves pairing the object or class with a message name in enclosing brackets. This is demonstrated in **Figure 13**.

```
JASAbstractWidget *widget = nil;

// Sending a message to the class causes
// a class method to be invoked.
widget = [JASConcreteWidget createInstance];

// Sending a message to an object will
// invoke an instance method.
[widget wreakHavocOnHumanity];
```

Figure 13 - Sending messages to invoke the methods declared in Figure 12

Here is a quick algorithm to convert calling a parameterless C# method into passing the equivalent message to an Objective-C object:

1. Begin with C# code: `object.Method();`

2. Convert parentheses to brackets: `object.Method[];`

3. Move the first bracket to the beginning: `[object.Method];`

4. Replace the '.' with a space: `[object Method];`

5. Make the first letter lowercase: `[object method];`

Objective-C uses a verbose, but highly readable, syntax for declaring methods with parameters and sending messages with parameters. The first parameter of a method is appended to the initial part of the method name. Each subsequent parameter is preceded by an optional label and a colon. The parameters are "woven into" the method name, as seen in **Figure 14**.

```
@interface JASAbstractWidget : NSObject

// In C# this method signature would be:
//
// public void stateManifesto(string manifesto,
//                                int volumeLevel);
//
- (void)stateManifesto:(NSString *)manifesto
          volumeLevel:(int)volumeLevel;

@end
```

Figure 14 - Declaring a method with two parameters

That method is defined in the class's implementation file, as seen in **Figure 15**.

```
- (void)stateManifesto:(NSString *)manifesto
          volumeLevel:(int)volumeLevel
{
    NSLog(@"manifesto = %@", manifesto);
    NSLog(@"volumeLevel = %d", volumeLevel);
}
```

Figure 15 - Defining a method with two parameters

The code in **Figure 16** shows how to pass a message to an instance of the JASAbstractWidget class that invokes the method declared above.

```
// In C# calling the method might look like this:
//
// widget.stateManifesto("DON'T PANIC", 11);
//
[widget stateManifesto:@"DON'T PANIC"
          volumeLevel:11];
```

Figure 16 - Sending a message with two parameters

The Objective-C code in **Figure 16** might look like named parameters in C#, but it is quite different because the name of an Objective-C method includes the labels that precede each parameter. The order in which parameters are listed when sending a message must match the order in which they are listed in the method declaration.

As mentioned earlier, a selector is used to identify which method of an object or class should be invoked. If two classes have methods with the same name, both methods can be invoked using the same selector. The method declared in **Figure 14** can be identified by the selector **stateManifesto:volumeLevel:** (notice that it includes a colon for each parameter). That selector is passed to an object in **Figure 17** to check if the object has a method that matches it. The Objective-C runtime represents selectors with the SEL data type.

```
SEL selector = @selector(stateManifesto:volumeLevel:);
if ([someObject respondsToSelector:selector])
{
    [someObject stateManifesto:@"DON'T PANIC"
                   volumeLevel:11];
}
```

Figure 17 - Checking if an object responds to a selector before sending it

There is a lot more to know about how message passing works in Objective-C. We have only scratched the surface of the internal details underpinning how the Objective-C runtime supports dynamic dispatch. I highly suggest reading Apple's documentation about this topic in <u>The Objective-C Programming Language</u> which is available for free online.

Method vs. Function

Since Objective-C is a strict superset of C it supports the use of *functions*. Like a method in a class, a function contains a set of executable instructions that provide functionality to an application. A function is unlike a method because it is not part of a class or struct. Nothing in C# is equivalent to functions. The closest approximation is a method in a `static` class.

Refer to **Figure 18** to see how a function is called. Functions can be called from methods and from other functions. Also, the code in a function can send messages to Objective-C objects.

```
// Calling a function in the Obj-C runtime.
Class aClass = NSClassFromString(@"JASNinja");
```

Figure 18 - Calling a function

As seen in the previous code example, Apple uses a prefix for function names. The **NSClassFromString** function's prefix is the same as that used for Objective-C class names, such as NSString and NSArray. Apple suggests that application developers use three-letter uppercase prefixes for functions. This is the same guidance given for class name prefixes. An example of a custom function with a proper prefix is shown in **Figure 19**.

```
void JASStateManifesto(NSString *manifesto,
                             int volumeLevel)
{
    // Smart stuff goes here...
}
```

Figure 19 - A function named with a prefix

Function declarations can be put into a header file (*.h*) and their definitions are put into a *.m* file with the same name, in the same manner as how classes are split up between the two files. By default a function is globally available to all source code files in an application. Use the `static` keyword before the function's return type to limit its scope to the file in which it is defined.

Constructor vs. Initializer

When an object is born there is often code that must execute to prepare it for life. If the object has a base class, the base class must also be given a chance to initialize the members it knows about. In C# programming this kind of code is typically found in a method referred to as a constructor. Objective-C classes have one or more *initializer* methods that serve the same purpose. By convention an initializer method name starts with *init* and returns an `id` (the most generic way to reference an object in Objective-C).

Every class should have one and only one *designated initializer*. The designated initializer of a class is the method responsible for ensuring that a new instance of that class is properly configured. All other initializers in a class should make use of the designated initializer. The designated initializer is typically the initializer that takes in the full set of initialization parameters needed to configure a new object. This implementation pattern is demonstrated in **Figure 20**.

```objc
@implementation JASAbstractWidget {
    BOOL enjoysMayhem;
    int deathRays;
    NSString *evilLaugh;
}
// A class inherits init from NSObject.
- (id)init {
    NSString *laugh = @"BUAHAHA!";
    return [self initWithEvilLaugh:laugh];
}
- (id)initWithEvilLaugh:(NSString *)laugh {
    return [self initWithEvilLaugh:laugh
                         deathRays:42];
}
// This is the designated initializer.
- (id)initWithEvilLaugh:(NSString *)laugh
              deathRays:(int)rays {
    // Use super's designated initializer.
    self = [super init];
    if (self != nil) {
        // Configure this object.
        self->evilLaugh = [laugh copy];
        self->deathRays = rays;
        self->enjoysMayhem = YES;
    }
    return self;
}
@end
```

Figure 20 - The designated initializer is always invoked

Operator new vs. alloc and init

Creating an object in C# typically involves using the new operator. When that operator is used to create an instance of a class, the allocation and initialization of memory occurs in a single, atomic operation.

In Objective-C creating an instance of a class is divided into two phases: allocation and initialization. First, the **alloc** message is sent to a class, causing memory to be allocated for a new instance. The return value of the **alloc** method is an uninitialized object, which is why an initializer message, such as **init**, should be sent immediately after **alloc** completes.

NSObject also declares a method named **new**. This is a convenience method that sends **alloc** and **init**. Whether to use the shorthand or not is often debated in the Objective-C development community. Some advocate using **new** because it is convenient and works just as well as manually sending **alloc** and **init**. Others say that it does not clearly express one's intentions, and it is limited to only using the standard **init** method. I personally prefer being explicit by sending the **alloc** and **init** messages. This also makes it easier to use a different initializer should the need arise. Sometimes in this book I send the **new** message for the sake of showing how it's used.

Initializing strings

The previous section reviewed methods involved with creating Objective-C objects. Here I show concrete examples of those methods in use. **Figure 21** demonstrates three ways to create an NSString. The first string is created using the same syntax that can be used to create a string in C#.

```
NSString *s1, *s2, *s3;

s1 = @"DON'T PANIC";

s2 = [[NSString alloc] initWithString:s1];

s3 = [NSString stringWithFormat:@"%@", s2];
```

Figure 21 - Three ways to create the same wise words

The first variable is created using the Objective-C @"..." syntax, which allocates and initializes an instance of NSString. Without the leading @ symbol the compiler would consider this to be a C string, not an Objective-C object. The second string is explicitly allocated and initialized. The **alloc** message is sent to NSString, and the return value is initialized using the **initWithString:** initializer. This clearly demonstrates the two phases of object creation.

The last string in **Figure 21** is created using the **stringWithFormat:** class method, which eliminates the need to send the **alloc/init** or **new** messages. Factory methods like this serve a special purpose related to memory management, which was more relevant before iOS 5 introduced Automatic Reference Counting. The fact that these factory methods return *autoreleased* objects will make more sense when memory management is explained in Chapter 5.

Static constructor vs. +initialize

A class in .NET can have a static constructor that is guaranteed to run before any instances of the class are created or any other static method in the class executes. Objective-C offers the same feature. A class should implement a class method named **initialize** to perform one-time setup work, as seen in **Figure 22**.

```
@implementation JASNinja

static NSString *motto;

// Class initializer
+ (void)initialize {
    // This can run more than once
    // if JASNinja subclasses do
    // not implement +initialize.
    if ([JASNinja class] == self)
        motto = @"(silence)";
}

// Instance initializer
- (id)init {
    NSAssert(motto != nil, @"Huh?");
    return [super init];
}
@end
```

Figure 22 - The initialize method is called once per class

Note the conditional logic in the **initialize** method. It checks to see if the **initialize** message was sent to JASNinja; the class in which the method is defined. This is important because if a JASNinja subclass does not define an **initialize** method then the JASNinja implementation will execute during initialization of the subclass. This is because class methods, like all methods in Objective-C, are virtual and can be overridden by subclasses. C# does not support the concept of virtual static methods, so this might seem strange at first.

Static field vs. Static variable

The 'motto' static variable seen in **Figure 22** is *not* a member of the JASNinja class. Objective-C classes do not have the equivalent of static fields in C#. A static variable is scoped to the implementation file in which it is defined. As a consequence, there is no designated method for dismantling and deallocating static variables in a class's implementation file. They are simply destroyed when the application terminates.

Finalizer vs. dealloc

If a .NET object holds onto system resources that must be released when the object is deleted by the garbage collector, the object should have a finalizer method. The .NET runtime invokes an object's finalizer, if it exists and has not been suppressed at run-time, just before reclaiming the memory it occupies.

Objective-C objects, on the other hand, inherit a method from NSObject named **dealloc**. The **dealloc** message is automatically sent to an object just before it dies. Before the memory management improvements introduced in iOS 5 (a.k.a. the bad old days) the **dealloc** method was where an object relinquished ownership of all objects it owned. In modern iOS apps the **dealloc** method is only used to do cleanup tasks, such as unsubscribing the object from notifications, seen in **Figure 23**. An application will crash if a notification is sent to the memory address of a deallocated object. Notifications are reviewed later in this chapter.

```
- (void)dealloc
{
    NSNotificationCenter *nc;
    nc = [NSNotificationCenter defaultCenter];
    [nc removeObserver:self];
}
```

Figure 23 - Unsubscribing from notifications before an object dies

Refer to Chapter 5 for more information about how **dealloc** fits into the memory management system in Objective-C programming.

Lambda expression vs. Block

Objective-C and C# both allow methods to be defined inside, or within, other methods. In both languages these "inner methods" can reference and mutate variables declared in an enclosing "outer method." They can also be passed to other methods as an argument. This language feature blurs the line between data and instructions, and is the foundation of *functional programming*.

In C# these nameless chunks of code are known as lambda expressions. In C, and by extension Objective-C, they are called *blocks*. A block can receive arguments and return a value, just like any other method. **Figure 24** demonstrates the basics of using blocks.

```objc
// In C# this would be the delegate declaration:
// delegate bool JASBlock(int arg1, string arg2);
typedef BOOL (^JASBlock)(int arg1, NSString *arg2);

- (JASBlock)createBlock {
    // This variable's value is used in the block.
    BOOL hasTowel = YES;
    JASBlock block = ^(int arg1, NSString *arg2) {
        BOOL result = arg1 != arg2.length;
        return (BOOL)(result && !hasTowel);
    };
    return block;
}
- (void)useBlock {
    // Retrieve a block from another method.
    JASBlock block = [self createBlock];

    // Invoke the block and pass it some arguments.
    BOOL panic = block(42, @"Gargle Blaster");

    // Prints out: DON'T PANIC
    NSString *firstWord = panic ? @"DO" : @"DON'T";
    NSLog(@"%@ PANIC", firstWord);
}
```

Figure 24 - Declaring, creating, and using a block

Note that the 'hasTowel' variable is captured by the block and available when the block is invoked by the **useBlock** method. This is an example of how blocks can reference variables declared in their enclosing scope. In order for a variable to be assignable from within a block, however, its definition must be prefixed by the __block keyword (note: there are two underscores before the word *block*).

There is a lot more to know about blocks. They are becoming commonly used in the iOS APIs, so blocks should be high on the list of things to learn in great depth for an aspiring iOS developer. Books about the Objective-C language normally have an entire chapter devoted to them. Also, Apple has published some excellent documentation about blocks on their Web site.

Extension method vs. Category method

In C# an extension method can be "added" to a type without modifying or subclassing it. Extension methods are defined in a static class that cannot add fields to the original class. The closest thing in Objective-C to an extension method is a method defined in a *category*.

A category blends the .NET concepts of a partial class and a static class containing extension methods. Sometimes categories are used to partition the code of a large class between multiple implementation files, similar to a partial class in C# programming. Other times a category is created to add methods to an existing class for which the source code is unavailable, such as classes that ship with iOS. Methods in a category are inherited by subclasses of the class targeted by the category. The methods in a category can even replace/override methods in the target class. A category cannot add ivars to a class, only methods.

Figure 25 shows the header file for a category on NSString that adds one utility method named **stringWithGusto**. Notice that the category file name is *NSString+Utilities.h* and the category declaration is *NSString (Utilities)*. This file naming pattern is a standard Objective-C convention and should be adhered to for the sake of your fellow iOS developers.

```
// NSString+Utilities.h
#import <Foundation/Foundation.h>

@interface NSString (Utilities)

// Returns a more emphatic
// version of this string.
- (NSString *)stringWithGusto;

@end
```

Figure 25 - Declaring a category on NSString

The implementation file for this category, named *NSString+Utilities.m*, is shown in **Figure 26**. The **stringWithGusto** method returns the string's value with a few exclamation marks on the end.

```
// NSString+Utilities.m
#import "NSString+Utilities.h"

@implementation NSString (Utilities)

- (NSString *)stringWithGusto
{
    return [self stringByAppendingString:@"!!!"];
}

@end
```

Figure 26 - Defining a method in a category on NSString

An instance method in a category has a `self` pointer that references an instance of the target class, just like any other instance method. Category methods are added to the target class by the Objective-C runtime, making them genuine members of that class. These methods can access private ivars of the object for which they execute, just like any other instance method. **Figure 27** demonstrates that invoking a category method on an object can be achieved using the same message passing syntax as usual.

```objectivec
#import "JASConcreteWidget.h"
#import "NSString+Utilities.h"

@implementation JASConcreteWidget

- (void)sayAngryWords:(NSString *)words
{
    NSString *rage = [words stringWithGusto];
    NSLog(@"%@", rage);
}

@end
```

Figure 27 - Using a method from a category on NSString

Property vs. @property

Objective-C and C# both support a naming convention that enables an object's accessor methods to be used as if directly accessing a variable of the object. In C# the naming convention is *get_Foo* and *set_Foo* for a getter and setter of the *Foo* property. The C# language and compiler conceal that convention from developers, treating it as an implementation detail. In Objective-C the accessors are named *foo* and *setFoo:* for a property named *foo*. This is one of the naming conventions with which iOS programmers must be familiar.

As seen in **Figure 28**, properties are declared in a header file via the `@property` directive. The `nonatomic` attribute means that the property's accessor methods will not be thread-safe. This attribute is often used because the code included for thread-safety has a minor affect on run-time performance, and it is not usually necessary to make accessors thread-safe.

```
#import "JASAbstractWidget.h"

@interface JASConcreteWidget : JASAbstractWidget

@property (nonatomic, copy) NSString *name;

@property (nonatomic, retain) NSArray *teeth;

@property (nonatomic, assign) BOOL isNocturnal;

@end
```

Figure 28 - Declaring properties in a class

The **name** property uses the `copy` attribute because some strings can be mutated, and the widget's name should not be accidentally modified by another object after it has been assigned. Having the compiler-generated setter method store a copy of the string prevents subsequent changes (mutations) to the string from affecting the widget's name.

The **teeth** property uses the `retain` attribute. This has to do with memory management, the topic of the next chapter.

The **isNocturnal** property data type is BOOL, which is a primitive value, not a class. Due to its data type this property uses the `assign` attribute. This means that the property's setter method should not perform any memory management, as discussed in Chapter 5.

As seen in **Figure 29**, the Objective-C compiler will generate accessor methods, and optionally an ivar with the same name as the property, if the `@synthesize` directive is used for a property in a class's implementation file. The `@dynamic` directive informs the compiler that a property's accessors are provided either at run-time or are defined in the class's implementation file. Technically, neither directive must be used if a class's implementation file contains the necessary accessor method(s) for a property. I prefer to use the @dynamic directive when explicitly defining all of a property's accessors because it acts as a reminder that those methods are used as a property. If I only need to explicitly define one of a property's two accessors I will use @synthesize so that the compiler generates the other one for me.

```objc
@implementation JASConcreteWidget
{
    BOOL sleepsAtNight;
}

// The compiler generates
// the accessors and ivar.
@synthesize name;

// The compiler generates
// the accessors and uses
// an ivar named 'chompers'.
@synthesize teeth = chompers;

// The accessors and ivar
// are explicitly provided.
@dynamic isNocturnal;
- (BOOL)isNocturnal
{
    return sleepsAtNight == NO;
}
- (void)setIsNocturnal:(BOOL)isNocturnal
{
    sleepsAtNight = !isNocturnal;
}

@end
```

Figure 29 - Defining properties in several ways

Properties can be accessed with dot notation, like in C#, or by explicitly sending messages to invoke accessor methods. **Figure 30** demonstrates how to use the **name** property defined above.

```
// These are equivalent
widget.name = @"Sal";
[widget setName:@"Sal"];

NSString *name;

// These are equivalent
name = widget.name;
name = [widget name];
```

Figure 30 - Using a property is the same as using its accessors

There is no quantifiable difference in run-time performance between using dot notation or directly using the accessor methods. Deciding which approach to use is a matter of personal preference. Coming from a long C# background, I prefer using dot notation simply out of habit.

Class extensions for hidden declarations

As shown previously, a class's members can be declared in an @interface block within the class's header file, and in a header file of a category on that class. There is another place where a class's members can be declared, but this one is for members that should only be known by the class itself. Hidden members of a class are declared in a *class extension*, which looks very much like a category, as seen in **Figure 31**.

```
/* Header File */

// Class interface
@interface JASNinja : NSObject

// Readonly property
@property (nonatomic, readonly) BOOL isAlive;

@end

/* Implementation File */

// Class extension
@interface JASNinja ()
{
    NSString *hiddenIvar;
}

// Property is given a non-public setter
@property (nonatomic, readwrite) BOOL isAlive;

@end

// Class implementation
@implementation JASNinja

@synthesize isAlive;

@end
```

Figure 31 - Adding a setter to a property in a class extension

A class extension is normally written above the class's @implementation block in an implementation file. It looks like a category with no name between the parentheses. Unlike a category, you can include ivars in a class extension. A common use of class extensions is adding a setter to a property that, in the header file, is declared as readonly.

The importance of class extensions has somewhat diminished over time. In the past, any method used in an implementation file needed to be declared or defined above the first place it was referenced. This caused a problem when two methods referenced each other and neither was declared in the header file, since only one method can be placed lexically above the other. It was common practice to declare all hidden methods in a class extension, which served as a workaround for what was essentially an artificial limitation of the compiler. Improvements made to Apple's LLVM compiler for Objective-C in early 2012 removed this limitation, making it unnecessary to declare methods in a class extension. The reason I mention this is because a lot of Objective-C code was written before that compiler improvement was introduced, so it is common to see methods declared in class extensions.

Interface vs. Protocol

In C# an interface is a group of related methods, properties, and events that a class can implement to support additional functionality. Other classes can reference an object through an interface without needing information about the object's class. This helps decouple objects, avoids the need for multiple inheritance, and reduces compile-time type dependencies.

In Objective-C this concept is known as a *protocol*. In earlier versions of the language it was loosely supported by what is known as an *informal protocol*. They were implemented as categories on NSObject without an implementation file. A class can "implement" an informal protocol by simply including some or all the protocol methods in the implementation file. This was far from ideal, particularly because there was really nothing the compiler could do to help (such as detecting typos in the method names). I only mention the old way because there are still some informal protocols used in old iOS APIs, and it is helpful to be aware of them.

The modern form of protocol is known as a *formal protocol*. It is declared using the @protocol directive in a header file, with no accompanying implementation file. A formal protocol can declare methods and properties that are required to be implemented by a class which *adopts* it. Classes that adopt a protocol are also said to *conform* to it. It is possible to declare optional members, which may or may not be implemented by a class that adopts the protocol. **Figure 32** demonstrates how to declare a formal protocol.

```
// JASDoubleAgent.h (there is no .M file)
#import <Foundation/Foundation.h>

// Most protocols implement the NSObject
// protocol. NSObject is both a protocol
// and a class, both with the same name.
@protocol JASDoubleAgent <NSObject>

// Methods are required by default.
//@required
- (void)reportSecretsAboutEmployer;

@optional
- (void)swallowPoison;

@end
```

Figure 32 - Declaring a formal protocol

A class declaration can include a list of one or more protocols it adopts between angle brackets (<>) immediately following the super class name. Refer to **Figure 33** for an example of this.

```
#import <Foundation/Foundation.h>
#import "JASDoubleAgent.h"

@interface JASSpy : NSObject <JASDoubleAgent>

- (void)interrogatePerson:(id)person;
- (void)reportSecrets;

@end
```

Figure 33 - Declaring a class that adopts a protocol

The **interrogatePerson:** method, seen in **Figure 34**, checks to see if the person being interrogated is a double agent by using the **conformsToProtocol:** method of NSObject and the `@protocol()` directive.

```objc
@implementation JASSpy
- (void)interrogatePerson:(id)person {
    BOOL kill = [person conformsToProtocol:
                  @protocol(JASDoubleAgent)];
    if (kill) {
        // Check if the optional method can be used.
        id<JASDoubleAgent> doubleAgent = person;
        SEL sel = @selector(swallowPoison);
        BOOL poison = [doubleAgent respondsToSelector:sel];
        if (poison) [doubleAgent swallowPoison];
        else        NSLog(@"Make it look accidental.");
    }
    else NSLog(@"Extract info from person.");
}
- (void)reportSecrets { NSLog(@"The eagle has landed!"); }

#pragma mark - JASDoubleAgent methods
- (void)reportSecretsAboutEmployer { NSLog(@"Secrets!"); }
// A class is not obligated to implement optional methods.
//- (void)swallowPoison { }
@end
```

Figure 34 - Working with objects via protocols

Code can refer to an object via a protocol by using the id<*ProtocolName*> syntax. This is equivalent to having a variable whose type is an interface in C#. In Objective-C one variable can be of several formal protocol types by using this syntax: id<*ProtocolName1, ProtocolName2*>.

In **Figure 34** the **swallowPoison** message is not sent unless the 'doubleAgent' object indicates that it responds to that selector. This extra step is necessary because the **swallowPoison** method is marked as optional in the JASDoubleAgent protocol.

Another point of interest in **Figure 34** is the use of the `#pragma` preprocessor directive. It can be used for several reasons, such as disabling a compiler warning for a line of code. In the example seen here, it is being used for the most common purpose, which is to mark and label a group of related methods. Xcode honors the `#pragma mark - XYZ` pattern and causes the code editor's drop-down list of class members to display a horizontal line with a label of *XYZ* to demarcate that region of code. This has no effect on a program at run-time.

Event vs. Delegation pattern

There is often a need for one object to notify another object when something interesting occurs, such as a user typing into a text field. In order for the text field to be reusable it cannot have any information about the type of object that it notifies of user input. In C# this problem is solved by having the text field raise events that are observed by application code. An event is a restricted multicast delegate, which is an object that can be used to invoke methods on one or more objects.

In Objective-C there is nothing directly equivalent to a .NET event or a multicast delegate. For a one-to-one relationship between a publisher object and a subscriber object it is common to use the Delegation pattern. The next section of this chapter reviews how to implement a one-to-many relationship between publisher and subscribers.

The Delegation pattern is commonly used in iOS frameworks. For example, delegates handle user interaction with cells in a UITableView, respond to user input in a UITextField, and facilitate network calls with an NSURLConnection. The real benefit of the Delegation pattern is that it enables an object's behavior to be customizable without the need for subclassing. Instead, an object's delegate is stored as an ivar and treated as a callback target for one or more well-known customizable operations.

Delegate methods often use the *Should, Will, Did* protocol pattern, which allow an object to respond to events that take the following forms:

- Should this thing do that?

- This thing is just about to do that.

- This thing just did that.

A delegate's list of supported operations is defined by a protocol, which was discussed earlier in this chapter. An object's class must adopt the protocol and implement its required methods to be used as a delegate. This is very different from .NET events, which cannot represent a set of related operations and do not require the event listener's type to implement an interface.

Refer to Chapter 7 for an example of how the Delegation pattern is used in practice.

Event vs. NSNotificationCenter

Another form of eventing in Objective-C relies on a class named NSNotificationCenter. It notifies multiple objects when something interesting occurs. Unlike C#, where subscriber objects get a reference to a publisher object and add a handler to its event, an NSNotificationCenter instance is where all subscribing and unsubscribing takes place. **Figure 35** shows how to subscribe and unsubscribe for notifications.

```
- (id)init {
    self = [super init];
    if (self) {
        [[NSNotificationCenter defaultCenter]
         addObserver:self
         selector:@selector(handleMemoryWarning:)
         name:UIApplicationDidReceiveMemoryWarningNotification
         object:nil];
    }
    return self;
}

- (void)handleMemoryWarning:(NSNotification *)notif {
    NSLog(@"Oh no! We're running out of memory!");
}

- (void)dealloc {
    // Be sure to unsubscribe from all notifications when being
    // deallocated, otherwise notifications will be sent to this
    // object after it is dead. Zombie hunting is not much fun!
    [[NSNotificationCenter defaultCenter] removeObserver:self];
}
```

Figure 35 - Listening for notifications about memory warnings

The NSNotification object passed into a handler method provides extra information about the notification. It has a property named **object** which (optionally) points to the object for which the notification was posted, just like the standard **sender** argument in a C# event handling method. If the notification has extra information associated with it, that data will be found in the **userInfo** dictionary property of the NSNotification. This is similar to the EventArgs passed into a C# event handling method.

Posting a notification is straightforward, as seen in **Figure 36**.

```
NSDictionary *info;
info = [NSDictionary dictionaryWithObject:@"Howdy!"
                                    forKey:MyInfoKey];


NSNotificationCenter *c;
c = [NSNotificationCenter defaultCenter];
[c postNotificationName:MyAwesomeNotification
                 object:self
               userInfo:info];
```

Figure 36 - Posting a notification

Posting a notification to the NSNotificationCenter is a synchronous, blocking operation. All handlers for a notification will execute before control returns to the code which posted the notification. More advanced options, such as enqueuing notifications on the main thread's run loop and coalescing similar notifications, can be achieved with the NSNotificationQueue class. Notification subscribers do not observe a queue, they always observe an NSNotificationCenter. This gives you the option to change how notifications are dispatched without affecting existing subscribers.

Summary

Getting a handle on the nuances of Objective-C is a critical step in the process of learning to write high quality iOS software. It is not something that happens overnight. For a developer accustomed to thinking in C# it will seem very strange at first. This chapter has shown how many of the concepts in C# are present in Objective-C, but are often surfaced in a different way. I highly suggest reading a book about Objective-C, such as <u>Objective-C Programming: The Big Nerd Ranch Guide</u> by Aaron Hillegass, to gain a more comprehensive understanding of how the language works and can be properly used.

Chapter 5: From Garbage Collection to ARC

The .NET runtime uses a garbage collector to reclaim memory by deleting unreferenced objects. This introduces ambiguity about exactly when an object will be deleted. The technical term for this ambiguity is *nondeterministic finalization*. When a .NET object is garbage collected its finalizer method is invoked so that it can perform cleanup work, such as releasing unmanaged resources. This will only occur if an object has a finalizer method which has not been explicitly suppressed at runtime.

There is no guarantee that a .NET object will ever be garbage collected. Once the GC frees up enough memory to meet its quota it goes to sleep, potentially leaving behind objects eligible for collection. If a .NET program must have control over when an object performs cleanup work, it might use the IDisposable interface to implement the Dispose pattern. That pattern can have far-reaching effects on how classes are designed and used.

All of this complexity was introduced for the sake of making software development easier. Whether or not that goal was achieved is debatable. Whether or not it engenders a false sense of security in many developers, which can lead to intellectual laziness and sloppy coding, is also debatable. What cannot be debated is that having a garbage collector makes software run less quickly and predictably than it otherwise could.

The Objective-C runtime in iOS does not have a garbage collector. When designing iOS, Apple decided not to include the garbage collector used by many OS X desktop apps. The processing power and battery life of today's mobile devices pale in comparison to desktop and laptop computers, making garbage collection a luxury not worth the price.

For a competent iOS developer memory management is, out of necessity, integral to the thought process of writing code. Mobile apps that work with large amounts of data are practically guaranteed to run out of memory and crash if memory is improperly managed. This problem becomes even more apparent if an app needs to support running on older device models, which have much less memory than the latest and greatest iDevices.

This chapter shows how memory management works and can be properly implemented in iOS software. It also reviews how memory management has become almost entirely automated starting in iOS 5, but why a professional developer must be able to manage memory without assistance.

Reference counting

Memory management in iOS is based on the simple concept of counting how many *references* to an object exist. This number is the object's *reference count*, also commonly referred to as its *retain count*. If an object's retain count is greater than zero, that means at least one other object in the program depends on it, so it gets to live. Once the object's retain count reaches zero it is no longer a valuable member of society and is immediately killed (the Objective-C runtime is cold-hearted)! Before the object is put to death, its **dealloc** method is invoked so that it can relinquish ownership of objects it references, potentially leading to their immediate demise. At that point the memory occupied by the object is freed and made available for other purposes.

In this context, a reference implies *ownership*. An owner *retains* an object on which it depends, and subsequently *releases* the object to relinquish ownership. All objects are born with a retain count of one, meaning that the code which creates an object implicitly owns it. Unlike in a garbage collected environment, where unreferenced objects can exist indefinitely, a reference counted object is immediately destroyed when its last owner releases it.

For example, suppose object A needs to use object B to get its job done. To ensure object B is not deleted while being used, object A must take ownership of object B until it is no longer needed. When object A is finished using object B it should release it. Object B might not be deallocated then, however, because it may have other owners keeping it alive.

A memory leak occurs when an owner neglects to relinquish ownership of an object on which it no longer depends. Similarly, an object can be released too many times, which can result in a **release** message being sent to a dead object or, worse, to a new object living at that memory address. Sending messages to the dead is just asking for trouble! There is a technique for troubleshooting this kind of problem, referred to as *zombies*, which uses the NSZombie class to detect and report messages sent to dead objects.

The code seen in **Figure 1** shows the fundamentals of managing memory in Objective-C. Note, this code is not using the Automatic Reference Counting compiler feature explained later in this chapter.

```
JASNinja *ninja;

// This code owns the new ninja.
// The ninja's retain count is 1.
ninja = [[JASNinja alloc] init];

//
// Do some badass ninja stuff...
//

// Relinquish ownership of the
// ninja, which will kill him
// if he has no other owners.
[ninja release];
```

Figure 1 - Managing the lifetime of an object

Figure 1 shows how an object can be created, used, and destroyed from within the same method. The object returned by NSObject's **alloc** method is guaranteed to have a retain count of one. If that was not the case, it would be impossible to instantiate a class because an object would be born with a retain count of zero and immediately be deallocated. After the JASNinja object is used and no longer necessary, it is sent the **release** message. This invokes the **release** method, defined by NSObject, which decrements the object's retain count. Assuming the ninja's retain count was not increased by other objects, that **release** message will cause the ninja's retain count to be decremented to zero. Then its **dealloc** method will run and the ninja object will cease to exist.

> Important: You should never send the **dealloc** message to an object, except when sending it to the super class from within the **dealloc** method of a subclass. Only the Objective-C runtime is supposed to initiate the deallocation of an object.

Often an object needs to take ownership of an object it did not create. This occurs frequently in object initializers, where method arguments need to be stored by ivars. To ensure that the object referenced by an ivar remains alive it must be retained, as seen in **Figure 2**.

```
- (id)initWithNinja:(JASNinja *)aNinja
{
    self = [super init];
    if (self)
    {
        // Take ownership of the ninja
        // so that it cannot be destroyed
        // while this object depends on it.
        self->ninja = [aNinja retain];
    }
    return self;
}

- (void)dealloc
{
    // Relinquish ownership.
    [self->ninja release];

    // The super implementation
    // must only be used after
    // this object is finished
    // releasing its ivars.
    [super dealloc];
}
```

Figure 2 - Managing ownership of an instance variable

The **dealloc** method in **Figure 2** releases the JASNinja object retained by the initializer. If it did not do this, the ninja's retain count would never reach zero (unless some other code accidentally over-released the ninja), and the ninja would never be deallocated. As mentioned earlier, memory leaks occur when an owner neglects to release an object it owns.

Transferring ownership

Object ownership is not always as straightforward as seen in the examples so far. Consider the problem described in **Figure 3**.

```
- (JASNinja *)makeNinja
{
    // The code that allocates an object
    // is its initial owner, but all this
    // method does is create and return
    // a new object. If this method
    // released the object before returning
    // it, the calling code would receive
    // a dead ninja.
    return [[JASNinja alloc] init];
}

- (void)assassinateSomeone
{
    JASNinja *ninja = [self makeNinja];

    // Silently assassinate someone...

    // This method does not own the ninja
    // so it should not release it.
    // Who should release the ninja?
    //[ninja release];
}
```

Figure 3 - Who should release the ninja?

The **makeNinja** method causes a JASNinja object to be allocated, which means that method is the ninja's initial owner. It would seem that the **makeNinja** method should be the one to send a **release** message to the ninja, to relinquish ownership before returning the object. That would, however, cause the new ninja to be immediately deallocated. Writing a method that returns a pointer to garbage in memory is a rather stupid thing to do. Clearly, there must be more pieces of the puzzle that I have not yet introduced.

It turns out that there are two more concepts related to memory management involved with solving this problem. The first is a rule based on a simple method naming convention.

You own an object if you created it using a method whose name begins with:

• alloc

• new

• copy

• mutableCopy

Figure 4 shows how the problem described in **Figure 3** can be solved by using this naming convention. The fact that the **makeNinja** method was renamed to **newNinja** means that it is no longer responsible for releasing the ninja object. That responsibility shifts to its caller; the **assassinateSomeone** method.

```
- (JASNinja *)newNinja
{
    return [[JASNinja alloc] init];
}

- (void)assassinateSomeone
{
    JASNinja *ninja = [self newNinja];

    // Silently assassinate someone...

    // The ninja object was created
    // using a method whose name
    // begins with 'new' so this
    // method owns the object.
    [ninja release];
}
```

Figure 4 - Following a naming convention to transfer ownership

Refer to **Figure 5** for more examples of this method naming convention in action.

```
NSURL *url, *url2;
NSArray *array;
NSString *string;
NSMutableString *mutableString;

// Not owned
url = [NSURL URLWithString:@"http://ijoshsmith.com"];

// Owned
array = [[NSArray alloc] initWithObjects:url, nil];

// Owned
string = [NSString new];

// Owned
url2 = [url copy];

// Owned
mutableString = [string mutableCopy];

// Release the objects that are owned.
[array release];
[string release];
[url2 release];
[mutableString release];
```

Figure 5 - Using the method naming convention for ownership transferal

The last four objects created in **Figure 5** are owned by the code that creates them, because the creation method names begin with *alloc*, *new*, *copy*, and *mutableCopy*. What about the first object created, the NSURL instance named 'url'? Who owns that object? When does that object get released?

The autorelease time-bomb

There is often no good time or place for an object's owner to send it the **release** message. A common example of this is a method that returns a new instance of a class, such as the URLWithString class method of NSURL, seen previously in **Figure 5**. The intention of such convenience methods is to create an object that can be used and discarded without burdening the caller with ownership responsibilities. Any method that returns an object it created faces this concern, unless the method's name begins with *alloc*, *new*, *copy*, or *mutableCopy* (as discussed in the previous section).

The solution to this problem is the NSObject **autorelease** method. Sending the **autorelease** message to an object is like strapping a time-bomb to it. The object will be destroyed, but not immediately. When the autorelease bomb detonates, a **release** message is sent to the object and its retain count is reduced by one. At that time the owner who strapped the bomb onto the object has officially relinquished ownership. An object can be autoreleased by multiple owners, if necessary.

Figure 6 shows how the problem introduced in **Figure 3** can be solved using the **autorelease** message.

```
- (JASNinja *)makeNinja
{
    // Send the ninja an autorelease message
    // so that this method can relinquish
    // ownership of the object without destroying
    // the ninja before it can be used.
    return [[[JASNinja alloc] init] autorelease];
}

- (void)assassinateSomeone
{
    JASNinja *ninja = [self makeNinja];

    // Silently assassinate someone...

    // There is no need to release the
    // ninja since it comes from a
    // method that autoreleased it.
}
```

Figure 6 - Strapping on the autorelease time-bomb

A natural question to ask at this point is, when does the autorelease time-bomb detonate? The answer is a bit complicated, but the general idea is that an object is autoreleased when the thread on which it was sent the **autorelease** message has nothing better to do. The next section reviews the technical underpinnings that make this work. Feel free to skip ahead if you don't care about that level of detail.

Autorelease pools

The mechanism that supports autoreleasing of objects is called an *autorelease pool*. This is represented in code by the NSAutoreleasePool class or, in modern Objective-C, via the @autoreleasepool directive. When an object is sent the **autorelease** message it is thrown into an autorelease pool on the current thread of execution. If that thread has an active runloop (i.e. the main/UI thread) the autorelease pool is *drained* after all events have been processed by the runloop. When more user events or device events arrive at the runloop, a new autorelease pool is opened to start collecting objects that are autoreleased while the application responds to those events. Draining the pool means sending a **release** message to each object in the pool once for every time it was added to the pool (remember, an object can be autoreleased by more than one of its owners).

It works differently for threads that do not have a runloop, such as background threads spawned by your code. It is the developer's responsibility to set up the autorelease pool for a background thread, which is now quite easy thanks to the @autoreleasepool directive. Using that directive leaves it up to the compiler to work out the implementation details. The background thread's pool is typically drained just before its main method completes. **Figure 7** shows the entry point function of an application, which pushes the root autorelease pool onto the stack.

```
int main(int argc, char *argv[])
{
    @autoreleasepool
    {
        NSString *class;
        class = NSStringFromClass([JASAppDelegate class]);
        return UIApplicationMain(argc, argv, nil, class);
    }
}
```

Figure 7 - Using the @autoreleasepool directive

Another use of autorelease pools has to do with loops that involve many iterations and create many autoreleased objects. To prevent a loop from eating up too much memory, it is sometimes necessary to use an autorelease pool that is drained periodically while the loop executes, such as every ten iterations. In practice, it is often sufficient to simply set up and drain a pool for every iteration of the loop. Note, this technique should be reserved only for loops that exhibit problematic behavior concerning memory usage. It is not something that should be used on a regular basis.

Property attributes control memory management

The declaration of a property in a class includes one of several available attributes that indicate the memory management policy for its setter method. The syntax for specifying these attributes was demonstrated in Chapter 4. The attributes are listed below. The ones tagged with ARC were introduced in iOS 5 as part of Automatic Reference Counting (more on that soon).

- **strong** - the property takes ownership of the destination object and relinquishes ownership of the object it previously referenced (ARC)

- **retain** - the **retain** message is sent to the destination object and **release** is sent to the object previously referenced by the property

- **weak** - the property does not take ownership of the destination object, and the property is set to nil if the destination object is deallocated (ARC)

- **assign** - the property does not take ownership of the destination object

- **copy** - the property stores the result of passing the **copy** message to the destination object and **release** is sent to the object previously referenced by the property

Most of the time a property that points to an object should retain the object assigned to it, otherwise it could be prematurely deallocated. In certain situations it is necessary to reference an object without retaining it, to avoid creating a *retain cycle*. Retain cycles exist when multiple objects retain each other in a circular manner; such as if object A retains, and is retained by, object B. This can cause a graph of objects to never be deallocated. The `assign` and `weak` property attributes can be used to create the equivalent of a WeakReference in .NET programming, which allows an object to be referenced without affecting its ability to be removed from memory.

In the past, the default setter semantic for a property was `assign`. With the latest compiler things get more complicated. According to the Clang documentation (which is written by the people who create the Objective-C compiler used in Xcode), when using ARC a property that points to an object is `strong` by default, except under certain obscure conditions. Note, properties of a scalar type, such as float or BOOL, always use the `assign` attribute since memory management does not apply to primitive values.

Reference counting guidelines

Managing memory with reference counting becomes a matter of routine after a while. It is important to have a good set of guidelines to follow, and to follow them all the time. I suggest reading the excellent guidelines published by Brent Simmons on his 'inessential' blog. The blog post I kept returning to until I finally "got it" is titled <u>How I Manage Memory</u>. I won't bother regurgitating that blog post here since it is well written, concise, and covers everything that needs to be covered.

Ignore the retainCount

NSObject has a method named **retainCount** that might seem useful when writing memory management code. It is definitely not useful and should never be relied on for any reason whatsoever. Even Apple's documentation about the method states that it is "typically of no value in troubleshooting memory management issues." There is no reason why a properly written iOS app should ever need to ask an object for its retain count.

Automatic reference counting

Manually managing memory is, at best, a tedious and repetitive chore. For newbies it can be a baffling source of runtime errors and memory leaks. That is why iOS developers were thrilled by Apple's introduction of Automatic Reference Counting (ARC) in iOS 5. ARC makes writing memory management code largely a thing of the past.

At first ARC might seem very similar to garbage collection since they both automate the task of deleting objects from memory. That similarity is merely superficial. ARC and garbage collection are fundamentally different technologies. Garbage collectors do their work at run-time, by butting in occasionally and cleaning up the heap for you. ARC is a compiler feature. It does not exist at run-time.

The LLVM compiler can be told to enable the Automatic Reference Counting feature through a build setting in Xcode. The easiest way to enable ARC is to make sure the "Use Automatic Reference Counting" checkbox is checked while creating a new project. When ARC is enabled the compiler enforces some new rules, such as prohibiting your code from sending the **retain**, **release**, and **autorelease** messages. Then, through a process indistinguishable from magic, the compiler inserts highly optimized memory management logic into your application's assembler code. In essence, ARC writes an application's memory management code for you.

Only use ARC if you don't need to

The title of this section is not a typo. I firmly believe that an iOS developer should only use ARC if he or she is capable of doing what ARC does. It must be very tempting to enable ARC on one's first few iOS projects and avoid learning how to manually manage memory. That is a terrible idea and will turn an otherwise promising iOS developer into an unhirable amateur.

The rationale behind my strong conviction is simple. You should understand the tools on which you rely. An iOS developer who does not bother to learn how to manually manage memory is equivalent to a .NET developer who has no idea what the garbage collector does or how it works. ARC and garbage collection are both leaky abstractions (no pun intended), requiring a developer to understand how they interact with a program to be properly used. This understanding can only be gained through hands-on experience with reference counting, retain cycles, autorelease pools, zombie objects, etc.

To understand what ARC is and how to properly use it, you should have firsthand experience doing what ARC does. Then, and only then, should ARC be used to eliminate the repetitive coding involved with memory management. Do yourself a big favor and avoid ARC until you don't need it.

Other forms of memory management in iOS

While a detailed overview is outside the scope of this book, it is worth noting that there are other forms of memory management in iOS. ARC cannot help you with any of them. The NSObject-based reference counting system reviewed in this chapter is the form with which many iOS developers are most familiar. More advanced scenarios might require direct use of the Core Foundation library, written in C. Core Foundation has its own memory management conventions that must be learned and adhered to.

In Objective-C it is also possible to use the standard C library functions for dynamic memory allocation: **malloc**, **realloc**, **calloc**, and **free**. While certainly not necessary in most situations, it is not unheard of to come across Objective-C code that makes use of these low-level functions.

Summary

This is the first chapter to introduce a concept foreign to many .NET developers. iOS has nothing similar to a garbage collector. Instead it has a few simple methods in NSObject, an autorelease pool, and some simple naming conventions. With some practice and patience, managing memory becomes second nature. Once it is merely a routine task for you, enable the ARC compiler feature to eliminate the drudgery and increase your productivity.

All code examples in the remaining chapters do not use ARC, unless I indicate otherwise.

Chapter 6: From System.* to NS*

Software development is all about small tasks, such as adding an object to a collection or comparing two strings. A developer's productivity is a function of the speed at which he or she can write code to perform such tasks. Naturally, the first step to becoming productive is learning the language in which a program must be written. Learning a language is largely an intellectual exercise, reinforced with hands-on experience. The next step is gaining familiarity with the APIs needed to get real work done. Many APIs must be learned to create even modest production software. This requires memorization through practical experience more than abstract contemplation.

Moving from the familiar APIs of .NET to the foreign APIs of iOS can be frustrating at first. A seasoned .NET developer might spend a few seconds on some trivial programming task in a .NET app, while in iOS it might require five to thirty minutes of searching the Web and browsing books, just to find the right method or class. Once found the task may take no more than a few seconds to complete. Good times!

The crux of the matter is that iOS terminology is often different from .NET terminology. Both platforms include the same concepts but give them different names. Overcoming this "vocabulary barrier" is one of the most significant challenges to becoming a productive iOS developer. This chapter provides terminology and concept mappings that make it easier for a .NET developer to understand and use the iOS APIs.

The title of this chapter indicates that it relates information about classes in the System.* namespaces to equivalent classes with the NS prefix. Apple uses the NS prefix for classes in the Foundation framework (it is also used by the Core Data framework, the topic of Chapter 10). The Foundation framework contains the most commonly used classes in iOS apps. In case you're curious, the NS class prefix was inherited by Apple when they acquired the NeXT company and its **NeXTSTEP** operating system, on which OS X and, by extension, iOS are based.

The code examples in this chapter include comments that show equivalent C# code using .NET objects, where applicable.

Object vs. NSObject

System.Object is the root base class for every class written in C#. It provides a handful of core methods used by almost all applications. In iOS, NSObject serves the same purpose. It is almost always included in the class hierarchy of other classes, though technically it is optional. NSObject, too, provides commonly used methods, as seen in **Figure 1**.

```
// Comments show the C# equivalent.

// Object obj = new Object();
NSObject *obj = [[[NSObject alloc] init] autorelease];

// string desc = obj.ToString();
NSString *desc = [obj description];

// int hsh = obj.GetHashCode();
NSUInteger hsh = [obj hash];

// Object obj2 = new Object();
NSObject *obj2 = [[[NSObject alloc] init] autorelease];

// bool eq = obj.Equals(obj2);
BOOL eq = [obj isEqual:obj2];

// Type cls = obj.GetType();
Class cls = [obj class];
```

Figure 1 - NSObject

String vs. NSString

Both System.String and NSString are immutable, meaning they cannot be modified after initialization. The .NET runtime manages string interning, which means that a pool of unique strings is used to avoid having duplicate strings in memory. The Objective-C runtime does not intern strings. Every NSString lives at its own memory address, even if it is a duplicate of another string. **Figure 2** shows some common string manipulations in action.

```
// String truth = "DON'T PANIC";
NSString *truth = @"DON'T PANIC";

// String str = String.Format(
//              "{0} = {1}", truth, 42);
NSString *str = [NSString stringWithFormat:
                 @"%@ = %d", truth, 42];

// int len = str.Length;
NSUInteger len = [str length];

// char letterD = str[0];
unichar letterD = [str characterAtIndex:0];

// String strLower = str.ToLower();
NSString *strLower = [str lowercaseString];

// int idx = truth.IndexOf(" ");
// String dont = truth.Substring(0, idx);
// String panic = truth.Substring(idx+1);
// Console.WriteLine(@"{0} {1}", dont, panic);
NSRange rng = [truth rangeOfString:@" "];
NSUInteger idx = rng.location;
NSString *dont = [truth substringToIndex:idx];
NSString *panic = [truth substringFromIndex:idx+1];
NSLog(@"%@ %@", dont, panic);
```

Figure 2 - Common string manipulations

NSString has an extensive API, which is further augmented by category methods. **Figure 3** shows a few more interesting methods defined by NSString, and the equivalent .NET code.

```
// String str = "Gargle Blaster";
// String str2 = "GARGLE BLASTER";
NSString *str = @"Gargle Blaster";
NSString *str2 = @"GARGLE BLASTER";

// bool equal = str.Equals(str2);
// Debug.Assert(equal == false);
BOOL equal = [str isEqualToString:str2];
NSAssert(equal == NO, nil);

// bool same = str.Equals(str2,
//    StringComparison.CurrentCultureIgnoreCase);
// Debug.Assert(same);
NSComparisonResult res;
res = [str localizedCaseInsensitiveCompare:str2];
BOOL same = NSOrderedSame == res;
NSAssert(same, nil);

// str = "        42                    ";
// str = str.Trim();
// int fortyTwo = int.Parse(str);
// Debug.Assert(42 == fortyTwo);
str = @"        42                    ";
str = [str stringByTrimmingCharactersInSet:
        [NSCharacterSet whitespaceCharacterSet]];
int fortyTwo = [str intValue];
NSAssert(42 == fortyTwo, nil);
```

Figure 3 - NSString comparison, trimming, and type conversion

The Objective-C compiler recognizes an NSString literal by the at symbol (@) immediately preceding the quoted value. A string declared without the at symbol is a C string, not an NSString. C strings are simply an array of characters in memory, without any methods to simplify their usage. Since Objective-C is a superset of C, many of the system APIs include methods that accept and return C strings. When working with object-oriented Objective-C code there is usually no need to work with C strings.

Be sure to visit the NSString documentation and learn more about its vast API.

StringBuilder vs. NSMutableString

Constructing a piece of text out of many strings can involve a series of memory allocations and data copying. This can lead to performance problems, especially in long-running loops. The StringBuilder class is used by .NET developers to construct a string in a resizable character buffer. iOS developers use an NSString subclass named NSMutableString when they need to modify a string after initializing it. Since NSMutableString derives from NSString there is no need to call a method to get the string out of a buffer, such as calling **ToString** on a StringBuilder.

> Note: It is common in iOS for a base class to represent an immutable object, and one of its subclasses to represent a mutable object. Examples include NSString/NSMutableString, NSArray/ NSMutableArray, and NSURLRequest/NSMutableURLRequest.

Figure 4 shows how an NSMutableString can be used.

```
// StringBuilder buffer;
NSMutableString *buffer;

// buffer = new StringBuilder("So long");
buffer = [NSMutableString stringWithString:@"So long"];

// buffer.AppendFormat(", and {0} ???", @"thanks");
[buffer appendFormat:@", and %@ ???", @"thanks"];

// buffer.Replace("???", "for all the");
NSRange range = NSMakeRange(0, buffer.length);
[buffer replaceOccurrencesOfString:@"???"
                        withString:@"for all the"
                            options:0
                              range:range];

// buffer.Append(" fish!");
[buffer appendString:@" fish!"];
```

Figure 4 - NSMutableString

Regex vs. NSRegularExpression

Text searching and replacement can be performed using regular expressions, which iOS supports via the NSRegularExpression class. This class is more cumbersome to use than .NET's Regex, but it works well and is thoroughly documented by Apple. See **Figure 5** for an example of searching for a pattern in some text.

```
/* The C# equivalent...

 String text = @"http://ijoshsmith.com";
 Match match = Regex.Match(text, MY_REGEX_PATTERN);
 if (match.Success)
    Console.WriteLine("match = " + match.Value);
*/

NSRegularExpression *regex;
regex = [NSRegularExpression
          regularExpressionWithPattern:MY_REGEX_PATTERN
          options:NSRegularExpressionCaseInsensitive
          error:NULL];

NSString *text = @"http://ijoshsmith.com";
NSRange searchRng, matchRng;
searchRng = NSMakeRange(0, text.length);
matchRng = [regex rangeOfFirstMatchInString:text
                                    options:0
                                      range:searchRng];

if (NSNotFound != matchRng.location)
{
    NSString *m = [text substringWithRange:matchRng];
    NSLog(@"match = %@", m);
}
```

Figure 5 - NSRegularExpression

DateTime vs. NSDate

Writing iOS software that handles date and time data can involve the use of several classes. NSDate is similar to the DateTime class in .NET programming, though not as convenient. Converting a date object to and from a string involves using an NSDateFormatter. Advanced tasks might require the use of NSDateComponents and NSCalendar. This topic is rather complicated, which is why Apple published their Date and Time Programming Guide on the Web. **Figure 6** shows some the most commonly needed date and time operations.

```
// DateTime now = DateTime.Now;
NSDate *now = [NSDate date];

// const int SECS_PER_WEEK = (60 * 60 * 24 * 7);
const int SECS_PER_WEEK = (60 * 60 * 24 * 7);

// var nextWeek = now.AddSeconds(SECS_PER_WEEK);
NSDate *nextWeek =
  [now dateByAddingTimeInterval:SECS_PER_WEEK];

// var earlier = now < nextWeek ? now : nextWeek;
// Debug.Assert(earlier == now);
NSDate *earlier = [now earlierDate:nextWeek];
NSAssert(earlier == now, nil);

// var later = now > nextWeek ? now : nextWeek;
// Debug.Assert(later == nextWeek);
NSDate *later = [now laterDate:nextWeek];
NSAssert(later == nextWeek, nil);

// var prettyDate = now.ToString("yyyy-MM-dd");
// Console.WriteLine("prettyDate = " + prettyDate);
NSDateFormatter *frm =
    [[[NSDateFormatter alloc] init] autorelease];
[frm setDateFormat:@"yyyy-MM-dd"];
NSString *prettyDate = [frm stringFromDate:now];
NSLog(@"prettyDate = %@", prettyDate);
```

Figure 6 - NSDate and NSDateFormatter

Boxing vs. NSValue

An object reference in C# can only refer to an instance of a reference type; such as an Object, String, or Button. If a reference is assigned an instance of a value type, such as an integer or double, the compiler automatically wraps a copy of that primitive value into an object on the heap. This is called *boxing*. The process of accessing the value in the box is called *unboxing*. Objective-C programming includes this concept, only the compiler does not implicitly box and unbox values.

The most basic form of box in which a primitive value can be stored is NSValue. It can store a single C data item, such as a structure or pointer. An example of NSValue can be seen in **Figure 7**.

```
// Point pt = new Point(42, -42);
// object box = pt;
// Point pt2 = (Point)box;
// bool equal = pt == pt2;
// Debug.Assert(equal);
CGPoint pt = CGPointMake(42, -42);
NSValue *box = [NSValue valueWithCGPoint:pt];
CGPoint pt2 = [box CGPointValue];
BOOL equal = CGPointEqualToPoint(pt, pt2);
NSAssert(equal, nil);
```

Figure 7 - NSValue boxes and unboxes a CGPoint struct

This is most often used when adding primitive values to a Foundation collection, because they can only contain pointers to Objective-C objects. Collections in the Foundation framework, such as NSArray and NSDictionary, are reviewed later in this chapter.

Nullable vs. NSNumber

NSNumber is an NSValue subclass that stores a C scalar value; such as an `int`, `long`, `BOOL`, `float`, etc. It can be used to achieve something similar to *nullable value types* in .NET programming, where a value type can be "missing" a value. This is particularly useful when working with a variable that cannot have an unset value, such as -1, because all possible values are valid. Representing that variable as an NSNumber object allows nil to be its unset value, as seen in **Figure 8**.

```
// int? num = this.FavoriteNumber();
// if (num.HasValue)
//     Print("Fav = {0}", num.Value);
// else
//     Print("Fav unknown");
NSNumber *num = [self favoriteNumber];
BOOL hasValue = num != nil;
if (hasValue)
{
    int value = [num intValue];
    NSLog(@"Fav = %d", value);
}
else
{
    NSLog(@"Fav unknown");
}
```

Figure 8 - Using NSNumber for a nullable number

Similarly, the .NET framework includes DBNull with its static Value property to represent a missing/nonexistent value. In iOS the NSNull class serves the same purpose. Its class method named **null** returns the singleton instance of NSNull, which represents the absence of a value. This is most often used when adding a missing/null value to a collection, because a nil pointer cannot be added to a collection.

Array vs. NSArray

C# has syntax dedicated to simplifying usage of the System.Array class, such as array declarations and element access via an indexer. The Objective-C syntax for working with arrays is inherited from C, which means it is built for working with C arrays. An array in C is just a block of memory that can be accessed by a pointer. The Foundation framework includes a class named NSArray that is very useful and convenient, but there is no syntax in Objective-C that makes it especially easy to use. An NSArray is immutable, meaning it cannot be modified after initialization. **Figure 9** demonstrates the basics of using NSArray.

```
// String[] array = { "A", "B", "C" };
NSArray *array = [NSArray arrayWithObjects:
                        @"A", @"B", @"C", nil];

// int len = array.Length;
NSUInteger len = array.count;

// foreach (String str in array)
//    Console.WriteLine(str);
for (NSString *str in array)
    NSLog(@"%@", str);

// int idxB = Array.IndexOf(array, "B");
// int idxZ = Array.IndexOf(array, "Z");
// Debug.Assert(idxB == 1, nil);
// Debug.Assert(idxZ == -1, nil);
NSUInteger idxB = [array indexOfObject:@"B"];
NSUInteger idxZ = [array indexOfObject:@"Z"];
NSAssert(idxB == 1, nil);
NSAssert(idxZ == NSNotFound, nil);

// String strA = array[0];
NSString *strA = [array objectAtIndex:0];
```

Figure 9 - NSArray

One point worth noting is that initializing an NSArray with multiple objects requires a sentinel value of nil, as seen at the top of **Figure 9**. This nil is not added to the array, but simply marks the end of a variable-length argument list. The compiler emits a warning if the sentinel nil value is omitted because initializing an array without it causes a runtime error.

Figure 10 shows a couple of the more interesting methods available in NSArray.

```
// String[] array = { "C", "A", "B" };
NSArray *array = [NSArray arrayWithObjects:
                     @"C", @"A", @"B", nil];


// Array.ForEach(array,
//   str => Console.WriteLine(str));
[array enumerateObjectsUsingBlock:
 ^(id obj, NSUInteger idx, BOOL *stop)
{
    NSString *str = obj;
    NSLog(@"%@", str);
}];


// Array.Sort(array,
//   CaseInsensitiveComparer.Default);
array = [array sortedArrayUsingSelector:
              @selector(caseInsensitiveCompare:)];
```

Figure 10 - Iterating and sorting an NSArray

Since Objective-C does not support generics there is no way to prevent a collection from containing different types of objects. This explains why the first parameter of the block used by the **enumerateObjectsUsingBlock:** method is of type id. As mentioned previously, id is the most general way to reference an Objective-C object.

In **Figure 10** a sorted version of an array is created using the **sortedArrayUsingSelector:** message. The selector passed to it is called **caseInsensitiveCompare:**, which is an instance method of NSString. This selector is passed to each string in the array to determine the sort order.

ArrayList vs. NSMutableArray

Working with a mutable array in iOS is similar to using a .NET ArrayList. NSMutableArray can store non-nil pointers to any type of Objective-C object (use [NSNull null] to represent a nil value). Unlike in C#, it is unnecessary to cast an object after retrieving it from the array. **Figure 11** shows commonly used NSMutableArray methods in action.

```
// ArrayList list;
// list = new ArrayList();
NSMutableArray *list;
list = [NSMutableArray array];

// var widget = new JASWidget();
// list.Add(widget);
JASWidget *widget = [JASWidget new];
[list addObject:widget];

/* Obj-C: Adding an object to a collection
 causes the collection to retain it,
 so we can release the widget now. */
[widget release];
widget = nil;

// widget = list[0] as JASWidget;
widget = [list objectAtIndex:0]; // no cast

// list.Insert(0, "Mr. Ed");
[list insertObject:@"Mr. Ed" atIndex:0];

// list.Remove(widget);
[list removeObject:widget];
/* Obj-C: 'widget' is now deallocated. */

// list.Clear();
[list removeAllObjects];
```

Figure 11 - NSMutableArray

The code in **Figure 11** demonstrates an important aspect of collection classes from the Foundation framework. A collection retains every object added to it, and releases every object removed from it. In other words, a collection owns the objects it contains. When a collection is deallocated it sends the **release** message to every object it contains, to relinquish ownership of those objects.

Hashtable vs. NSMutableDictionary

NSDictionary is an immutable collection of key-value entries that store non-nil pointers to Objective-C objects. An instance of NSMutableDictionary, which derives from NSDictionary, can be modified after initialization. This class is similar to a Hashtable collection in the .NET framework, which fell out of favor when the generic Dictionary<TKey, TValue> class was introduced. These collections allow for arbitrary key-value associations to be made between objects. **Figure 12** shows the basics of using NSMutableDictionary.

```
// Hashtable dict = new Hashtable();
// dict["truth"] = 42;
// dict["url"] = "http://ijoshsmith.com";
NSMutableDictionary *dict;
dict = [NSMutableDictionary
          dictionaryWithObjectsAndKeys:
          // Objects                  Keys
          [NSNumber numberWithInt:42], @"truth",
          @"http://ijoshsmith.com",   @"url",
          nil];

// int num = (int)dict["truth"];
// dict[num] = "gargle blaster";
NSNumber *num = [dict objectForKey:@"truth"];
[dict setObject:@"gargle blaster" forKey:num];

// dict.Remove("url");
[dict removeObjectForKey:@"url"];

// var keys = dict.Keys;
// var vals = dict.Values;
// Debug.Assert(keys.Count == values.Count);
NSArray *keys = [dict allKeys];
NSArray *vals = [dict allValues];
NSAssert(keys.count == vals.count, nil);
```

Figure 12 - NSMutableDictionary

HashSet<T> vs. NSMutableSet

When a programming task calls for an unordered collection of distinct objects, a *set* is an appropriate collection type to use. Set collections are a programmatic actualization of a mathematical set, central to Set Theory. NSSet and NSMutableSet are used quite often when working with Core Data, which is the topic of Chapter 10. NSMutableSet is similar to .NET's HashSet<T> class. Refer to **Figure 13** to see the basics of using NSMutableSet.

```
// var mset = HashSet<String>();
NSMutableSet *mset;
mset = [NSMutableSet set];

// mset.Add("Arthur");
// mset.Add("Dent");
// mset.Add("Dent");
[mset addObject:@"Arthur"];
[mset addObject:@"Dent"];
[mset addObject:@"Dent"];

// Debug.Assert(mset.Count == 2);
NSAssert(mset.count == 2, nil);

// bool inSet = mset.Contains("Dent");
// Debug.Assert(inSet);
BOOL inSet = [mset containsObject:@"Dent"];
NSAssert(inSet, nil);

// mset.Remove("Arthur");
[mset removeObject:@"Arthur"];
```

Figure 13 - NSMutableSet basics

This code tries to add the string "Dent" twice to the set but it only ends up being added once. This is what I meant by describing a set as an unordered collection of *distinct* objects.

There are several binary operations that can be performed on sets, such as taking an intersection or a union of two sets. **Figure 14** demonstrates only a couple of these operations. Refer to the NSSet and NSMutableSet documentation to learn about other available operations.

```
// var mset = HashSet<String>(new String[]
//   { "Arthur", "Dent" });
NSMutableSet *mset =
  [NSMutableSet setWithObjects:
   @"Arthur", @"Dent", nil];

// var other = HashSet<String>(new String[]
//   {"Dent", "Beeblebrox", "Arthur"});
NSSet *other =
   [NSSet setWithObjects:
   @"Dent", @"Beeblebrox", @"Arthur", nil];

// bool isSubset = mset.IsSubsetOf(other);
// Debug.Assert(isSubset);
BOOL isSubset = [mset isSubsetOfSet:other];
NSAssert(isSubset, nil);

// mset.IntersectWith(other);
// Debug.Assert(mset.Count==2, "Arthur+Dent");
[mset intersectSet:other];
NSAssert(mset.count == 2, @"Arthur + Dent");
```

Figure 14 - Performing set operations

Exception vs. NSException

iOS programming does not involve much throwing and handling of exceptions. The philosophy is that exceptions should not be used for general flow-control or simply to signify errors. The APIs generally use return values and out parameters to indicate when something failed, instead of throwing an exception.

However, exceptions are sometimes used and must be accounted for by callers. Using an API that can throw an exception looks very similar to exception handling code in C#, as seen in **Figure 15**. Exception objects are instances of NSException or one of its subclasses.

```objc
NSArray *empty = [[NSArray alloc] init];
@try
{
    id obj = [empty objectAtIndex:0];
    NSLog(@"Object: %@", obj);
}
@catch (NSException *ex)
{
    NSLog(@"name: %@", ex.name);
    NSLog(@"reason: %@", ex.reason);
}
@finally
{
    NSLog(@"This always executes");
    [empty release];
}
```

Figure 15 - Handling an NSException

Assembly vs. NSBundle

The fundamental unit of deployment in .NET is referred to as an *assembly*, which is either an executable (EXE) or a dynamic link library (DLL). An iOS app is deployed as a *bundle*, which is a set of folders that contain an executable and various resource files. Bundles can be accessed in code via the NSBundle class, as seen in **Figure 16**.

```
/* Ask the main bundle for the path of the property
   list file named Truth.plist and read it into a
   dictionary. Then grab a property named The Answer
   from it and write that out to the console. */
NSBundle *bundle = [NSBundle mainBundle];
NSString *path = [bundle pathForResource:@"Truth"
                                   ofType:@"plist"];
NSDictionary *settings =
  [NSDictionary dictionaryWithContentsOfFile:path];

NSNumber *box = [settings valueForKey:@"The Answer"];
int answer = [box intValue];
NSLog(@"The Answer is %d", answer);
```

Figure 16 - Using NSBundle to look up a config value

Reflection vs. Introspection

The ability to access information about objects and their classes at run-time is known as *reflection* in the .NET world. The .NET framework makes extensive type metadata easily accessible to application developers. That metadata can be used to invoke nonpublic methods and directly access an object's fields. Reflection is a sanctioned backdoor into the strongly typed fortress of the .NET runtime.

The Objective-C runtime is like the Matrix. It gives reality to classes and objects in a language otherwise devoid of object orientation. The runtime is what creates and stores every bit of metadata about each class and object within it. Like the Matrix, it does not make much of that information known to objects living within it. The information it makes available supports a programming technique known by iOS developers as *introspection*. **Figure 17** shows a few of the type-centric introspection methods available for an NSObject.

```
// Type myClass = this.GetType();
// Type widgetClass = typeof(JASWidget);
Class myClass = [self class];
Class widgetClass = [JASWidget class];

// bool kindOf = (this is JASWidget);
BOOL kindOf = [self isKindOfClass:widgetClass];

// bool subclassOf = kindOf ||
//   myClass.IsSubclassOf(widgetClass);
BOOL subclassOf =
  [myClass isSubclassOfClass:widgetClass];

// Debug.Assert(kindOf == subclassOf);
NSAssert(kindOf == subclassOf, nil);
```

Figure 17 - Using introspection to learn about an object

In addition to the "Who are you?" methods seen in **Figure 17** there are a handful of methods that allow objects to be asked "What can you do?" These methods are demonstrated in **Figure 18**.

```
id obj = [self findSomeObject];

// In C# this would require the use of reflection
// to query an object's type and see if it has
// a method with a certain name, and then invoke it.
BOOL responds = [obj respondsToSelector:@selector(doIt)];
if (responds)
    [obj performSelector:@selector(doIt)];

// In C# this is equivalent to checking if an object
// implements an interface, such as:
// var conformist = someObj as ISomeInterface;
// if (conformist != null)
//     conformist.SomeMethod();
BOOL conforms =
  [obj conformsToProtocol:@protocol(SomeProtocol)];
if (conforms)
{
    id<SomeProtocol> conformist = obj;
    [conformist someMethod];
}
```

Figure 18 - Discovering an object's capabilities at run-time

On occasion it is necessary to transcend the limited view of reality conferred by the convenient Objective-C introspection methods. In those situations one can tap into the Objective-C runtime itself and directly interact with its C structs and functions. This low-level programming is not standard fare for most iOS developers, but it is useful to know what's possible. For more information about interacting with the Objective-C runtime, including mind-bending tricks such as *method swizzling*, check out the blog named 'NSBlog' by Mike Ash.

Reflection vs. Key-Value Coding

A common use of .NET reflection is to read and write properties by name. That technique treats an object like it's a dictionary whose keys are property names and values are property values. Until the introduction of the dynamic keyword in C#, implementing this required extra work because it had to be done using .NET's reflection API. In contrast, this is a fundamental and intrinsically supported technique in iOS programming, referred to as *Key-Value Coding*, or *KVC* for short.

Broadly speaking, KVC consists of two related topics:

1. Naming conventions that ensure an object is *KVC-compliant*
2. Methods that enable any KVC-compliant object to be used like a dictionary

In this section I focus on that second aspect of KVC, using an object like it's a dictionary. A full review of KVC is outside the scope of this book. Refer to Apple's Key-Value Coding Programming Guide online for all the details. At the time of this writing, the PDF version of the programming guide is fifty-four pages long. There is a lot to know about KVC.

The Foundation framework includes an informal protocol named NSKeyValueCoding that declares methods used for KVC. NSObject implements these methods, which means that any KVC-compliant NSObject subclass can be generically accessed with them. **Figure 19** shows two commonly used KVC methods in action.

```
/* Two equivalent ways to set a property value. */
// Direct access
widget.battleCry = @"Grrr!";
// KVC
[widget setValue:@"Grrr!" forKey:@"battleCry"];

/* Two equivalent ways to get a property value. */
// Direct access
double radius = widget.blastRadius;
// KVC
NSNumber *box = [widget valueForKey:@"blastRadius"];
radius = [box doubleValue];
```

Figure 19 - Accessing properties via KVC

This example code shows how KVC methods are used, but not why they are useful. There are many situations in which treating objects like a dictionary provides a simple and elegant solution to a programming problem. Examples include configuring objects with name-value data from a JSON dictionary, and displaying arbitrary properties of an object in a user-defined table or chart.

Collection classes support some KVC messages by redirecting them to each object in the collection and accumulating the results; a technique known as *Higher-Order Messaging*. Also, some KVC methods use a collection to get or set the value of multiple properties at once. **Figure 20** demonstrates how to use these features of the platform.

```objc
// Configure both widgets.
widget1.battleCry = @"ROOOOAAARRRRR!";
widget2.battleCry = @"Save yourself!";
widget1.blastRadius = 42.0;
widget2.blastRadius = 69.0;

// Put the widgets into an array.
NSArray *array = [NSArray arrayWithObjects:
                     widget1, widget2, nil];

// Collect their battle cries in an array.
NSArray *cries = [array valueForKey:@"battleCry"];
NSLog(@"Battle cries = %@", cries); // show'em all

// Create a dictionary that contains property
// names and values for a widget object.
NSDictionary *dict =
   [NSDictionary dictionaryWithObjectsAndKeys:
    @"Run for the hills!",            @"battleCry",
    [NSNumber numberWithDouble:99], @"blastRadius",
    nil];

// Assign multiple properties of the widget.
[widget1 setValuesForKeysWithDictionary:dict];
```

Figure 20 - Using collections with KVC

Another convenient feature of KVC is known as *collection operators*. These operators are specialized key paths that can be used by the **valueForKeyPath:** method of a collection. Collection operators can perform tasks such as summing and averaging a group of numbers. They are not nearly as efficient as writing the equivalent loop by hand, but for small collections of data the difference is negligible. When working with Core Data (see Chapter 10) these operators are very efficient because they can be executed by a SQLite database. A couple of the collection operators, **@avg** and **@max**, are seen in **Figure 21**.

```
// Give each widget a blast radius.
widget1.blastRadius = 69.0;
widget2.blastRadius = 42.0;
widget3.blastRadius = 8675309.0;

// Put the widgets into an array.
NSArray *array = [NSArray arrayWithObjects:
                    widget1, widget2, widget3, nil];

// Determine the average blast radius.
NSNumber *box;
box = [array valueForKeyPath:@"@avg.blastRadius"];
NSLog(@"Average radius = %f", [box doubleValue]);

// Determine the largest blast radius.
box = [array valueForKeyPath:@"@max.blastRadius"];
NSLog(@"Largest radius = %@", box);
```

Figure 21 - Using KVC collection operators

There is a lot more to know about KVC than what is presented here. I urge you to read Apple's documentation on the subject, and learn more about how KVC can simplify the way iOS software is written.

Data binding vs. Key-Value Observing

Several .NET UI programming platforms, such as WPF and Windows Forms, include classes that make it possible to bind one property to another. This is commonly used to synchronize the state of data objects with what is shown by user interface controls. Changes made to one property get pushed to another property and vice versa, if the binding is bidirectional.

iOS does not have a data binding API, but it does have the infrastructure used to support bindings in Cocoa desktop applications. Part of that infrastructure is Key-Value Coding, reviewed in the previous section. The other part is known as *Key-Value Observing*, or *KVO*. The "Key-Value" part of KVO refers to the same keys and values discussed in the section about KVC: *keys* are property names and *values* are property values. The "Observing" part of KVO is where things get interesting...

If you are familiar with the INotifyPropertyChanged interface in .NET programming, you already understand the basic idea of KVO. The idea is that an object notifies other objects when its property values change. Which objects does it notify? Whichever objects subscribed for notifications from it. For this to work, the observed object must be *KVO-compliant*, which basically means that it is KVC-compliant and emits notifications when property values change. More on that later.

KVO is a general-purpose mechanism for observing changes to properties of any KVO-compliant object. It is often used by a View Controller to listen for changes made to Model objects. View Controllers and Models are reviewed in Chapter 7.

The following example assumes the existence of a simple class named JASCitizen with one property called **name** which points to an NSString. The **name** property of a JASCitizen object will be observed via KVO. There is no code in that class's implementation file that emits property change notifications, it all happens automatically. I will return to this point later.

A JASCitizen object is monitored by a class named JASBigBrother. **Figure 22** shows the code that registers Big Brother as an observer of a citizen.

```
// This is a method of JASBigBrother.
- (void)monitorCitizen:(JASCitizen *)aCitizen
{
    // Big Brother needs to keep a pointer to
    // all monitored citizens in order to stop
    // observing them when he is deallocated.
    [citizens addObject:aCitizen];

    // Big Brother wants to know your old name
    // and new name when your name changes.
    NSKeyValueObservingOptions oldAndNew =
    NSKeyValueObservingOptionOld |
    NSKeyValueObservingOptionNew;

    // Big Brother is watching you!
    [aCitizen addObserver:self
            forKeyPath:@"name"
              options:oldAndNew
              context:self];
}
```

Figure 22 - Subscribing for property change notifications

Take note that the code passes the self pointer as the 'context' argument. That argument value is used by the code in **Figure 23**, which shows how Big Brother is notified when the citizen's **name** property value changes. The **observeValueForKeyPath:ofObject:change:context:** method, inherited from NSObject, is invoked when any observed property changes value.

```
// This is a method of JASBigBrother.
- (void)observeValueForKeyPath:(NSString *)keyPath
                      ofObject:(id)object
                        change:(NSDictionary *)change
                       context:(void *)context
{
    BOOL sentToMe = (context == self);
    if (sentToMe)
    {
        NSLog(@"%@ changed from %@ to %@",
               keyPath,
               [change objectForKey:NSKeyValueChangeOldKey],
               [change objectForKey:NSKeyValueChangeNewKey]);
    }
    else
    {
        // The notification must have been sent
        // for a property that one of my parent
        // classes observes, so pass it on.
        [super observeValueForKeyPath:keyPath
                             ofObject:object
                               change:change
                              context:context];
    }
}
```

Figure 23 - Getting notified when a citizen's name changes

Note: When the ARC compiler feature is enabled this code becomes slightly more complicated. Using the 'context' argument, which is a void pointer, requires what's known as a *bridged cast*. That is a special form of type cast which involves the `__bridge` keyword to inform ARC how ownership of the object should be managed. This is one of countless examples of why understanding memory management is critical, even though ARC exists to help ease the burden.

It is important to remove observers when they are finished observing property changes because the KVO infrastructure retains neither observers nor the observed. If an observer is not removed from the KVO system, property change notifications might be sent to it after being deallocated. That will cause an application to crash if you're lucky (the alternative is running in an undefined state with corrupt data)! This important step is shown in **Figure 24**.

```
// This is a method of JASBigBrother.
- (void)dealloc
{
    for (JASCitizen *citizen in citizens)
    {
        [citizen removeObserver:self
                     forKeyPath:@"name"
                        context:self];
    }
    [citizens release];
    [super dealloc];
}
```

Figure 24 - Big Brother stops observing citizens before he dies

There is a significant difference between property change notifications using INotifyPropertyChanged in .NET and KVO in iOS. Any KVO-compliant object can send property change notifications without the need for a developer to write a single line of code. Sure, there are IL weaving techniques in .NET that allow an object to emit property change notifications without someone manually writing the boilerplate code. In contrast, with KVO a property setter of an object only contains the executable instructions to emit a notification if the property is currently being observed on that particular object. If a property on an object is not being observed for changes, its setter/mutator method does not contain or execute any KVO-related instructions whatsoever. Those instructions are added on-demand, thanks to a technique known as *isa swizzling*, where an object's type is replaced by a dynamically generated class which overrides the mutator methods of observed properties. The overridden mutators execute instructions that emit a notification to observers.

This discussion quickly veered into rather advanced and esoteric concepts. The reason I mention all of this is because KVO looks like magic. Most reasonable developers detest magic, and prefer not to use things they cannot explain. There is no magic in KVO, just some *very* clever engineering. KVO is a powerful tool worth learning.

KVO is yet another important topic whose scope vastly exceeds what a book like this should rightly cover. Be sure to read more about it in Apple's Key-Value Observing Programming Guide online (note: this is not the same programming guide mentioned in the section on KVC). Another great source of information about KVO, and many other topics, is the book iOS 5 Programming - Pushing the Limits by Rob Napier and Mugunth Kumar.

Summary
The Foundation framework contains a wide variety of indispensable classes for iOS developers. There are many parallels between what Foundation and the .NET Base Class Library have to offer, though many of the concepts often go by different names. Learning how to translate between the two vocabularies is an essential step in becoming a productive iOS developer.

Chapter 7: From XAML to UIKit

People expect iOS apps to be beautiful, intuitive, and responsive. It is in Apple's best interest to help application developers meet those expectations. A significant aspect of creating a great iOS app is making it visually consistent with Apple apps; such as Settings, Calendar, and Mail. The iOS development platform makes it easy for developers to use the same UI controls Apple uses. This is certainly not a foolproof means for ensuring an app will have an excellent user experience, but it is a big step in the right direction.

This chapter reviews UIKit, the most popular and high-level UI programming platform for iOS. It explains UIKit to a .NET developer familiar with WPF or Silverlight (hereafter referred to as WPF/SL). Don't worry if you have no experience with those UI platforms, there is plenty of information to absorb in this chapter regardless of your UI programming background. The following chapter builds upon knowledge gained here by showing how to build UIKit-based user interfaces via drag-and-drop.

Before starting our guided tour of UIKit, I want to point out that Apple is very restrictive about allowing UI controls to be customized by application developers. This is in stark contrast to WPF/SL, which support almost unlimited UI customization. Apple's controls are highly opinionated whereas Microsoft's are simply suggestive. Perhaps their emphasis on consistency explains, in part, why Apple's mobile platform has become so popular. Food for thought...

The major drawing systems

iOS has several drawing systems, each specialized for a certain kind of rendering work, that can be mixed together in one user interface. All of them are built on top of the core operating system and services, which includes the Foundation framework reviewed in the previous chapter. Refer to **Figure 1** to see where a few of the most commonly used drawing systems reside in the iOS stack.

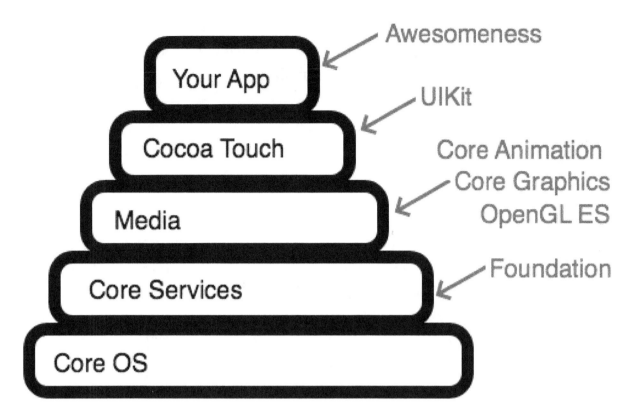

Figure 1 - Drawing systems in the iOS stack

The following list describes the four drawing systems referenced in the preceding diagram.

• **UIKit** is what most iOS developers use to create user interfaces. It supports drawing, images, layout, input focus, animation, text, and more. Classes in UIKit are prefixed with *UI*, such as UIButton. The user interface controls in iOS are part of UIKit.

• **Core Animation** provides an object-oriented API for creating two and three-dimensional animations, which are integrated with UIKit. Its architecture is based on the concept of a *layer hierarchy*, analogous to the view hierarchy design used by UIKit. Classes in this system are prefixed with *CA*.

• **Core Graphics**, also known as *Quartz*, offers an API exposed as C structures and functions whose names are prefixed with *CG*. It is commonly used for rendering custom user interfaces and PDF documents. UIKit uses Core Graphics extensively under the hood.

- **OpenGL ES** is a subset of OpenGL optimized for embedded systems. This book does not review OpenGL ES at all. It is typically used for high-performance games and extremely demanding data visualizations.

The rest of this chapter focuses on UIKit.

UIKit rendering

The way UI rendering works in UIKit is similar to how it works in WPF/SL. A UIView can contain other UIViews, known as its *subviews*, and be occluded by them (i.e. visually covered over by them). The View that contains another View is known as its *superview*. This nested arrangement of Views forms a hierarchy. All Views in a hierarchy are rendered in memory and composited into an image. That image is sent to a render target such as the screen, an image file, or a PDF document.

Every View has a backing *layer* which contains an image of the View, but not its subviews. When a View needs to be rendered, the system checks if that view's layer contains an up-to-date image of the View. It prefers to make use of a device's **GPU** to composite the cached image in a layer. This is much more efficient than having the View render itself again, which requires using the **C**PU to execute the View's drawing code.

UIKit rendering is much more complicated than what I've described here. To learn more about this important topic, refer to Apple's <u>View Programming Guide for iOS</u> on the Web.

Points and pixels

Similar to WPF/SL, all drawing and layout logic in UIKit uses points, not pixels. A *point* is an abstract unit of measurement, which allows an iDevice with a Retina display to render a user interface at the same size as a non-Retina display, but with more clarity and detail. Most iOS applications do not require code that takes the device's screen resolution into account. That information is easily accessible, however, should the need arise. Simply access the **scale** property of the

`[UIScreen mainScreen]` object. It will return 1.0 on non-Retina devices, and 2.0 on Retina devices.

There is not always a one-to-one relationship between points and pixels. On an iPhone 3, whose display has 320x480 pixels, one point is rendered by one pixel. For an iPhone 4's Retina display, which has the same screen size as iPhone 3 but a resolution of 640x480, one point is rendered by four pixels (because a Retina display has twice as many pixels in each dimension).

An app that supports devices with and without a Retina display should include two versions of every image shown in the UI. The dimensions of the image for Retina should be twice as large as the image for non-Retina. Having twice as many pixels in both dimensions enables the Retina display to show a higher-quality image in more detail. The image for Retina should have "@2x" appended to the file name, just before the file extension. For example, the following two image files would be added to a project:

- Non-Retina
  - File Name: SomeImage.png
  - Image Size: 100 x 150
- Retina
  - File Name: SomeImage@2x.png
  - Image Size: 200 x 300

When an image is loaded at run-time, the appropriate image file is used based on whether or not the device has a Retina display. If a Retina-specific version of an image is not available, UIKit falls back to loading the smaller image.

UIKit uses Model-View-Controller
UIKit is fundamentally based on the Model-View-Controller (MVC) design pattern. Apple promotes MVC extensively through their APIs, tools, and documentation. Some developers might be turned off by Apple making an

architectural decision about their app for them, but in practice having pervasive support in the platform for creating well-structured applications is a godsend.

Having rich MVC support in UIKit means application developers don't need to reinvent the wheel. It is common for WPF/SL developers to roll their own system for navigating between different user interface Views. In iOS that would be an unusual thing to do because UIKit provides a system for navigating between Views and Controllers. This navigation system includes visual transitions, such as sliding a View in from an edge of the screen or flipping the UI over to present a modal View. Apple's iOS apps use the same navigation system and transitions, which means your apps can look and feel like "real iOS apps" with minimal effort.

UserControl vs. UIView

In WPF/SL it is common to build a View by adding UI elements, such as buttons and labels, to a UserControl. For example, building a View in WPF that allows the user to type in their evil plans to destroy the solar system might involve adding a multiline TextBox and a couple of Button controls to a UserControl. In iOS that task would be performed by adding a UITextView and two UIButtons to a UIView. The code in **Figure 2** demonstrates how to add a UITextView to the user interface of an iOS app.

```
// This method is in a UIViewController subclass.
- (void)viewDidLoad {
    [super viewDidLoad];

    // Create a multi-line editing control.
    CGRect frm = self.view.bounds;
    UITextView *textView = [[[UITextView alloc]
                            initWithFrame:frm]
                            autorelease];

    // This Controller adopts UITextViewDelegate,
    // which enables responding to editing events.
    textView.delegate = self;

    // Show the editor in this Controller's view.
    [self.view addSubview:textView];

    // Give input focus to the text editor,
    // causing the virtual keyboard to appear.
    [textView becomeFirstResponder];
}
```

Figure 2 - Adding a UITextView to a View

This code example includes two common properties used to arrange Views on a screen: **frame** and **bounds**. The 'frm' variable is a CGRect structure that stores a point and size to represent a rectangle. That variable is initialized with the **bounds** of the Controller's **view**, which is a property that returns the root UIView object managed by the Controller. The *bounds* of a View stores its size and location within its own coordinate system, which means the location coordinate defaults to the top-left corner.

Remember: In UIKit the origin coordinate (0, 0) is at the top-left corner of a View. The X axis increases from left-to-right, and the Y axis increases from top-to-bottom. This is the same as in WPF/SL and many other Windows UI platforms. However, in Core Graphics and Core Animation the coordinate system is flipped, which can be confusing at first!

The UITextView in **Figure 2** is initialized via the **initWithFrame:** message. The 'frm' variable is passed to this initializer to set the View's **frame** property. The *frame* of a View represents its size and location within the coordinate system of its superview. The **frame** property can be used to determine where a View should be placed on the screen. By assigning the superview's **bounds** to the UITextView's **frame** causes it to completely occlude the superview. Note, the distinction between a View's **frame** and **bounds** grows more complicated when transforms are used, but for the most common scenarios these two properties are very similar.

Code-behind vs. UIViewController

Most .NET UI platforms include a source code file for each View in an application. They are referred to as *code-behind* files and are intended to be the place where View management code lives. Code-behind files are typically implemented as partial classes that get combined, at compile-time, with a View's designer file(s); such as a XAML file. The result is that a code-behind file is inextricably tied to the View with which it is associated.

In the WPF/SL world it is common to put a View's state management and user interaction logic in a ViewModel class, instead of its code-behind file. A ViewModel is similar to a Controller in that, when properly implemented, they both avoid taking a hard dependency on the View being managed. The type of View managed by a ViewModel or Controller object can be determined at run-time, because they are not tightly coupled to a View at compile-time.

A ViewModel indirectly modifies a View using property change notifications to update data bindings, whereas a Controller directly updates a View using pointers to UI objects. In that sense, Controllers are similar to code-behind files because both directly reference and manipulate UI objects. Later in this chapter I demonstrate how Controllers use *outlets* to reference controls in a View without needing any information about the type of View being managed. This enables a Controller to work directly with a View but avoid being tightly coupled to it.

The loose coupling between Controller and View can be leveraged by universal apps. An app is *universal* if it supports being run on both iPhone and iPad. Each device requires Views to be designed for a specific screen size and form factor. Ideally, the same Controller class can be used with different device-specific Views.

Navigation controller

A major component of the navigation system in UIKit is the UINavigationController class. It manages a stack of UIViewControllers, allowing Controllers to be pushed onto and popped off of the stack by application code. Like all Controllers, it manages a View, accessible through its **view** property, that contains a navigation bar on top, an optional toolbar on bottom, and a content area that fills the remaining space. The View of the Controller on top of the navigation stack is shown in the content area.

The screenshot in **Figure 3** shows a View being presented by a UINavigationController. The navigation bar with the back button titled "Evil Overlords" is part of the UINavigationController's user interface. The image, label, and gray background is the View of the top Controller on the navigation stack.

Figure 3 - Displaying a View using UINavigationController

The back button on the left of the navigation bar is created automatically by UINavigationController. The title of the button defaults to the **title** property of the previous Controller in the navigation stack. The code in **Figure 4** shows how to push a Controller onto the stack, so that its View is displayed to the user.

```
/* This controller code executes in response to
   the user tapping on a table cell or button. */

// Create the controller to show info about Thor.
JASViewController *thorVC =
   [[[JASViewController alloc] init] autorelease];

// Configure the controller with some data.
thorVC.title = @"Thor";
thorVC.evilOverlordData = thorData;

// Any UIViewController managed by a navigation
// controller can access it via the inherited
// navigationController property.
[self.navigationController pushViewController:thorVC
                                    animated:YES];
```

Figure 4 - Pushing a Controller onto the navigation stack

The most common use of UINavigationController is to present a set of hierarchical screens to the user. For example, the first screen shows a list of data items and tapping on a data item pushes a details screen onto the stack. Popping a Controller off the stack, and its View off the screen, can be done in code by sending the **popViewControllerAnimated:** message to a UINavigationController object.

iPad-specific controllers

Before the iPad, iOS apps were only supposed to display the View of one Controller at a time. Violating this rule lead to various problems, such as not all Controllers getting notified when the device was rotated and its orientation changed. With the iPad came more screen real estate and the need to show the Views of multiple Controllers on the screen simultaneously. This problem was addressed by the introduction of the UISplitViewController and UIPopoverController classes, which are only available for the iPad, as of iOS 5.1.

The UISplitViewController class derives from UIViewController and provides two panes in which the Views of two other Controllers can be displayed. The first pane has a fixed width of 320 points and a height that fits the window at its current orientation. The other pane fills the remaining space. The first pane is normally used to display a list of data items, and the second pane displays information about the selected item in the list.

When a UISplitViewController is displayed in landscape orientation both Views are shown next to each other. When the user rotates the device to portrait orientation the first view is shown in a popover by default. This is done by using the UIPopoverController class, which derives directly from NSObject. A popover floats above other Views on the screen, similar to a context menu. Unlike a context menu, a popover can display an arbitrary View. An example of UIPopoverController in action can be seen in **Figure 5**.

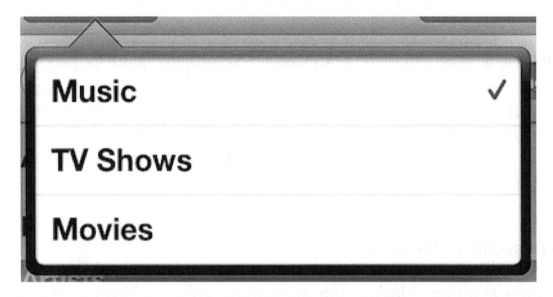

Figure 5 - Displaying a UITableView with a UIPopoverController

The UIPopoverController class can be used on its own, independent of the UISplitViewController. For example, it can provide functionality similar to a .NET ComboBox.

Container view controllers

There are two general Controller categories in UIKit: content and container. *Content View Controllers* present a subset of an application's data to the user, collect user input, display animated activity indicators, etc. Most Controllers written for an iOS app fall into this category. The other category, *Container View Controllers*, manage a collection or hierarchy of other Controllers. The UINavigationController and UISplitViewController classes reviewed earlier fall into this category.

Until iOS 5 the UIViewController API did not make it possible for application developers to create their own Controller that contains other Controllers. Now it is possible to implement custom containers that use additional methods exposed by UIViewController. This involves sending **addChildViewController:** to a container and **removeFromParentViewController:** to a Controller in a container, as well as a handful of other messages documented online. This is useful in situations where an app requires a UI navigation scheme that none of the built-in Container View Controllers support.

Control field vs. Outlet

In a WPF/SL UserControl an element with an x:Name attribute value in XAML is easily referenced by code in the control's code-behind file. At compile-time a field is added to the UserControl subclass. That field's name matches the x:Name attribute value assigned in XAML. At run-time the field is assigned a reference to the UI object for which it was generated. As usual, things work a bit differently in iOS.

As explained in the 'Code-behind vs. UIViewController' section, a Controller is loosely coupled to a View even though it can have pointers to the View's subviews. This is possible because Controller code is not combined with a View at compile-time. Instead, it relies on UIKit infrastructure to plug UI objects into its outlets at run-time. An *outlet* is just a normal property or ivar decorated with the `IBOutlet` symbol, which makes it assignable at design-time using Interface Builder. The next chapter shows how to hook up outlets in Interface Builder. For now, refer to **Figure 6** to see various ways an outlet can be declared.

```
// NOTE: This code assumes ARC is enabled.

// Class declaration
@interface JASSomeViewController : UIViewController
@property (strong, nonatomic) IBOutlet UIView *theView;
@property (weak, nonatomic) IBOutlet UIButton *button;
@end

// Class extension
@interface JASSomeViewController ()
@property (weak, nonatomic) IBOutlet
  UIActivityIndicatorView *activityIndicator;
@end

// Class implementation
@implementation JASSomeViewController {
    __weak IBOutlet UIDatePicker *datePicker;
}
@synthesize activityIndicator, button, theView;
- (void)viewDidUnload {
    [self setTheView:nil];
    [self setButton:nil];
    [self setActivityIndicator:nil];
    datePicker = nil;
    [super viewDidUnload];
}
@end
```

Figure 6 - Declaring four outlets in a UIViewController subclass

There are several places where an outlet can be declared. Many tutorials and books demonstrate creating an outlet by adding a property to the `@interface` in a Controller's header file. I consider this to be a bad practice because it puts what are essentially private properties into a class's public-facing header file.

If ARC is not being used, a reasonable place to declare outlet properties is in a class extension, found in the class's implementation file. This keeps outlet declarations out of the header file, and does not in any way reduce their ability to be used in Interface Builder.

When ARC is enabled for an app that targets iOS 5 and later, however, the most streamlined approach to declaring and using outlets is to make them ivars, not properties. This can be done by adding them directly to the `@implementation` of a class between braces, where ivars should normally be declared. The reason this approach makes the most sense when ARC is enabled has to do with the `__weak` keyword seen previously in **Figure 6**. It ensures that when the UI object is deallocated, the ivar outlet will immediately be set to nil. This is the same behavior exhibited by the two property outlets in the example marked **weak** in their property declarations. Weak references in ARC make it next to impossible to accidentally send a message to the memory address of a dead object. It is important to note that even though ARC was back-ported to iOS 4, weak references are *not* automatically set to nil in iOS 4. This is a major drawback to using ARC when an app must support running on iOS 4.

Before iOS 5, it was standard practice in iOS programming to make an outlet property retain the UI object to which it points. This guidance was based on intricacies of how UI objects are loaded and configured at run-time. Apple has improved the situation, however. When using ARC and the latest version of Xcode and Interface Builder, outlets created by the IDE are almost always **weak**. This improvement prevents Controllers from accidentally not releasing UI objects, which was a common source of memory leaks.

The IDE does not *always* generate weak outlets. Take another look at **Figure 6** and look carefully at the outlet property named **theView**. This outlet is intended to reference the top-level UIView object in a View hierarchy. Since that top-level UIView is not owned by any other object in its View hierarchy, and is autoreleased when created by UIKit, it could be problematic to have an outlet weakly reference it. The UIView might be released and deallocated before the Controller gets a chance to use it! That is why the outlet property named **theView** has the **strong** modifier, which causes its mutator method to retain the UIView object. Note, this is a contrived example since the UIViewController's **view** property is automatically wired up to point at and retain that top-level UIView. **theView** outlet merely demonstrates how memory management affects outlets.

Another point of interest in **Figure 6** is the **viewDidUnload** method. It contains code that sets outlets to nil. This code is automatically inserted into the method by the IDE when it creates an outlet for you, which is reviewed in the next chapter. Actually, the only outlet in this example that needs to be set to nil is **theView**, since it is the only property that retains the UI object assigned to it. The fact that Xcode continues to generate this boilerplate code for projects using ARC and targeting iOS 5 or above seems unnecessary, because outlets declared as weak properties and ivars will not prevent their UI objects from being deallocated. Unless it was intentional, I hope Apple improves this aspect of Xcode in a future release.

Control event handling method vs. Action

As mentioned in Chapter 4, Objective-C does not support the equivalent of .NET events. It does, however, offer several means of notifying objects when something interesting has occurred elsewhere in the program. One of these mechanisms is the Delegation pattern, which causes certain methods of an object to be invoked in response to another object being used. The Delegation pattern was reviewed in Chapter 4, and is shown in greater depth later in this chapter. Another commonly used mechanism is known as an *action*, which is used in a manner very similar to a .NET event.

Every UIControl subclass has a set of touch input events that it can send out to other objects. As seen in **Figure 7** an object can register to be notified about input events by sending a control the **addTarget:action:forControlEvents:** message. This method is equivalent to using the += operator in C# to attach an event handler.

```
- (void)viewDidLoad {
    [super viewDidLoad];

    UIButton *btn =
      [UIButton buttonWithType:UIButtonTypeRoundedRect];

    //                       { x,  y,  width, height}
    btn.frame = (CGRect) { 10, 10, 200,    40};

    [btn setTitle:@"DON'T PANIC!"
        forState:UIControlStateNormal];

    btn.tag = 42;

    // Add a target and action for when the user
    // taps the button, by lifting a finger off
    // the button while inside its bounds.
    [btn addTarget:self
            action:@selector(handleButtonTapped:)
   forControlEvents:UIControlEventTouchUpInside];

    [self.view addSubview:btn];
}

- (IBAction)handleButtonTapped:(id)sender {
    NSAssert([sender tag] == 42, @"What the deuce?");
}
```

Figure 7 - Handling a UIButton event with an action

The return type of the **handleButtonTapped:** method is IBAction. This is simply a #define symbol that gives another name for void. When hooking up an action in code it is not necessary to use IBAction as the method's return type. The presence of the macro is detected by Interface Builder when it determines which methods in a class are eligible to be invoked in response to a control event. In the next chapter I show how to work with actions using Interface Builder.

XAML controls vs. iOS controls

UIKit includes many user interface controls that are similar to controls used in WPF/SL programs. Their names are sometimes quite different, so it can take some investigation to figure out which control to use to perform a particular UI task. The following table maps WPF/SL controls to their iOS equivalent, if one exists. Items marked with an asterisk (*****) are only available on the iPad. Items marked with an exclamation mark (**!**) require custom coding to emulate the behavior of the associated WPF/SL control. If a WPF/SL control is not in the list, there is no equivalent control in iOS, though there might be an open-source implementation that fits your needs. This table reflects the state of available UIKit controls as of iOS 5.1.

WPF/SL	Closest iOS Equivalent
Button	UIButton
CheckBox	UISwitch
ComboBox	UIPickerView
ContextMenu	UIPopoverController (*)(!)
DataGrid	UITableView
DatePicker	UIDatePicker
Image	UIImageView
ItemsControl	UITableView
Label	UILabel
ListBox	UITableView
ListView	UITableView
MediaElement	MPMoviePlayerViewController
MessageBox	UIAlertView
PasswordBox	UITextField
Popup	UIPopoverController (*)
ProgressBar	UIProgressView

WPF/SL	Closest iOS Equivalent
RadioButton	UISegmentedControl
RichTextBox	UITextView
ScrollViewer	UIScrollView
Slider	UISlider
TabControl	UITabBar
TextBox	UITextField
ToolBar	UIToolbar
TreeView	UITableView (!)
UserControl	UIView
WaitCursor	UIActivityIndicatorView
WebBrowser	UIWebView

For more information about iOS controls refer to the 'iOS UI Element Usage' section of Apple's iOS Human Interface Guidelines document, commonly referred to as the "HIG." That is a very important document because it explains the UI design principles and guidelines that Apple promotes for creating high-quality iOS applications.

Layout panels vs. Autoresizing

Managing the size and location of UI elements in WPF/SL is based on the use of layout panels. A layout panel is a special type of UI element. Other UI elements are added to a panel, which then applies its unique layout strategy to the elements within it. One example is the DockPanel, which positions and sizes its child elements so that they are either attached to a particular side of the panel or fill the remaining space in the panel. Another example is Canvas, which simply arranges child elements using (x, y) coordinates and does not modify their sizes.

There is nothing in iOS equivalent to layout panels. Managing the size and position of UI objects in iOS is a task entirely left up to the application developer.

In practice this task is often accomplished by assigning a CGRect to a View's **frame** property, which in turn specifies its (x, y) coordinate, width, and height. Resizing and relocating a View to accommodate a different layout, such as when the device's orientation changes, can typically be managed by setting its **autoresizingMask** property to an appropriate value. This provides adaptive layout behavior similar to the WPF/SL DockPanel. An example of a user interface layout that is preserved between both orientations is seen in **Figure 8**.

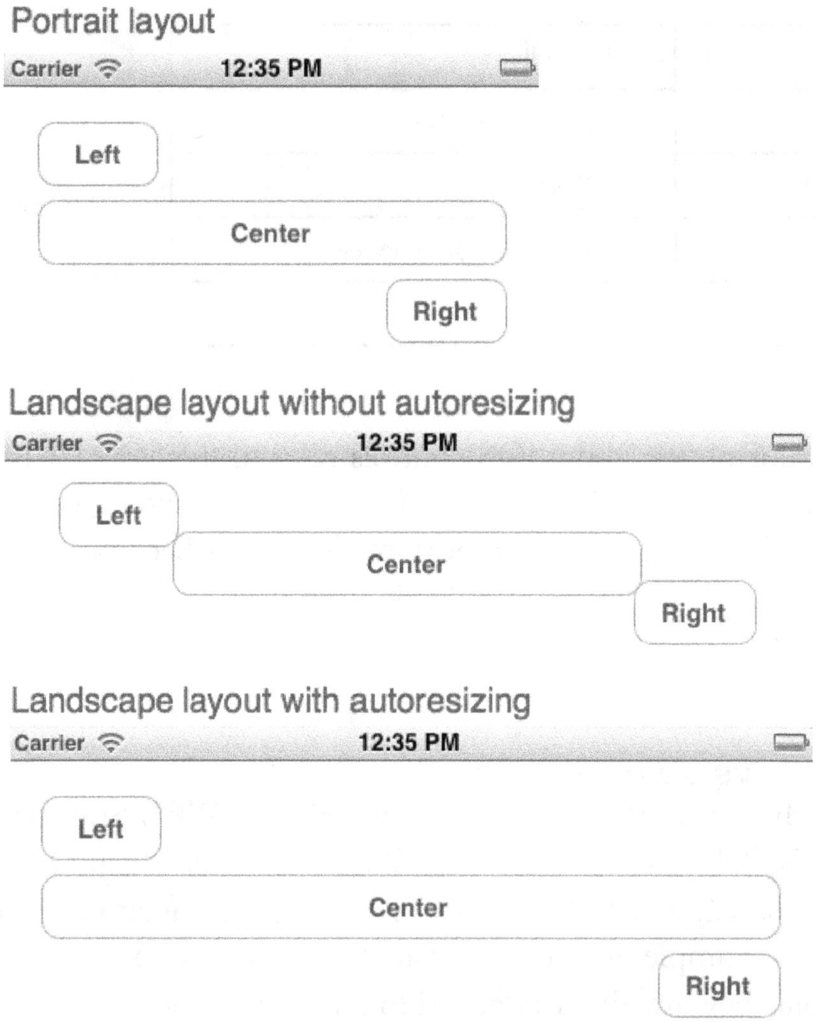

Figure 8 - Maintaining a UI layout via autoresizing

Notice how the relative locations of the buttons are not maintained in landscape orientation when autoresizing is not used. Also note that when autoresizing is enabled the Center button's width increases to accommodate the extra horizontal space available in landscape orientation. **Figure 9** shows the code that configures the autoresizing masks for each button. In the next chapter I show how to configure autoresizing masks using a graphical tool in Interface Builder.

```
self.leftButton.autoresizingMask =
UIViewAutoresizingFlexibleBottomMargin |
UIViewAutoresizingFlexibleRightMargin;

self.centerButton.autoresizingMask =
UIViewAutoresizingFlexibleBottomMargin |
UIViewAutoresizingFlexibleWidth;

self.rightButton.autoresizingMask =
UIViewAutoresizingFlexibleBottomMargin |
UIViewAutoresizingFlexibleLeftMargin;
```

Figure 9 - Configuring the autoresizing masks of three buttons

In some situations the autoresizing feature does not provide the layout adaptation logic a View needs. Maintaining highly customized layouts between both portrait and landscape orientations can involve responding to orientation change notifications and manually updating the **frame** of various Views in code. Autoresizing is a big timesaver, and should be preferred over manually adjusting Views whenever possible.

Style vs. UIAppearance

In iOS 5 Apple introduced a centralized means of theming an application's user interface, known as *appearance proxies*. An appearance proxy is similar to a WPF/SL Style because it allows all instances of a certain control type to be given the same visual treatment, such as a common background image and tint color for a UINavigationBar. Each View in an application can opt to override the appearance settings on any control object, if necessary, by simply setting the relevant properties to a new value. Lastly, the appearance proxy API makes it possible to specify the appearance of a certain type of control when it is contained in another type of control. For example, this makes it easy to give all UIActivityIndicatorView instances a brown tint when displayed in a UITableViewCell. **Figure 10** shows the code involved with leveraging this UIKit feature.

```
// Set the default tint color of all navigation bars.
UIColor *tint = [UIColor colorWithRed:0.2
                                green:0.4
                                 blue:0.6
                                alpha:1];
[[UINavigationBar appearance] setTintColor:tint];

// Set the color of activity indicators in a table cell.
Class<UIAppearanceContainer> class = [UITableViewCell class];
id proxy = [UIActivityIndicatorView appearanceWhenContainedIn:
            // This is a nil-terminated list of arguments...
          class, nil];
[proxy setColor:[UIColor brownColor]];
```

Figure 10 - Applying a UI theme with appearance proxies

The **appearance** and **appearanceWhenContainedIn:** messages passed in the previous code example are members of the UIAppearance protocol. A control class must adopt that protocol to be used by the appearance proxy API. Just because a control adopts that protocol does not mean that every property and method in it can be assigned through an appearance proxy. To support appearance customization, a class must conform to the UIAppearanceContainer protocol and relevant accessor methods must be marked with UI_APPEARANCE_SELECTOR. Since the UIView class adopts both UIAppearance and UIAppearanceContainer, all Views are eligible to have their appearance customized. To determine which messages can be sent to an appearance proxy it is necessary to look at a View class's header file and see which of its property and method declarations have been tagged with the UI_APPEARANCE_SELECTOR symbol. Some people have also posted listings of these declarations online, which is only useful if the listings are updated shortly after each new release of iOS.

Tip: To view the header file of a class in Apple's frameworks, hold the Command key while clicking on the class name in an Editor window in Xcode.

Attached property vs. Associative reference

In WPF/SL it is possible to read and write properties on an object that are not defined by that object's class. This is known as an attached property, because the property's value is "attached" to the object on which it is set. In iOS this concept exists but is supported for all NSObjects; it is not limited to objects intended for use in the UI layer. This feature of the Objective-C runtime is known as *associative references*. It can be used by apps compiled with and without ARC. When setting an associative reference on an object you must specify whether the object being stored should be retained. This is yet another example of why learning memory management is so important for iOS developers. Refer to **Figure 11** for an example of how to implement an associative reference.

```objc
// Required: #import <objc/runtime.h>
// Note: This works with and without ARC.

// The memory address of this char is used as an ID.
static char theAnswerKey;

- (void)setAssociativeReference {
    objc_setAssociatedObject(self,
                             &theAnswerKey,
                             [NSNumber numberWithInt:42],
                             OBJC_ASSOCIATION_RETAIN);
}

- (void)readAssociativeReference {
    NSNumber *theAnswer =
      objc_getAssociatedObject (self, &theAnswerKey);

    NSAssert(42 == [theAnswer intValue], @"No way!");

    objc_setAssociatedObject (self,
                              &theAnswerKey,
                              nil, // Remove the value
                              OBJC_ASSOCIATION_ASSIGN);
}
```

Figure 11 - Assigning and reading an associative reference

Event Routing vs. Responder chain

WPF/SL and UIKit both send user input events up the UI hierarchy to find handler methods. WPF/SL has routed events, and UIKit has the responder chain. Routed events bubble up the element tree when user input occurs. The same concept is the basis for the responder chain in iOS.

Both of these concepts exist, primarily, to process input events in a hierarchical user interface built of elements that can opt to handle an input event. In the .NET world, the implementation consists of UI element trees and routed events. In iOS, where MVC is built into the framework, things are a little different. If a View is managed by a Controller then it also is given a chance to respond to an input event. If a Controller has a parent Controller, the parent gets a chance to handle the event as well. If an event is not handled by any View, Controller, or the window, the UIApplication singleton object gets a shot. This is depicted by the diagram in **Figure 12**.

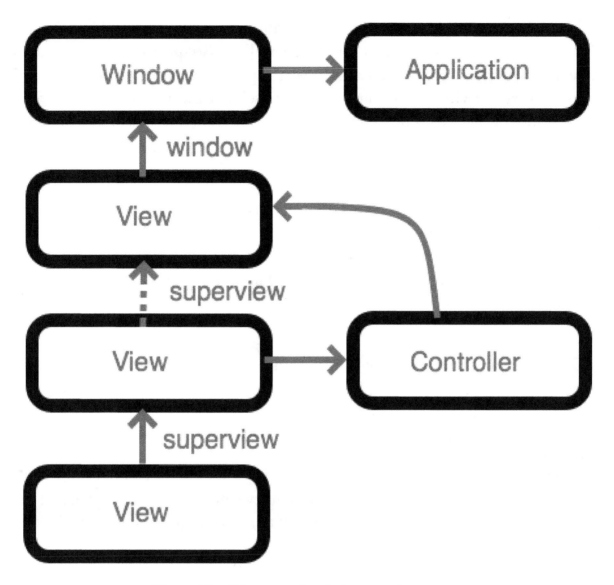

Figure 12 - The responder chain routes input events

In the .NET world a control is said to have input focus when it is the initial target of user input. UIKit has the concept of *first responder*, which is essentially the same thing. For all input events, other than touch events, the first responder in the responder chain gets notified first. Input events that traverse the responder chain include such things as when the user shakes the iPhone or presses the Pause button on their headset. If the first responder can't handle the event, UIKit carries it up the chain notifying other responders, just like a bubbling routed event in WPF/SL. The responder chain is traversed by sending the **nextResponder** message to the first responder and every subsequent responder encountered until reaching the end of the chain.

The first responder is also involved with text editing. A UITextField or UITextView control can be sent the **becomeFirstResponder** message to be made the first responder, which will give it input focus. Giving focus to a text control causes the virtual keyboard to appear so that the user can begin typing. UIKit automatically asks a text editing control to become the first responder when the user taps on it.

When a user touches the screen UIKit performs hit-testing to determine which element is the initial responder for the event. It will send touch events to the first eligible responder under the user's finger(s). This makes sense because the user touches on whatever control they are interested in using, regardless of what the first responder happens to be.

To learn more about the event infrastructure check out Apple's Event Handling Guide for iOS online.

Responding to touch gestures

UIKit includes a set of objects that figure out what the user's fingers are doing and allow your application to respond to high-level gestures, such as pinching and panning. These clever little objects are known as *gesture recognizers* and they all derive from the UIGestureRecognizer class.

There are conventional semantics for gestures that your apps should adhere to. For example, pinching two fingers together should make something on the screen smaller, while dragging a finger around should make a UI object follow along. The latter is known as *panning*, which is demonstrated in **Figure 13**. In this code example a UIImageView is added to a user interface and given a UIPanGestureRecognizer that is used to move the image when the user drags their finger over it.

```
- (void)viewDidLoad {
    [super viewDidLoad];
    // Create an image to drag around the screen.
    CGRect frm = self.view.bounds;
    UIImageView *imgView = [[[UIImageView alloc]
                                initWithFrame:frm]
                               autorelease];
    imgView.image = [UIImage imageNamed:@"Thor"];
    [self.view addSubview:imgView];

    // An image does not support touch input by default.
    imgView.userInteractionEnabled = YES;

    // Create and add the gesture recognizer for panning.
    UIPanGestureRecognizer *recognizer =
      [[UIPanGestureRecognizer alloc]
       initWithTarget:self action:@selector(pan:)];
    [imgView addGestureRecognizer:recognizer];
    [recognizer release];
}
- (void)pan:(UIPanGestureRecognizer *)recognizer {
    // Update the center point of the panned view and reset
    // the recognizer's translation to avoid accumulation.
    CGPoint trans = [recognizer translationInView:self.view];
    CGPoint center = recognizer.view.center;
    recognizer.view.center = CGPointMake(center.x + trans.x,
                                         center.y + trans.y);
    [recognizer setTranslation:CGPointMake(0, 0)
                        inView:self.view];
}
```

Figure 13 - Using a gesture recognizer to pan a UIImageView

For more sophisticated scenarios requiring more control of an application's response to gestures, a class can adopt the UIGestureRecognizerDelegate protocol and be assigned to the **delegate** property of the recognizer object. One situation in which this is necessary is when a View must allow the user to perform multiple gestures at the same time. The delegate object must return YES from the **gestureRecognizer:shouldRecognizeSimultaneouslyWithGestureRecognizer:** protocol method to allow this to occur.

Controlling a UITableView with the Delegation pattern

UITableView is the workhorse of many iOS applications. It presents a scrollable list of data to the user. Unlike the ItemsControl subclasses in WPF/SL, such as ListBox and ListView, a UITableView intrinsically supports reordering and deleting the items in its user interface. Application code has control over which items can be moved or deleted, and can be notified as the user makes changes to the table. An animated transition can be specified when an item is added to or removed from the table, such as fading or sliding it in a certain direction.

Each item in a table is rendered by an instance of UITableViewCell. The default user interface offered by a cell contains two UILabels and a UIImageView. These Views are exposed to application code via the **textLabel**, **detailTextLabel**, and **imageView** properties. The UITableViewCell class honors several cell styles which determine the layout of these Views within the cell. If none of the predefined layouts suit your needs it is possible to create a custom UITableViewCell subclass and design its layout in Interface Builder, or write code that configures a cell's subviews.

A cell can display an *accessory view* on the righthand side, such as a checkmark or disclosure indicator. It also allows for a custom view to be displayed instead of a standard accessory view. This is demonstrated in **Figure 14**, which shows a UITableView from my *Master WPF* app. The first three cells display a disclosure indicator on the righthand side and the bottom cell uses a custom view.

Figure 14 - UITableView is used as a menu in the Master WPF app

The API for using a UITableView relies heavily on the Delegation pattern, which was introduced in Chapter 4. One of the objects to which a table delegates is known as its *data source*, which must conform to the UITableViewDataSource protocol. The data source supplies a table with information about what to display and determines what actions the user can perform on its data, such as deleting and reordering cells. A table also relies on an object that conforms to the

UITableViewDelegate protocol known as its *delegate*, which responds to user interactions with the table.

The UI in **Figure 15** is a UITableView managed by a UITableViewController subclass named JASTableViewController. The UITableViewController class adopts the two aforementioned protocols that enable it to be used as a data source and delegate.

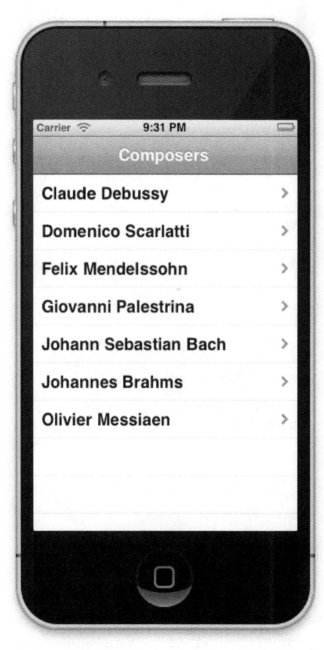

Figure 15 - Listing composers in a UITableView

Figure 16 demonstrates the Controller preparing an array of data items to present to the user, in this case the names of musical geniuses.

```
- (id)init
{
    self = [super initWithStyle:UITableViewStylePlain];
    if (self)
    {
        composers = [[NSArray alloc] initWithObjects:
                    @"Claude Debussy",
                    @"Domenico Scarlatti",
                    @"Felix Mendelssohn",
                    @"Giovanni Palestrina",
                    @"Johann Sebastian Bach",
                    @"Johannes Brahms",
                    @"Olivier Messiaen",
                    nil];

        self.title = @"Composers";
    }
    return self;
}
```

Figure 16 - Creating the data items shown in a UITableView

Shortly after a UITableView is loaded it asks its data source about the data to display. The first step is figuring out how many sections of data there are. A flat list of data will only have one section, but grouped data can have multiple. For example, if the composers were grouped by the era during which they lived there would be several sections, with titles such as "Baroque" and "Romantic." Once the number of sections is known, the next task is determining how many data items exist in each section. This data source code from the JASTableViewController class is shown in **Figure 17**.

```
- (NSInteger)numberOfSectionsInTableView:(UITableView *)tv
{
    // Only one section since the data is not grouped.
    return 1;
}

- (NSInteger)tableView:(UITableView *)tv
 numberOfRowsInSection:(NSInteger)section
{
    // All data items are in the first and only section.
    return composers.count;
}
```

Figure 17 - UITableViewDataSource methods

Another task of a table's data source is creating UITableViewCell objects and configuring them to display attributes of a data item. This is performed on-demand as the user scrolls through the table, which improves performance when working with large lists of data. Since creating UITableViewCells has an associated cost of CPU time and memory consumption, it is strongly encouraged that cell objects be recycled by application code. This is easy to implement, especially considering that when you create a UITableViewController subclass in Xcode it creates an implementation file that contains most of the code needed to properly recycle cells. This is demonstrated in **Figure 18**.

```
- (UITableViewCell *)tableView:(UITableView *)tv
        cellForRowAtIndexPath:(NSIndexPath *)indexPath
{
    static NSString *CellID = @"Whatever";

    // Try to use a recycled cell, or create a new one.
    UITableViewCell *cell =
      [tv dequeueReusableCellWithIdentifier:CellID];
    if (!cell)
    {
        cell = [[UITableViewCell alloc]
                initWithStyle:UITableViewCellStyleDefault
                reuseIdentifier:CellID];

        // Show an arrow on the righthand side indicating
        // that the user can tap on this cell for details.
        cell.accessoryType =
          UITableViewCellAccessoryDisclosureIndicator;
    }

    // Configure the cell to show a composer's name.
    cell.textLabel.text =
      [composers objectAtIndex:indexPath.row];

    return cell;
}
```

Figure 18 - Creating, recycling, and configuring UITableViewCells

When the user interacts with a UITableView, it consults its **delegate** property. The delegate is given the opportunity to respond to user input and take appropriate action. A common response to the user tapping a cell is to navigate to details about that data item. **Figure 19** shows how the **tableView:didSelectRowAtIndexPath:** protocol method can be used to navigate in response to the user tapping on a cell.

```
#pragma mark - Table view delegate

-       (void)tableView:(UITableView *)tv
didSelectRowAtIndexPath:(NSIndexPath *)indexPath
{
    // Make the tapped cell no longer selected.
    [tv deselectRowAtIndexPath:indexPath animated:YES];

    // Get the composer on which the user tapped.
    NSString *composer = [composers objectAtIndex:indexPath.row];

    // Create a Controller to display details about the composer.
    JASComposerDetailController *detailsVC =
      [[[JASComposerDetailController alloc]
        initWithComposer:composer] autorelease];

    // Push the details Controller onto the screen.
    [self.navigationController pushViewController:detailsVC
                                        animated:YES];
}
```

Figure 19 - Navigating to a details screen in response to tapping a cell

Considering how often UITableView is used, and how many features it has to offer, I highly suggest reading more about it. As usual, Apple provides great documentation about this topic in the Table View Programming Guide for iOS online.

Application vs. AppDelegate

When a WPF/SL application starts up it creates an instance of your Application subclass and invokes methods on it to load a Window or Page onto the screen. The Application class exposes virtual methods and events that notify the world when it is gains or loses the active window, when it is about to exit, and other lifecycle-related points of interest. The default project templates in Visual Studio for WPF/SL include a XAML and C# file for an Application subclass; App.xaml and App.xaml.cs. The equivalent of this in iOS is known as an *app delegate*.

An app delegate is an object that conforms to the UIApplicationDelegate protocol, and is assigned to the **delegate** property of the singleton UIApplication object at start up. The purpose of an app delegate is twofold: set up the application's initial user interface and then respond to application lifecycle state changes, such as when the app is interrupted by a phone call and subsequently brought back to the foreground when the call completes.

All too often the app delegate turns into a dumping ground for an assortment of miscellaneous methods and data objects. This might be due, in part, to the fact that many iOS programming tutorial authors put code in an app delegate to make their examples easier to understand. Maybe it's because developers new to iOS are not sure where else to put those assorted bits of code. Regardless of the reason, it's a mistake that should be avoided because it can quickly make a project difficult to understand, maintain, and extend. Follow the same object-oriented design principles you apply in .NET applications to avoid having the app delegate become a black hole of code.

iOS project templates in Xcode include an AppDelegate class full of comments explaining the UIApplicationDelegate protocol methods. For additional information about this aspect of an iOS app, refer to the 'Managing App State Changes' section of Apple's <u>iOS App Programming Guide</u> online.

Working with threads

Well-written apps are responsive to user interactions. If the user performs an action that causes a long-running task to occur, such as calling a Web service or solving a very large set of complex equations, the application should perform the task on a background thread. This prevents the main thread, which drives the user interface, from becoming blocked and unresponsive. In WPF/SL this technique is commonly implemented by using a thread from the ThreadPool to perform the long-running operation, and then the result is marshaled back to the main thread via the **BeginInvoke** method of a Dispatcher object. Returning to the main thread to update the user interface is important because UI objects, such as labels and buttons, have thread affinity. In other words, they must only be accessed by the thread on which they were created. Violating this rule causes run-time exceptions.

The situation is very similar in iOS programming. UI objects have thread affinity. Sometimes accessing UI objects from a background thread will not cause an error, but relying on luck is never a good plan. The iOS threading APIs allow the same classes to be used to execute code on background threads and the main thread. For example, instead of using ThreadPool and Dispatcher, as described above, in iOS you can use the **performSelectorInBackground:withObject:** and **performSelectorOnMainThread:withObject:waitUntilDone:** methods, both declared by NSObject, as seen in **Figure 20**.

```
- (IBAction)handleButton:(id)sender {
    [self performSelectorInBackground:@selector(doWork)
                           withObject:nil];
}

- (void)doWork {
    NSAssert([NSThread isMainThread] == NO, nil);

    // Simulate a long task by sleeping for five seconds.
    sleep(5);

    // Perform the UI updating logic on the main thread.
    [self performSelectorOnMainThread:@selector(showResult:)
                           withObject:@"The answer is 42"
                        waitUntilDone:NO];
}

- (void)showResult:(NSString *)result {
    NSAssert([NSThread isMainThread] == YES, nil);
    self.resultLabel.text = result;
}
```

Figure 20 - Performing selectors on different threads

Operation Queues are another threading API in iOS, with many more features than the simple NSObject methods in the previous example. This is the threading model in iOS most similar to .NET's ThreadPool. An operation queue represents a set of tasks that run on one or more threads. The main thread has a dedicated NSOperationQueue, which runs NSOperation objects on that thread. **Figure 21** shows how to work with operation queues.

```
NSOperationQueue *opQueue =
  [[[NSOperationQueue alloc] init] autorelease];

[opQueue addOperationWithBlock:^{
    NSAssert([NSThread isMainThread] == NO, nil);

    // Simulate a long task by sleeping for five seconds.
    sleep(5);

    // Marshal back to the main thread in order to update
    // the UILabel's text, because Views are not thread-safe.
    [[NSOperationQueue mainQueue] addOperationWithBlock:^{
        NSAssert([NSThread isMainThread] == YES, nil);
        self.resultLabel.text = @"The answer is 42";
    }];
}];
```

Figure 21 - Using operation queues to marshal between threads

The most powerful threading model is *Grand Central Dispatch* (GCD). This is the C API which underlies Operation Queues. GCD offers the widest range of threading capabilities; such as concurrent and serial queues, executing code after a specified time interval, dispatch semaphores, treating a set of asynchronous tasks as a group, and much more. All of this sits on a foundation of algorithms that optimize throughput based on hardware capabilities. The code example in **Figure 22** shows a simple use of GCD.

```
// Dispatch to a worker thread to perform a big task.
dispatch_queue_t backgroundQueue =
  dispatch_get_global_queue(DISPATCH_QUEUE_PRIORITY_DEFAULT, 0);

dispatch_async(backgroundQueue, ^{
    NSAssert([NSThread isMainThread] == NO, nil);

    // Simulate a long task by sleeping for five seconds.
    sleep(5);

    // Dispatch back to the main thread in order to update
    // the UILabel's text, because Views are not thread-safe.
    dispatch_queue_t mainQueue = dispatch_get_main_queue();
    dispatch_async(mainQueue, ^{
        NSAssert([NSThread isMainThread] == YES, nil);
        self.resultLabel.text = @"The answer is 42";
    });
});
```

Figure 22 - Threading with Grand Central Dispatch

Guidance on which threading API to use varies. Some suggest using the most high-level API that satisfies your needs, which normally means using Operation Queues. Others suggest always using the same API throughout an app, for the sake of having a consistent code base, which might mean using GCD if one part of an app requires it. I see merit in both lines of reasoning, but generally prefer using the high-level API of Operation Queues, unless I need the power of GCD. Using a simpler API means writing less code, which means fewer chances to make a mistake.

Threading is a huge, complicated, and important topic. While looking for information about threading, keep in mind that in the iOS world it is sometimes referred to as *multitasking*. Apple has published two programming guides that are required reading for iOS developers: Threading Programming Guide and Concurrency Programming Guide, both of which are available on the Web. Another good source of information about threading, amongst many other topics, is the book Beginning iOS 5 Development - Exploring the iOS SDK by Dave Mark, Jack Nutting, and Jeff LaMarche.

Are ViewModels relevant?

Developers working with WPF/SL often use a design pattern called Model-View-ViewModel (MVVM) to structure their applications. MVVM is a specialization of the Presentation Model pattern espoused by Martin Fowler. It takes advantage of WPF/SL-specific features, such as data binding, to reduce the amount of coupling and coding needed to keep the UI up-to-date. The ViewModel component of that pattern is similar to a Controller in MVC, only it does not usually have a direct reference to a View. Instead of directly informing a View how to update itself in response to data modifications, it uses property change notifications to alert Binding objects, which then update the View.

Does it make sense to use MVVM in an iOS project? Not really. There is no iOS equivalent to .NET data bindings, and without it MVVM does not really work as a presentation pattern. Using Key-Value Coding and Key-Value Observing, reviewed in Chapter 6, might seem like an alternative to data binding but the amount of code involved with setting that up and tearing it down is prohibitive.

I do, however, find that the more generic Presentation Model pattern can be useful in iOS programming. A complicated View might include separate areas that must all be synchronized with View-specific data, such as the currently selected item(s) in a list. It can be helpful to have another object that manages UI state changes and triggers domain logic processing, removing that kind of logic from the Controller.

It is important to keep in mind that iOS programming is very different from .NET programming. Just because a design pattern works well on one platform does not mean it should be used on another. If you are a fan of MVVM, try to keep it out of your mind while learning UIKit and how it leverages MVC. When in Rome...

Summary

Making a great impression on your users means having a great user interface that looks and feels like an iOS app. The UIKit framework equips an iOS developer with the tools needed to create attractive, responsive, touch-friendly user interfaces. It is built on top of several low-level frameworks, such as Core Graphics and Core Animation, that can be used directly, if necessary. Since all iOS apps must have a user interface, learning these APIs is a necessity (especially UIKit).

This chapter has been another whirlwind tour of a very large and important topic. It has shown some ways in which UIKit is quite similar to WPF and Silverlight, and other ways in which they differ significantly. There is no substitute for experience, so I highly suggest experimenting with the UIKit controls in Xcode to see how they can be configured and used. Also, be sure to read Apple's <u>iOS Human Interface Guidelines</u> (the "HIG") to better understand their philosophy about UI design and user experience. Understanding their philosophy helps explain certain aspects of UIKit's API.

Chapter 8: Building UIs with Interface Builder

While understanding the design principles and programmatic interface of UIKit is essential to being a competent iOS developer, it is equally important to have the know-how needed to make use of it. This chapter shifts focus from a conceptual overview of UIKit to a more practical guide to the tool in which user interfaces are created: Interface Builder (IB).

For many years IB was a separate program, loosely integrated with Xcode. Starting in Xcode 4 the two merged, with IB now seamlessly incorporated into the IDE. For a .NET developer familiar with Expression Blend, this can be thought of as Blend being made part of Visual Studio.

IB is your friend

Some iOS developers use IB, others don't. There are certainly some situations in which IB should not be used, which I mention later, but many of the reasons stated for not using it are ill-conceived. These reasons tend to fall into one of the following three categories.

1. Loading Views from designer-generated files is too slow.

2. IB cannot be trusted and might corrupt View files.

3. "Real" developers don't need a drag-and-drop designer.

I disagree with each of these reasons, as explained below.

Loading a View from a designer-generated file (called a *NIB*) is fast. Apple optimized NIB loading to the point where speed is a non-issue. I work on large, complex enterprise iOS applications that rely extensively on Views created in IB. Never once have I seen a performance problem in any way related to the speed at which Views are loaded from NIBs. I doubt that many Views can be constructed in code noticeably faster than being loaded from a NIB file. Perhaps there are some edge cases where building UIs in carefully optimized code is necessary to squeeze additional speed out of the system, but in those extreme conditions it is probably more appropriate to draw the UI directly in code rather than creating a hierarchy of View objects.

I suspect that people who don't trust IB have been burned in the past by low-quality UI design tools. While no tool is perfect, IB is excellent at what it does. After years of using IB on a regular basis to create complicated Views for both iPhone and iPad apps, I have never seen it corrupt a View. IB has been nothing but reliable. Even if IB were to one day corrupt a file, I would just grab a previous version from the source control repository and carry on.

The last, and most childish, objection to using IB is that it isn't for "real" developers. This type of misguided machoism has no place in a professional software development environment. While I agree with the sentiment that a developer should be able to create UIs in code, without help from IB, it is foolish to refuse to use a tool that can significantly enhance your team's productivity. "Real" developers use tools that save their employer or client money. IB can reduce the time needed to develop and maintain Views, which translates into more time for implementing features that add value for the business.

Although IB can and should be used to create Views, there are situations in which it is advantageous, or necessary, to create them in code. If a View is highly customized, perhaps including nonstandard layouts and complex animated transitions, it might only be possible to create the View in code. Like any tool, IB can only be used to solve certain kinds of problems.

XAML is to BAML as XIB is to NIB

XML is easy for developers and computer programs to read and write. This makes it a suitable serialization format for UI files generated by a tool. The ability to edit a file and view it in a diff tool makes it easier to work with. Figuring out the differences between two XML documents is much easier than between two binary blobs.

.NET developers who use WPF spend a lot of time reading and writing XAML, a flavor of XML used to declare and configure UI objects. When a WPF project is compiled its XAML files are parsed and converted into a compact binary format known as BAML. At run-time BAML is extracted from an assembly and used to quickly create live objects. This is very similar to what happens with files created by IB.

XIB (pronounced *zib*) files are XML documents that adhere to a schema understood by IB and the XIB compiler. All changes made to a View at design-time are stored in its XIB file. Unlike working with XAML, an iOS developer almost never sees the XML in a XIB file. The only time the XML in a XIB might be seen is when looking at it in a source control repository, such as when comparing two versions of the same file. When an iOS project is compiled, the XIB files are parsed and converted into NIB files. A NIB file contains binary data optimized for quick conversion into live UI objects. Since a XIB is parsed at compile-time the performance impact associated with using XML as a serialization format is entirely mitigated. The terms NIB and XIB are often used interchangeably. In this book I make sure to use them properly, to avoid confusion.

I speculate that, unlike in WPF/SL development, iOS developers almost never need to look at a View's XML because IB does not try to support the wide range of features offered by Blend. For instance, IB does not enable designing animations, visual state transitions, or other complex aspects of a user interface. iOS developers must implement those features of a user interface in code. IB was designed to only support features that could be fully encapsulated.

Views are created on the canvas

When a XIB file is opened in Xcode, typically by clicking on it in Project navigator, it is rendered on a design surface known as a *canvas*. A canvas is shown in the same area of Xcode where code files are viewed and edited. The background of a canvas looks like graph paper, but that is merely decorative. There is no support for aligning UI objects with the lines of the graph paper, nor is there any need for such a feature. It is possible, however, to drag a View around on the canvas by clicking on the translucent blue border surrounding the root UIView. **Figure 1** shows a View on a canvas.

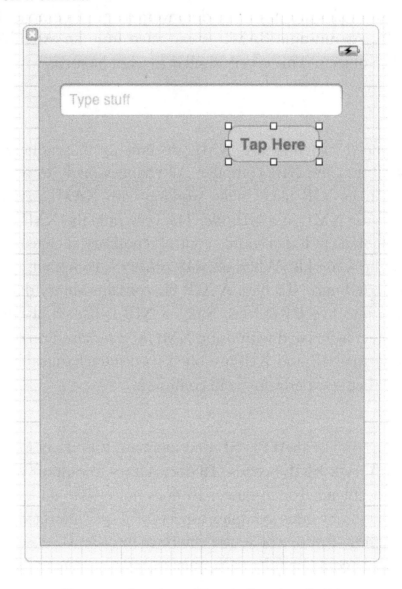

Figure 1 - Creating a View in Interface Builder

Document outline in the dock

On the left side of the canvas is a thin vertical strip called the *dock*. This part of the IB editor area displays placeholder objects and top-level objects in a XIB file. A *placeholder object* represents an object that exists at run-time, but is unavailable at design-time. The next two sections of this chapter review the File's Owner and First Responder placeholder objects. A XIB can contain multiple *top-level objects* but by default has only one: the UIView being designed. It is possible to add any type of top-level object to a XIB and reference it from code, which is a feature I have never found particularly useful.

By default the dock shows unlabeled icons that represent each placeholder and top-level object. A far more useful and intuitive way to view items in the dock is to show the *document outline*. The outline displays helpful labels next to each object in the dock and, what is more important, provides an interactive view of the entire UI hierarchy. The document outline can be opened by clicking the arrow button on the bottom of the dock, or via the *Show Document Outline* item in the *Editor* menu. The lefthand side of **Figure 2** shows the dock when only displaying icons. The center part of that image demonstrates how to show the document outline, a screenshot of which is on the righthand side.

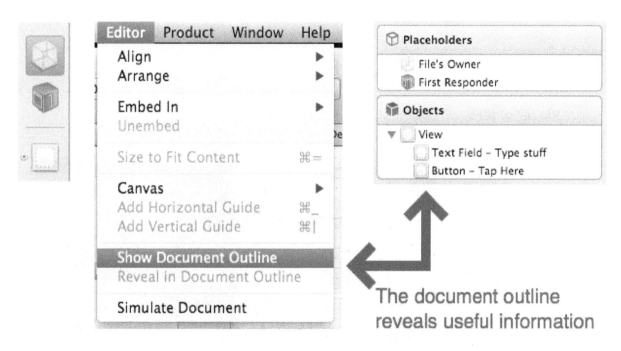

Figure 2 - Showing the document outline

The Objects hierarchy shown in the document outline is very useful. Clicking an item in the hierarchy causes the corresponding UI object on the canvas to be selected. Right-clicking on an item in the hierarchy causes a popup to appear, showing information about connections between the UI object and a Controller object, which is reviewed later in this chapter. Also, items can be dragged and dropped to change where in the hierarchy they appear, which is useful for affecting the Z-order of UI objects (i.e. which Views appear "behind" or "in front of" other Views).

The File's Owner placeholder

The most commonly used placeholder object in IB is called the *File's Owner*. This is a vague name for a very specific thing. The "owner" of a View is the Controller object that manages it. When a View is loaded from a NIB it is given a Controller object that links its UI objects into the rest of the app. The File's Owner icon shown in the IB dock represents that object. Since the class of the File's Owner is known at design-time it is possible to connect Views to actions and outlets of the owning Controller within IB. Working with actions and outlets is reviewed in detail later. **Figure 3** shows the popup tool displayed after right-clicking on the File's Owner item in the dock.

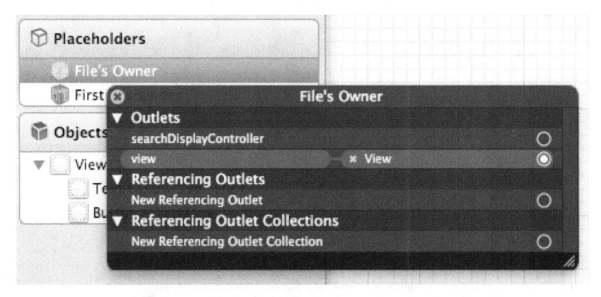

Figure 3 - Inspecting the Controller that owns a View

The **view** outlet of that Controller is connected to a View object on the canvas, as depicted by the short connector line between the left and right sides and the filled-in bubble on the righthand edge. That connection indicates the Controller's **view** property will automatically be assigned a pointer to the View loaded from that NIB file at run-time. It is also possible to load a View from a NIB file in code, specify its owner, and assign it to a Controller's **view** property, as seen in **Figure 4**.

```
NSArray *nib;

// Load top-level objects in the MyView NIB file.
// Pass self (a Controller) as the file's owner.
nib = [[NSBundle mainBundle] loadNibNamed:@"MyView"
                                    owner:self
                                  options:nil];

// This code assumes the NIB file only contains
// one top-level object; a UIView instance.
UIView *view = [nib lastObject];

// Just because a Controller is passed as the
// owner of a UIView in a NIB does not mean its
// 'view' property will point to that UIView.
NSAssert(self.view != view, nil);

// Show the new UIView for this Controller.
self.view = view;
```

Figure 4 - Specifying the File's Owner in code

I suspect that the term "file's owner" is based on the fact that it represents the object that retains, and thus owns, the top-level object(s) in a NIB file. Recall from Chapter 5, an object that retains another object is said to be one of its owners, in terms of memory management. Considering that the **view** property of UIViewController is declared to retain the object assigned to it, a Controller is an owner of a View. This is only conjecture on my part, but it seems like a reasonable explanation for the odd name that confuses so many iOS novices.

The First Responder placeholder

Beneath the File's Owner icon in the dock is another placeholder object named *First Responder*. This placeholder is less commonly used than File's Owner, and even more confusing for new iOS developers. This placeholder represents whatever object happens to be the first responder when a control sends an action message to an unspecified target. The target object for the action message is resolved at run-time to be the current first responder.

For example, this enables a UIButton, when tapped by the user, to send an action message to the current first responder, such as a UITextField. The action message might be the built-in **undo:**, which would allow the user to undo edits made to whichever UITextField on the screen currently has input focus (i.e. the first responder). This also allows the action message to travel up the responder chain to find an appropriate handler, if necessary. Refer to Chapter 7 for more information about the concepts of responders and the responder chain.

Figure 5 shows the popup displayed after right-clicking on the First Responder item in the dock. Each of these items represents an action message that the first responder can receive at run-time.

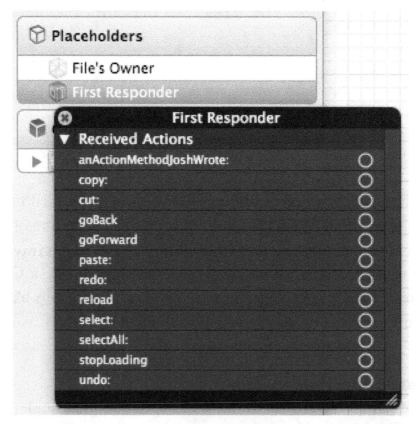

Figure 5 - Inspecting the First Responder placeholder

Object library

The Object library, seen in **Figure 6**, serves the same purpose as the Toolbox window in VS. Adding a control to a View being designed on a canvas is simply a matter of dragging it from the Object library and dropping it onto the View. It is found on the bottom-right corner of the Xcode workspace window. The search box at the bottom of the Object library can be used to filter the list, making it easy to quickly find a certain control.

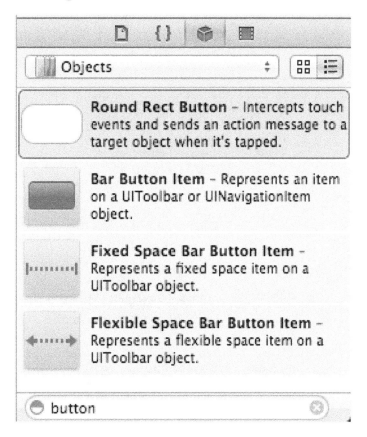

Figure 6 - Searching for a control in the Object library

Attribute inspector

Attribute inspector is used to graphically configure a UI object, similar to the Properties window in VS. Like all inspectors in Xcode, Attribute inspector appears on the righthand side of the workspace window. It displays groups of editable attributes for the UI object currently selected in a canvas. As seen in **Figure 7**, the groups are sorted by their depth level in the selected UI object's inheritance hierarchy. Attributes specific to the selected UI object appear in the top group, and attributes shared by all UIView objects are in the bottom group.

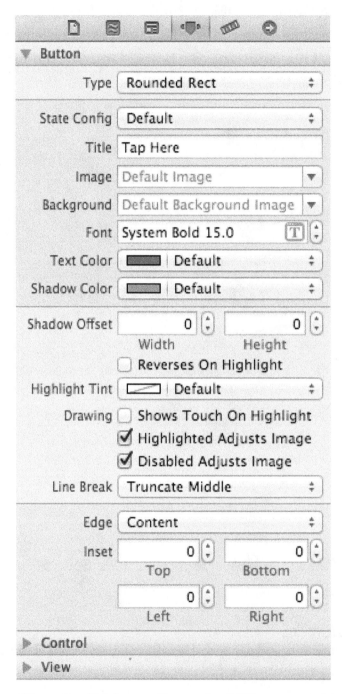

Figure 7 - Editing attributes of a UIButton control

Size inspector

Adjusting the size and position of a UI object on a canvas can be done with drag-and-drop, but sometimes more precision is needed. That's what Size inspector is for. It allows for detailed editing of a UI object's frame, which defines its position and size in the superview's coordinate space.

Size inspector is also where the **autoresizingMask** property on a UI object can be graphically edited. The area labeled "Autosizing" in **Figure 8** provides an interactive editor for adjusting a UI object's autoresizing behavior. Next to the editor is an animated example of what effect the selected value(s) will have on the object. This concept was demonstrated in code in the 'Layout panels vs. Autoresizing' section of Chapter 7.

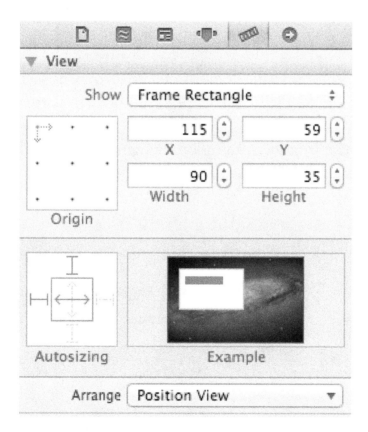

Figure 8 - Editing a UI object's frame and autoresizing mask

The "Autosizing" editor contains four *struts* and two *springs*. Struts look like I-beams that surround a square, which represents the currently selected UI object.

When a strut is enabled it turns red. A red strut indicates that the UI object has a fixed margin on that side of its superview (i.e. the UIView in which it is a subview). In other words, a red strut means the UI object is docked to that side. Clicking on a strut toggles it on and off.

Similarly, clicking on either of the two springs inside the box toggles them on and off. A red enabled spring means that the UI object will resize in the dimension represented by the spring. For example, enabling the vertical spring causes the UI object's height to automatically accommodate changes made to its superview's height.

Identity inspector

The type of objects added to a View in IB can be changed by using Identity inspector. This inspector contains several groups of editable fields, but most of them are very obscure and are not reviewed in this book. The most commonly used field in Identity inspector is in the "Custom Class" group, as seen in **Figure 9**. The "Class" field determines which class will be instantiated at run-time to create the currently selected UI object. As the following example shows, using a custom control subclass in IB is simply a matter of changing the "Class" field to the custom class name. This example assumes that a UIButton is the currently selected object on a canvas.

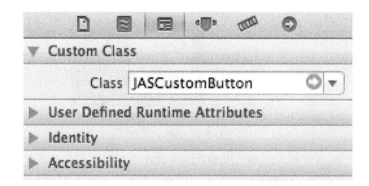

Figure 9 - Using a custom UIButton subclass

Connections inspector

Outlets and actions were introduced in Chapter 7. To summarize, an *outlet* is a property or ivar on a Controller that is assigned a UI object at run-time, enabling the Controller to interact with parts of a View but avoid being tightly coupled to it. An *action* is like an event on a .NET UI control because it causes a Controller method to execute in response to user interaction. Connections inspector in the Utilities area in Xcode displays an editable list of actions and outlets for the currently selected UI object. **Figure 10** shows Connections inspector when a UIButton object is selected.

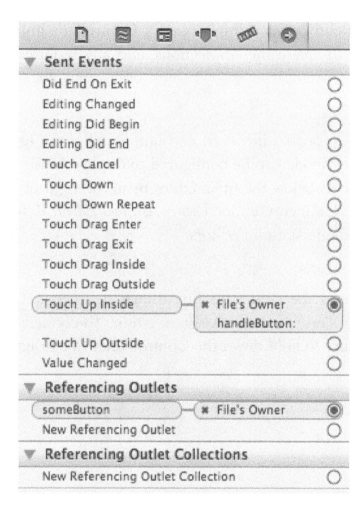

Figure 10 - Inspecting a UIButton's actions and referencing outlets

At the bottom of Connections inspector is a group titled 'Referencing Outlet Collections.' An *outlet collection* is an IB feature that makes it possible to have a collection of UI objects treated as a single outlet of a Controller. This allows a Controller to conveniently update a set of related controls, such as setting a group of UISwitch controls to the 'off' position, by iterating over each control in the collection.

Connecting to a new action method

There is more than one way to connect a UI object to an action method in a Controller. The most tedious way is to write a method in a Controller class to handle an action and then use IB to connect a UI object to that method. In Xcode 4 a streamlined workflow was introduced that makes it very easy to quickly accomplish this repetitive task. Simply open a Controller's implementation file in an Assistant editor to create the connections, and any required code, using drag-and-drop.

The easiest way to open a file in an Assistant editor is to Option+Click that file in Project navigator. Xcode can be configured to display Assistant editors in one of several layouts, such as below the main editor or to the right of it. This option can be selected via Xcode's menu, under *View | Assistant Editor*. Refer to Chapter 3 for more information about Assistant editors.

Figure 11 shows the connector line drawn between a UI object in an IB canvas and a Controller class in an Assistant editor. To connect a UI object in this manner it is necessary to hold down the Control key while dragging from IB to the Assistant editor.

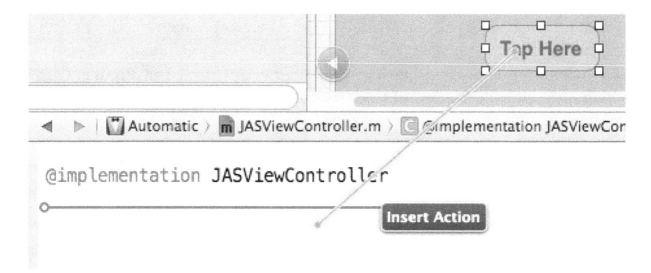

Figure 11 - Ctrl+Dragging from a control in IB to an Assistant editor

Note that in **Figure 11** the connection is being dragged into the Controller's implementation file. Many IB tutorials promote connecting to a Controller's header file, but I think that's bad advice. Action methods are not normally intended to be part of a class's public-facing API. Therefore, it does not make sense to drag the connection into a Controller's header file, which will create a method declaration in the `@interface` of the class.

When the mouse cursor is over an Assistant editor and the mouse button is released, a popup window, seen in **Figure 12**, is displayed.

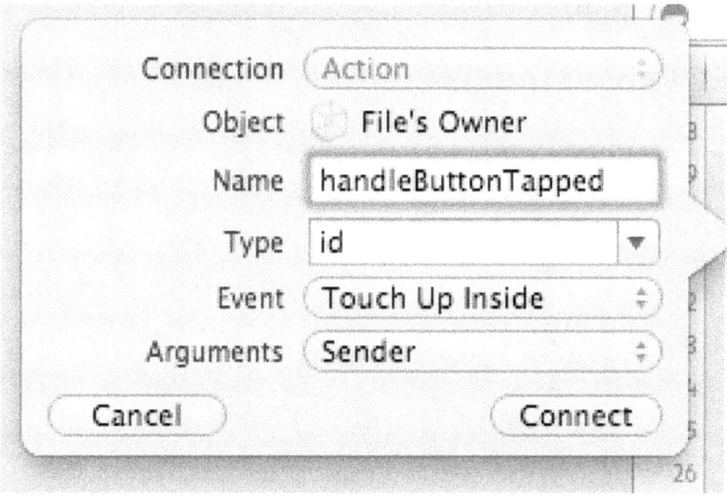

Figure 12 - Configuring a new action method before connecting to it

After typing in the action method's name, and optionally modifying other information about it, press the Enter key or click the Connect button. This causes a new method to be inserted into the Controller class. As seen in **Figure 13**, an action method that is connected to a UI object in a XIB file has a filled-in dot on the left side of the code editor. An empty dot, on the other hand, signifies that Xcode is not aware of any connection made with that action method. This provides a convenient means of visually verifying that all action methods in a Controller class are wired up as expected.

```
19    @implementation JASViewController
20
21  - (IBAction)handleButtonTapped:(id)sender {
22    }
```

Figure 13 - An action method created by IB

To summarize, the steps involved with connecting a UI object in a XIB to a new action method in a Controller class are as follows:

1. Click on a XIB file in Project navigator to open it on an IB canvas

2. Option+Click on a Controller class's implementation file in Project navigator to open it in an Assistant editor

3. Control+Drag from a UI object on the canvas to the `@implementation` section of code in the Assistant editor

4. Release the mouse button when the connector line is at the desired insertion point in the code file

5. Type the name of a new action method into the popup window, and adjust other settings about the action method as necessary

6. Press Enter or click the Connect button to generate the action method and establish a connection with the UI object

Connecting to an existing action method

Developing a screen in an app is sometimes a nonlinear process. For example, an action method is defined but later the UI objects connected to it are replaced and the new objects must be connected to the existing action method. Xcode accommodates the messy reality of life by making it easy to connect UI objects to action methods that already exist.

An easy way to reestablish a connection with an action method on a View's owning Controller is by right-clicking on the View to summon a list of its sent events and referencing outlets. As seen in **Figure 14**, a connection can be made by dragging from a dot on the righthand side of the popup window to the File's Owner placeholder object in the dock.

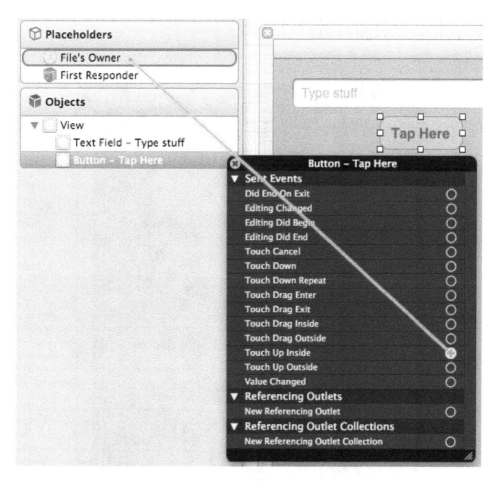

Figure 14 - Dragging from a control event to the File's Owner

After releasing the mouse button, a list of available action methods defined by the Controller is displayed. This is seen in **Figure 15**, which displays the sole action method defined by that Controller.

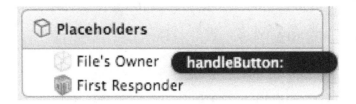

Figure 15 - Connecting to a preexisting action method

Click on the action method name shown in the popup list to establish a connection between the UI object and that method. Once the connection is made, the popup window summoned for the UI object on the canvas is updated to reflect the change, as seen in **Figure 16**.

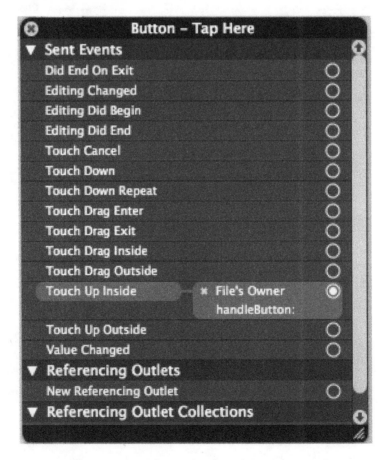

Figure 16 - The action has been connected

Connecting outlets to a Controller

The workflow for creating and connecting a UI object to an outlet on a Controller is very similar to the process reviewed earlier for actions. Hold down the Control key while dragging from a UI object to a Controller's implementation file to create the connector line seen in **Figure 17**.

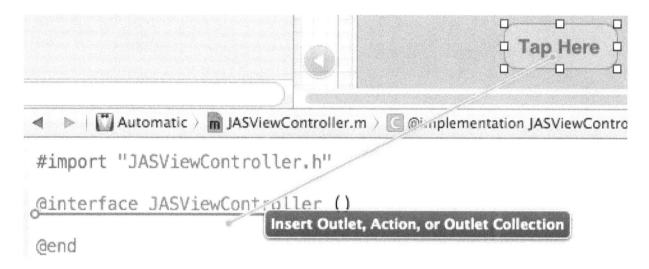

Figure 17 - Ctrl+Dragging from a control in IB to an Assistant editor

After releasing the mouse button a popup window appears, allowing the outlet's name to be specified, as seen in **Figure 18**.

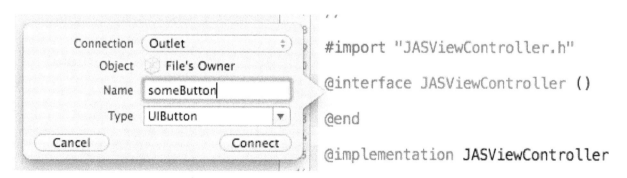

Figure 18 - Configuring a new outlet before connecting to it

After pressing the Enter key, or clicking the Connect button, Xcode generates code to implement the outlet and updates the XIB to connect it to the selected UI object. The example in **Figure 19** shows the code generated for an outlet property declared in the Controller's class extension.

```
11   @interface JASViewController ()
12   @property (retain, nonatomic) IBOutlet UIButton *someButton;
13
14   @end
15
16   @implementation JASViewController
17   @synthesize someButton;
18
19   - (void)viewDidUnload {
20       [self setSomeButton:nil];
21       [super viewDidUnload];
22   }
23
24   - (void)dealloc {
25       [someButton release];
26       [super dealloc];
27   }
```

Figure 19 - The code generated for an outlet property

The code example in **Figure 19** is in a project that does not use ARC. As discussed in Chapter 7, when the ARC compiler feature is enabled it is preferable to create outlets as ivars defined in the class's @implementation section.

In **dealloc** the 'someButton' ivar is released, but in **viewDidUnload** the property's mutator method is used instead. Setting a retained property to nil is usually the correct way to release the object to which it points, because it ensures the property no longer points at what might be a dead object's old memory address. However, properties should not be set in an object's **dealloc** method. This avoids problems that can arise if the object is being observed with Key-Value Observing. If an observer sends the dying object a message in response to a property change notification, the object might be unable to properly respond because some of its ivars have already been released by the partially completed **dealloc** method.

Storyboards

One of the most publicized new features for developers in iOS 5 is *storyboards*. iOS storyboards are nothing like storyboards in WPF and Silverlight, even though both are involved with coordinating animations. In iOS a storyboard is a file that can be viewed and edited in Interface Builder. It contains multiple Views, called *scenes*, that are connected to each other by animated transitions, referred to as *segues*. The terminology of storyboard, scene, and segue suggests that Apple thinks of using this feature as being analogous to planning a movie or television show. I suppose that's what happens when a tech company is headquartered in the same state as Hollywood!

As seen in **Figure 20**, a storyboard is shown on the IB canvas, like an individual XIB file. Each scene in a storyboard can be connected to other scenes via segues. A segue is rendered as a line between two scenes. It represents a navigation path between them.

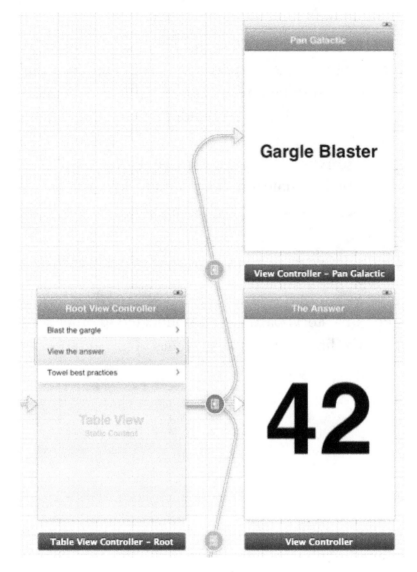

Figure 20 - Scenes connected by segues in a storyboard

The point of using storyboards is that you can easily view all screens in an app and how they are connected to each other. This is great for quickly throwing together a functioning prototype or proof-of-concept app. For small apps, using storyboards can make developing the UI layer easier.

Unfortunately, I have serious doubts about the viability of storyboards in medium or large sized apps worked on by more than one developer at a time. A storyboard file is essentially a collection of XIBs with metadata about relationships between them. Working with individual XIB files often creates source control merge conflicts that should generally not be resolved by hand. Storyboards amplify this problem to the point where only one developer on a team can edit the user interface at a time. In other words, storyboards are a productivity bottleneck for development teams.

One way to mitigate this problem is to break an app's functional areas into separate storyboards, each containing only the screens needed for that module of the app. This is not a very good solution, however, because it defeats the purpose of using storyboards, which is to view an app's entire UI workflow in one place. Also, this is not a great solution because there can still be merge conflicts if two developers edit the same "sub-storyboard" at the same time.

When working alone on an iOS app, using a storyboard might be a big help. It has several great features worth learning about. However, when starting a new project with a development team, carefully consider if using storyboards will be more hindrance than help.

Summary

It is important for new iOS developers to first learn how to create a user interface in code, without the help of a tool. Once that skill has been acquired, however, it is much more efficient to use Interface Builder. A development team that leverages IB can quickly create user interfaces without writing much code. When it comes to code, less is more.

[Part III: Alien Technology]

Creating complex software requires more than just knowledge of a programming language, an IDE, and the common libraries. Most applications need to share data with other computers over the Internet, store and retrieve complex data quickly, and a host of other complex tasks. As the size and complexity of an application grows, so does the job of troubleshooting and fixing problems. This part of the book shows how these tasks can be accomplished with Apple's tools and APIs, along with some third-party code libraries.

Chapter 9: Calling Web Services

Most mobile apps are not deployed with all the data they will ever display to a user. They rely on other computers to provide them with interesting and relevant data for the user to view, hear, touch, and edit. Many apps provide the user with a means of creating data that must be transmitted from their iDevice and received by another computer for further processing. This client-server architecture is nothing new for most .NET application developers.

The .NET framework and tooling provide layer after layer of abstraction that make interacting with server data dead simple. That is not the case with iOS programming. Apple does not appear to have made this aspect of their development platform a high priority. For example, it was not until iOS 5 that the platform supported reading and writing JSON, a very popular lightweight data format used by Web services for mobile apps. Fortunately, there are some community projects that can help make life easier. This chapter shows how to work with Web services using APIs from Apple and community projects.

The basics of NSURLConnection

The .NET framework offers HttpWebRequest for working with data on the Web. In iOS there is NSURLConnection, which manages sending data to, and receiving it from, other computers. Information being sent to a server, such as the HTTP Method and Body, is put into an NSURLRequest or NSMutableURLRequest object. The code example in **Figure 1** shows these classes being used to download an image.

```
// This Web request fills an NSData object with the
// bytes of an image. The image data is later read
// into a UIImage and displayed in the UI. This is
// somewhat contrived because filling an NSData with
// remote data is possible by using the class method
// +dataWithContentsOfURL:options:error: of NSData.
NSURL *url = [NSURL URLWithString:SOME_IMAGE_URL];
NSURLRequest *req = [NSURLRequest requestWithURL:url];
[NSURLConnection
   sendAsynchronousRequest:req
                     queue:[NSOperationQueue mainQueue]
         completionHandler:handler];
```

Figure 1 - Downloading an image from the Web

The previous code example uses NSURLConnection to create an asynchronous Web request that downloads a photograph from the Web. The NSURLRequest object wraps an NSURL, which itself holds a string that points to an image file. When the request completes, and the image data has been downloaded (or not), the NSURLConnection needs a way to inform the caller. This is what the 'handler' variable is for. NSURLConnection invokes the completion handler by placing a task into the operation queue specified by the 'queue' argument. This example uses the 'mainQueue' queue, which is on the main thread. This means the completion handler will be invoked on the main thread, enabling it to safely update the user interface. The completion handler is defined in **Figure 2**.

```
// Create a block that is invoked when the Web request completes.
void(^handler)(NSURLResponse *, NSData *, NSError *);
handler = ^(NSURLResponse *resp, NSData *data, NSError *error) {
    if (error) {
        // If the Web request utterly failed, just report the error.
        [self processError:error.localizedDescription];
    }
    else {
        // Check if the Web request made it to the server but there
        // was a problem with a known error code, such as 404.
        // 200 is the HTTP status code for OK. Ignoring only 200
        // might be too broad of a filter for some apps that rely
        // on HTTP status codes to determine what action to take.
        NSInteger code = ((NSHTTPURLResponse *)resp).statusCode;
        if (200 != code) {
            NSString *message =
                [NSHTTPURLResponse localizedStringForStatusCode:code];
            [self processError:message];
        }
        // Convert the raw binary data into an image and display it.
        self.imageView.image = [UIImage imageWithData:data];
    }
};
```

Figure 2 - The completion handler of a Web request

Most of the code involved with processing the server's response checks for errors. If the Web request was unable to be processed, the 'error' argument will be non-nil. This might happen if the device's Internet connection suddenly dropped, or perhaps the server was engulfed in flames thanks to a disgruntled ex-employee.

If a request makes it to the server and back to the device, the 'error' argument will be nil and the 'data' argument will be non-nil. This doesn't mean everything went well, though. It is often necessary to check for an HTTP status code, such as the infamous 404 'not found' error. Not all status codes indicate that an error occurred, however, and not all apps need to care about responding to these codes. In any case, if an app needs to check the status code of an HTTP response it can do so by casting the response to an NSHTTPURLResponse and then checking its **statusCode** property. Oddly, Apple does not define HTTP status code constants for application developers to use.

The previous example demonstrated downloading raw bytes from the Web and converting them into a UIImage object displayed by a UIImageView. In practice, it can be easier to use the **dataWithContentsOfURL:options:error:** NSData class method. This method is a synchronous call, so it should be made on a background thread to avoid freezing the user interface. Also, it is not appropriate in situations where the request must be configured with metadata, such as HTTP headers.

Alternative Web request implementations

NSURLConnection does not offer a broad set of features. Before iOS 5 it did not even have a convenient method to make an asynchronous Web request. To make a non-blocking network call, application code had to provide the NSURLConnection with a delegate object that manually appended raw binary data as it was downloaded. This was tedious and a nuisance. Limitations in Foundation's networking API spurred the development of open-source projects to fill the gaps.

The most popular Web request implementation used to be ASIHTTPRequest. In September of 2011 the owner of that project, Ben Copsey, announced he was no longer supporting it. There are several alternatives, one of which is a project named AFNetworking. Here are just a few features of AFNetworking that make it so appealing.

• A convenient API for interacting with Web services including features such as authentication, query string parameter serialization, and multipart form requests

• Methods for transforming data into formats such as XML, JSON, and images

• Networking operations can be canceled, suspended, and resumed

• Support for handling authentication challenges

• Caching behavior can be controlled

• Uploads and downloads can be streamed

• Upload and download progress can be monitored

The AFNetworking project currently lives on GitHub and is released under the MIT license.

For applications with simple networking requirements it makes sense to use NSURLConnection. Now that it supports easy asynchronous requests there is no reason not to use it. If an application has, or is likely to have, demanding requirements for making Web requests then a more powerful tool should be used. AFNetworking is a solid choice and has a lot to offer. The remaining examples in this chapter use NSURLConnection.

Working with JSON

JavaScript Object Notation (JSON) is a lightweight data format commonly used to send data between a server and a Web page or mobile app. Prior to iOS 5 there was no support in the platform for reading and writing JSON documents. Several popular open-source projects filled the gap, such as SBJson and JSONKit. Now the Foundation framework includes the NSJSONSerialization class, which can turn an NSArray or NSDictionary into an NSString containing JSON, and vice versa. The JSON serializer can read and write a well-defined set of Objective-C objects. Here are the rules for what NSJSONSerialization can process.

- The top-level object must be an NSArray or NSDictionary collection

- Objects in the collection must be an NSString, NSNumber, NSNull, NSArray, or NSDictionary

- All dictionary keys must be NSStrings

- NSNumbers cannot have the value NaN or infinity

One of the features offered by most open-source JSON implementations, which is unavailable in NSJSONSerialization, is the ability to convert instances of custom classes to and from JSON objects. For example, SBJson will send the **proxyForJson** message to any object so that it can save its state to a dictionary, which is then added to the JSON document being created. When using NSJSONSerialization it is necessary to first convert all objects into collections of simple values and then serialize those collections, which is less convenient.

A Web request can send or receive JSON data. The following example shows how to process JSON data from Google's free Geocoding service. It demonstrates passing parameters in a query string, instead of in the request's HTTP Body. Refer to **Figure 3** to see how the Web request is constructed using classes from the Foundation framework.

```
// Build a request using a query string to
// specify the street address to geocode.
NSString *host, *address, *path;
host    = @"maps.googleapis.com";
address = @"30 Rockefeller Plaza, New York, NY";
path    = [NSString stringWithFormat:
   @"/maps/api/geocode/json?address=%@&sensor=false",
   address];
NSURL *url = [[NSURL alloc] initWithScheme:@"http"
                                      host:host
                                      path:path];

NSURLRequest *request = [NSURLRequest
   requestWithURL:url
      cachePolicy:NSURLRequestUseProtocolCachePolicy
 timeoutInterval:30]; // 30 second timeout
[url release];
```

Figure 3 - Creating a request that returns JSON data

This code example relies on NSURL to encode the query parameters, such as whitespace in the street address. Working with query strings is safer when using a third-party HTTP request library, such as AFNetworking, because NSURL is known to fail to encode the complete set of characters that should be encoded. Improperly encoded URLs cause service calls to fail, making this a serious issue for apps that rely on Web services accepting parameters via query strings.

The code in **Figure 4** uses the request object created in **Figure 3**. It makes an asynchronous request using NSURLConnection, as seen in the previous section. Unlike the previous example, where the completion handler block was defined separately, the **sendAsynchronousRequest:queue:completionHandler:** message is passed with a block defined inline.

```
[NSURLConnection
  sendAsynchronousRequest:request
                   queue:[NSOperationQueue mainQueue]
       completionHandler:^(NSURLResponse *response,
                           NSData        *data,
                           NSError       *error) {
    if (error) return;
    NSDictionary *json = [NSJSONSerialization
                            JSONObjectWithData:data
                                       options:0
                                         error:NULL];
    // Log the status value of the JSON result.
    NSString *status = [json objectForKey:@"status"];
    NSLog(@"Service call status: %@", status);
    // Use KVC to grab a sub-object from the JSON.
    NSDictionary *addressComponents =
      [json valueForKeyPath:@"results.address_components"];
    // Display the dictionary of JSON data in a UITextView.
    self.textView.text = [addressComponents description];
}];
```

Figure 4 - Working with a JSON response

The JSON data received from Google's Web service is converted into an NSDictionary by the NSJSONSerialization class. It contains several other dictionaries and data objects, mirroring the schema of the JSON document. Working with JSON data is simply a matter of using standard Foundation classes.

Working with XML

The Foundation framework has supported reading eXtensible Markup Language (XML) data for a long time, but unfortunately Apple's API is tedious and does not support creating or modifying XML documents. The NSXMLParser class uses the SAX parsing model, as opposed to creating a DOM that can be queried. The SAX parsing model notifies a delegate object about XML nodes encountered while parsing the document. Your delegate object must keep track of which elements have been encountered, and, ideally, extract all the data it needs in one pass of the document.

Apps that need to work with a lot of XML data should almost definitely use a third-party library that provides a document-based API. There are several open-source XML libraries available, such as KissXML and GDataXML. I have used the excellent KissXML library, which is released under the MIT license. The code example in **Figure 5** shows how to parse the result of the Geocoding Web service seen in the previous section, only this time the app is consuming a version of the service that returns XML data, instead of JSON.

```
[NSURLConnection
  sendAsynchronousRequest:request
                    queue:[NSOperationQueue mainQueue]
        completionHandler:^(NSURLResponse *response,
                            NSData        *data,
                            NSError       *error) {
    if (error) return;
    // Use the KissXML API to have an XML document.
    NSError *err = nil;
    DDXMLDocument *doc = [[[DDXMLDocument alloc]
                              initWithData:data
                                   options:0
                                     error:&err] autorelease];
    if (err) return;
    // Use XPath to select a group of XML elements.
    NSArray *nodes = [doc.rootElement
                nodesForXPath:@"result/address_component"
                        error:&err];
    if (err) return;
    // Display formatted XML text in a UITextView.
    NSMutableString *text = [NSMutableString string];
    for (DDXMLElement *elem in nodes)
        [text appendFormat:@"%@\n", [elem prettyXMLString]];
    self.textView.text = text;
}];
```

Figure 5 - Using KissXML to query an XML document

Passing data in the HTTP Body

Many Web services expect the request's HTTP Body to contain data, such as a JSON or XML document. **Figure 6** shows the KissXML API being used to create an XML document that is added to an NSMutableRequest object.

```objc
// Create a Web request.
NSString *endpoint = [self lookUpServiceEndpoint];
NSURL *url = [NSURL URLWithString:endpoint];
NSMutableURLRequest *request =
  [NSMutableURLRequest requestWithURL:url];
[request setHTTPMethod:@"POST"];

// Put a SOAP message in the request's Body.
DDXMLDocument *soapDoc = [self makeSOAPDocument];
NSString *soap = [soapDoc XMLString];
NSData *body =
  [soap dataUsingEncoding:NSUTF8StringEncoding];
[request setHTTPBody:body];

// Add HTTP headers to the request.
NSString *contentLength =
  [NSString stringWithFormat:@"%u", [soap length]];
[request addValue:contentLength
forHTTPHeaderField:@"Content-Length"];
 [request addValue:@"text/xml; charset=utf-8"
forHTTPHeaderField:@"Content-Type"];
 [request addValue:@"SomeSOAPAction"
forHTTPHeaderField:@"SOAPAction"];
```

Figure 6 - Creating a request that posts SOAP data

Generating SOAP proxies with WSDL2ObjC

JSON is lightweight and easily parsed, making it a great format for sending data to and from a mobile device. Unfortunately, many companies are heavily invested in SOAP-based Web service APIs. When working with SOAP services, consider using the *WSDL2ObjC* open-source OS X app to generate Objective-C code based on a WSDL document. This is similar to the "Add Service Reference" feature in

VS, which creates classes for consuming Web services by using a file that describes the service API.

Basing service URLs on a build configuration

Developing an app that communicates with Web services typically requires using different servers at various times. Professional development shops do not develop and test new services and apps in a live production environment, for obvious reasons. Deploying Web services into Production is a phased process; starting on a Development server while many changes are expected to occur, next graduating to a Staging server for integration and user acceptance testing, followed by deployment to Production. Each server exists at a different URL, which means that applications must have a means of deciding which URL to use when invoking Web services. The part of a Web service URL that changes with respect to the server on which it exists is known as the *base URL*.

A common way for a .NET program to choose a base URL is to use an app config file. A config file is an XML document that adheres to a certain schema and can be accessed through a convenience API. In iOS this can be implemented by using a PLIST file, which stands for *property list*. A PLIST file is an XML document whose values can be accessed through an NSDictionary object. Reading from a PLIST was demonstrated in the 'Assembly vs. NSBundle' section of Chapter 6. This chapter shows another example of reading from a PLIST, to determine the base URL for invoking a Web service.

The following walkthrough explains how to construct the URL needed to invoke a Web service. Unlike previous examples of building request objects in this chapter, the base URL can point to one of three servers: Development, Staging, or Production. The determination of which server to use is controlled by the build configuration applied during compilation. Since a project has Debug and Release configurations by default, a third configuration must be added to accommodate all three deployment environments.

Click on the project item in Project navigator, which displays a properties page for the project. In the "Configurations" area on the right, click the add (+) button to duplicate the Debug configuration, as seen in **Figure 7**.

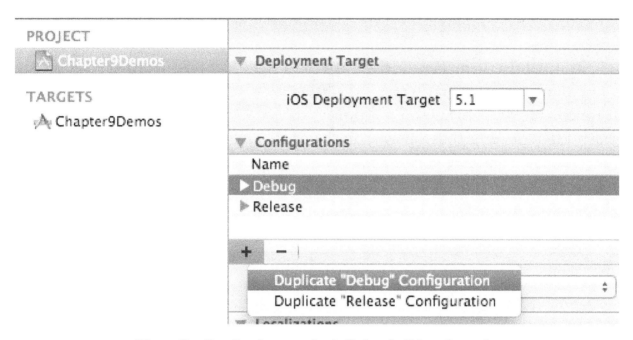

Figure 7 - Duplicating a project's Debug build configuration

Duplicating a build configuration allows a copy of it to be modified and renamed. In this scenario, only the name of the duplicate configuration will change. **Figure 8** shows the new configuration after it has been renamed to "Staging."

Configurations	
Name	Based on Configuration File
▶ Debug	No Configurations Set
▶ Staging	No Configurations Set
▶ Release	No Configurations Set
+ −	

Figure 8 - The duplicate configuration is named "Staging"

Next the app's PLIST file must be edited so that it can be used to discover two things at run-time:

- The active build configuration

- The host name of the server for the active build configuration

Xcode project templates include a PLIST file in the Supporting Files group. The naming convention used for that file is *ProjectName*-Info.plist, such as GargleBlaster9000-Info.plist for a project named GargleBlaster9000. Clicking on that PLIST file in Xcode opens it in the PLIST editor. **Figure 9** shows the two rows I added, named "Configuration" and "Hosts."

Key	Type	Value
Localization native development region	String	en
Bundle display name	String	${PRODUCT_NAME}
Executable file	String	${EXECUTABLE_NAME}
Bundle identifier	String	iJoshSmith.${PRODUCT
InfoDictionary version	String	6.0
Bundle name	String	${PRODUCT_NAME}
Bundle OS Type code	String	APPL
Bundle versions string, short	String	1.0
Bundle creator OS Type code	String	????
Bundle version	String	1.0
Application requires iPhone environmer	Boolean	YES
▶ Required device capabilities	Array	(1 item)
▶ Supported interface orientations	Array	(3 items)
Configuration	String	${CONFIGURATION}
▼ Hosts	Diction...	(3 items)
Debug	String	dev.acme.com
Staging	String	staging.acme.com
Release	String	production.acme.com

Figure 9 - Storing configuration and host name info in a PLIST

The "Configuration" entry has a string value, which is resolved during the build process thanks to the ${CONFIGURATION} build setting. In this example, the setting will resolve to either Debug, Staging, or Release; depending on the active build configuration. The "Hosts" entry references a dictionary that maps a build configuration name to a host name. The keys and values in that PLIST are easily accessed via the **infoDictionary** method of the NSBundle class, as seen in **Figure 10**.

```
- (NSURL *)urlForService:(NSString *)servicePath {
    // Since the host will not change during one run of the
    // app, cache it in a string with static storage.
    static NSString *host = nil;
    if (!host) {
        // Look up a host name based on the build configuration.
        NSDictionary *info =
          [[NSBundle mainBundle] infoDictionary];
        NSString *config, *keyPath;
        config  = [info objectForKey:@"Configuration"];
        keyPath = [NSString stringWithFormat:@"Hosts.%@", config];
        host    = [[info valueForKeyPath:keyPath] copy];
    }
    // Construct a URL using the resolved host name.
    NSURL *url = [[NSURL alloc] initWithScheme:@"https"
                                          host:host
                                          path:servicePath];
    return [url autorelease];
}
```

Figure 10 - Resolving the host name using a PLIST

Note that in **Figure 10** the keys "Configuration" and "Hosts" are used to look up values from the info dictionary. These are the same keys that were added to the PLIST file in **Figure 9**. Another point of interest in that example is the 'keyPath' variable, whose value can either be "Hosts.Debug", "Hosts.Staging", or "Hosts.Release". It is used to retrieve the host name for the active build configuration. The **valueForKeyPath:** message, part of the Key-Value Coding API, uses 'keyPath' to look up a value from the nested Hosts dictionary. Once the host has been retrieved, it is referenced by a string named 'host' declared with the `static` storage specifier. This variable is not destroyed when the **urlForService:** method completes and is only accessible from within that method.

Figure 11 shows how to use the method defined previously to create a Web request object pointing to the correct server.

```
NSURL *url = [self urlForService:@"/GetFooByID"];

NSURLRequest *request =
  [NSURLRequest requestWithURL:url];

[NSURLConnection
  sendAsynchronousRequest:request
                    queue:[NSOperationQueue mainQueue]
        completionHandler:^(NSURLResponse *response,
                            NSData        *data,
                            NSError       *error) {
    // TODO: Process the response...
}];
```

Figure 11 - Sending a request to the correct server

The last piece of the puzzle is selecting which build configuration to use. This can be done by editing the active scheme. The scheme editor is available via Xcode's menu under *Product | Edit Scheme...* or by pressing Command+Option+R. **Figure 12** shows the "Staging" configuration selected for the Run action.

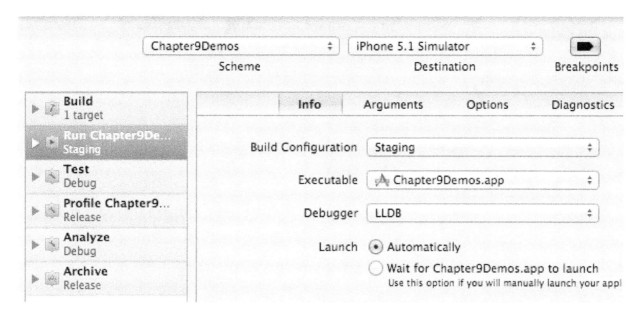

Figure 12 - Selecting a build configuration

Some applications have more complicated configuration requirements than using one option for each deployment environment. For example, it might be necessary to run a Release build of the app against a Staging server, which is not accounted for in this demonstration. The Xcode build system is flexible enough to handle most scenarios. For more information about the build system refer to Chapter 3.

Checking for an Internet connection with Reachability

Like any computer, a mobile device can lose Internet connectivity. Checking for an Internet connection on an iOS device can be done using a helper class published by Apple in a sample project titled *Reachability*. It contains a class named Reachability that should be added to your project. As of this writing, Apple has not updated the code to support ARC. It is possible, however, to mark a file added to an ARC project as being non-ARC-compliant. Search the Web for "-fno-objc-arc" (including the quotes) to learn how that can be done in Xcode. Alternatively, consider using the open-source Reachability implementation that was modified to support ARC, by Tony Million on GitHub.

Building a project after the Reachability class has been added will generate a set of linker errors. These cryptic errors, seen in **Figure 13**, are not indicative of the underlying problem.

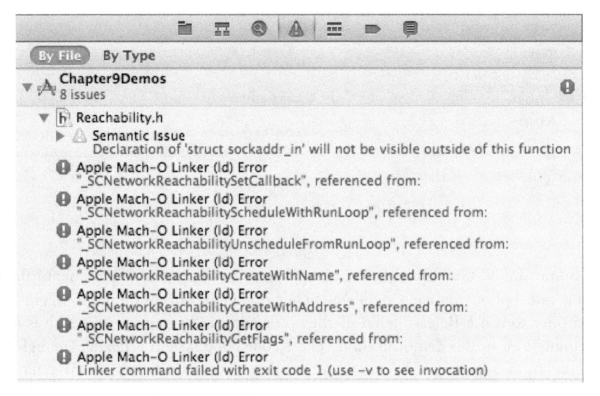

Figure 13 - Linker errors caused by adding the Reachability class

To make those errors go away simply link your project to the *SystemConfiguration* framework. Adding a framework is similar to adding an assembly reference in VS. This is accomplished in Xcode by following these steps:

1. Click on the project item in Project navigator to show a properties page for the project.

2. Select the target that must link to the SystemConfiguration framework.

3. View the "Linked Frameworks and Libraries" group, seen in **Figure 14**.

4. Click the add (+) button at the bottom of the group to open a list of available frameworks and libraries.

5. Type into the text field at the top of the list to filter the items, as seen in **Figure 15**.

6. Select the SystemConfiguration framework and click the *Add* button.

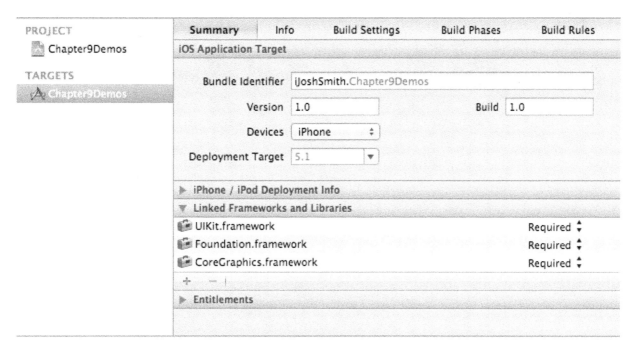

Figure 14 - Not yet linked to the SystemConfiguration framework

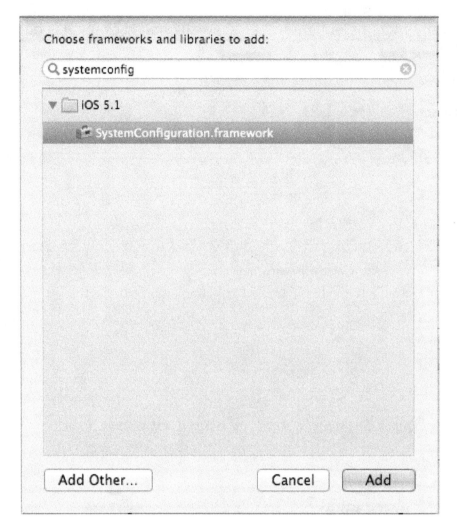

Figure 15 - Linking to SystemConfiguration.framework

Using the Reachability class is straightforward. **Figure 16** shows a C function that uses a Reachability object to detect if the device can reach one of Google's servers.

```
#import "Reachability.h"

BOOL JASIsInternetReachable()
{
    Reachability *r =
      [Reachability reachabilityWithHostName:@"google.com"];
    NetworkStatus status = [r currentReachabilityStatus];
    return status != NotReachable;
}
```

Figure 16 - A helper function that uses Reachability

This helper function can be used throughout an app to conditionally execute code that requires Internet connectivity, as seen in **Figure 17**.

```
if (JASIsInternetReachable())
{
     // Use the InterWebs...
}
```

Figure 17 - Checking if the Internet is reachable

Refer to the Reachability sample code from Apple for more advanced techniques, such as subscribing to device connectivity status change notifications.

Inspecting HTTP traffic with Charles

Troubleshooting Web service calls can be difficult and involve guesswork. In some situations it is helpful to see all the details about data being sent from and received by an iOS app. This is what the *Charles* tool is for. Charles runs on your Mac and acts as a proxy between an iDevice and the Internet. It records all HTTP and HTTPS traffic that flows between your app and Web servers, similar to the Fiddler application popular amongst .NET developers.

The screenshot of Charles in **Figure 18** shows information about a Web request made to Google's Geocoding service, examined previously in this chapter.

The service call was made from an iPad and recorded by Charles on a MacBook Pro.

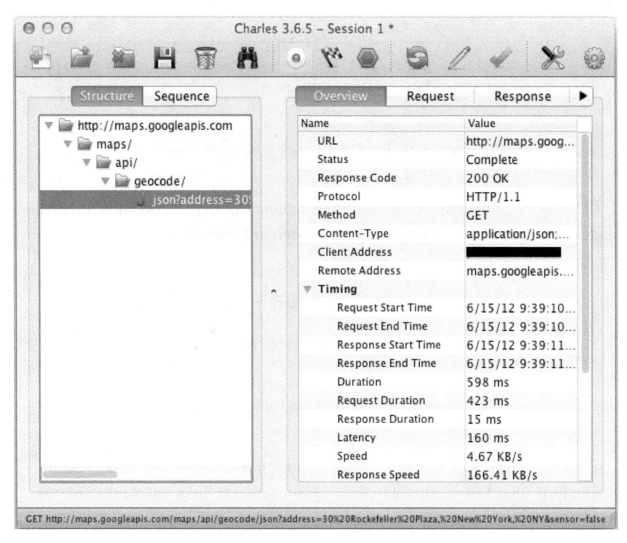

Figure 18 - Viewing information about a Web service call

The query string sent to the Geocoding service is displayed in an easy-to-read format, as seen in **Figure 19**.

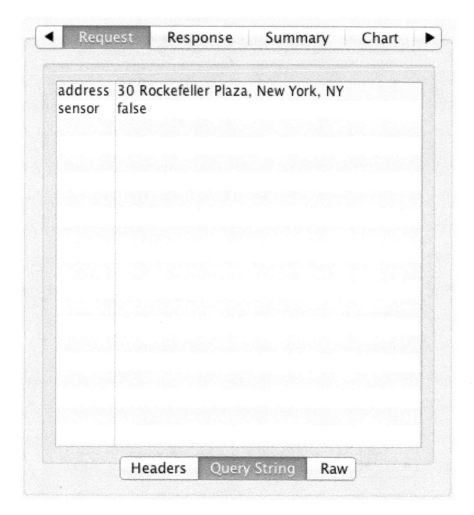

Figure 19 - Inspecting the query string of a Web request

Figure 20 shows one of the views available for inspecting the response data from the Web service call.

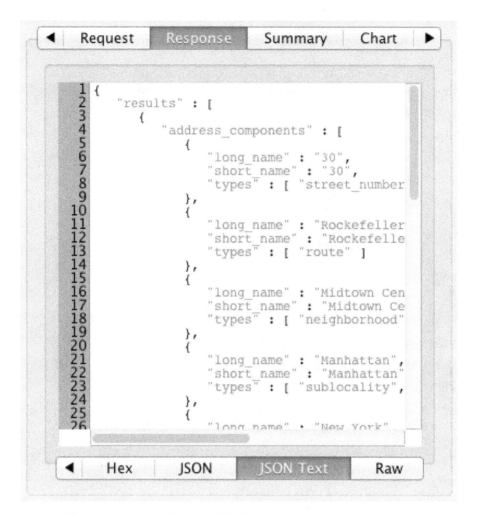

Figure 20 - Viewing the JSON response of a Web request

Do yourself a favor and download a free trial or purchase a copy of Charles at http://www.charlesproxy.com/ Follow these instructions for configuring an iDevice to work with Charles http://blog.mediarain.com/2009/08/iphone-http-connection-debugging/

Summary

Getting data to and from a server is critical for most mobile apps. The support in iOS for working with data on the Web is low-level compared to what is available for .NET developers. Despite the platform's lack of luxuries, what is provided gets the job done. This aspect of iOS programming typically involves using third-party APIs and tools; such as AFNetworking, KissXML, and Charles.

Chapter 10: Overview of Core Data

Manually incorporating a database into an app is boring, tedious, error-prone work. Imagine, for example, having to write properties in eighty-four classes so that they exactly match the schema of eighty-four database tables used by an app. Then suppose all eighty-four of those classes must have custom code that saves their properties to, and retrieves them from, a database. In that scenario the likelihood of a developer introducing mistakes, or leaping out of the nearest window, is extremely high. Computers are excellent at quickly performing boring, tedious, error-prone work. Developers, being such a clever bunch, have leveraged that fact by writing frameworks to automate as much of the tedium as possible.

This chapter reviews the Core Data framework that Apple provides to iOS developers to simplify working with data. It is somewhat similar to the Entity Framework and NHibernate framework used by many .NET developers. Every large, enterprise-scale iOS app I have worked on uses Core Data to manage the data layer. Even smaller apps, such as my pet projects, benefit from Core Data because it reduces the amount of code I must write, test, and maintain. Using the Core Data framework is certainly not a requirement, but it has so much to offer to application developers that to not learn about it is doing yourself a disservice.

Fundamental architecture

The purpose of Core Data is **not** to make it easier for application developers to work with databases. It is an object graph persistence framework whose main purpose is to save data objects and fetch them back into memory when requested. How it goes about doing this should be considered an implementation detail.

The standard persistent store to which Core Data persists object graphs is a SQLite database file. SQLite is similar to the SQL Server Compact database used by mobile and desktop .NET apps. It is a cross-platform, in-process database engine that exposes its functionality through a C API. When working with Core Data it is not necessary to program directly against SQLite. In fact, it is advisable not to do so because the database, and it's schema, is considered to be an implementation detail of how Core Data works. It is possible for Core Data to use a persistent store other than a SQLite database, such as an in-memory store or even a custom store, should the need arise.

Applications interact with data in a persistent store by using a small number of Core Data classes, as depicted in **Figure 1**.

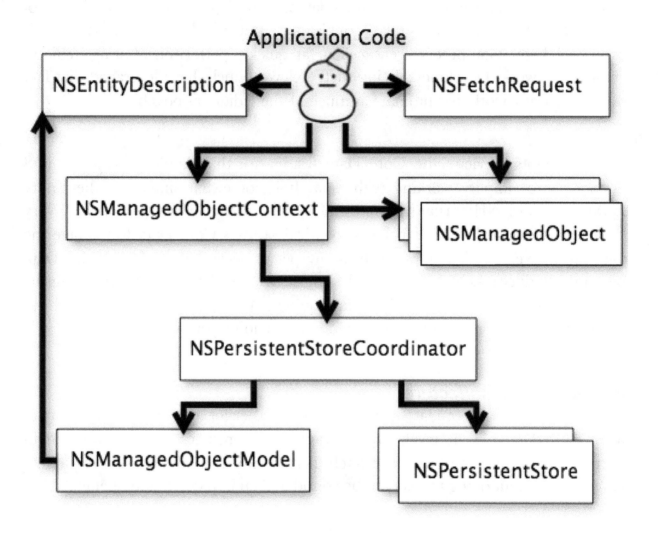

Figure 1 - Essential Core Data objects

A persistent store is represented in Core Data by an instance of NSPersistentStore. An application's data can be kept in multiple persistent stores, though it is common to use only one store for an entire app. Persistent stores are managed by an instance of NSPersistentStoreCoordinator. This class uses an application's data schema, represented by NSManagedObjectModel, to make sense of the data found in persistent stores and coordinate create/read/update/delete (CRUD) operations.

Application code does not often directly use an NSPersistentStoreCoordinator, NSPersistentStore, or NSManagedObjectModel object. These classes are infrastructure configured when an application starts up, and then promptly ignored. As seen in **Figure 1**, application code mostly uses the following four classes from the Core Data framework:

- **NSManagedObject** - Every data object persisted and loaded by Core Data is an instance of NSManagedObject, or an NSManagedObject subclass. An instance of NSManagedObject is commonly referred to as a *managed object*. Every managed object in an application adheres to an entity description (i.e. schema) loaded by an NSManagedObjectModel. A managed object can have *attributes* that store a single value and *relationships* that reference other managed objects. For example, a managed object that represents a spy might have an attribute named 'codeName' that is used when communicating with the spy, and a relationship named 'informants' that refers to a set of entities who provide intel to the spy. NSManagedObject uses a technique known as *faulting* to delay loading related managed objects, such as a spy's informants, until they are needed. This prevents an entire object graph from being loaded into memory when only one object in the graph is in use.

- **NSManagedObjectContext** - A managed object exists in one and only one managed object context, commonly abbreviated as *MOC*. A MOC is not thread-safe, meaning it should only be used by the thread on which it was created. MOC's are often described as a "scratchpad" because managed objects can be created, modified, and deleted in a MOC without affecting managed objects in other MOCs until the changes are committed. Changes made to managed objects are not committed to a persistent store until the **save:** message is passed to the MOC in which they exist.

- **NSFetchRequest** - Retrieving objects from a persistent store involves having a MOC execute a fetch request. An instance of NSFetchRequest contains the information used to decide which object(s) to retrieve from a persistent store. This can include using NSPredicate, a class from the Foundation framework that provides support for simple SQL-like expressions. Fetch requests can also specify the order in which objects are returned, by sorting on one or more attributes, using instances of NSSortDescriptor. Fetching objects is simply a matter of including an NSFetchRequest object as the first parameter for the **executeFetchRequest:error:** message passed to a MOC. Fetching objects is reviewed later in this chapter.

• **NSEntityDescription** - A managed object adheres to the "schema" defined by an entity description, which is represented in code by an instance of NSEntityDescription. This class is used to insert a new managed object into a MOC. It also provides type metadata and methods that can be used in a way similar to the .NET reflection API.

There are a few other classes in Core Data that application developers should know about, such as NSFetchedResultsController and NSManagedObjectID, which are outside the scope of this introductory chapter. If you plan on using Core Data, be sure to put these classes on your radar and learn how they can simplify data management.

Including Core Data in a project

The easiest way to configure an app to use Core Data is to make sure there is a checkmark in the *Use Core Data* checkbox when creating the project, as seen in **Figure 2**.

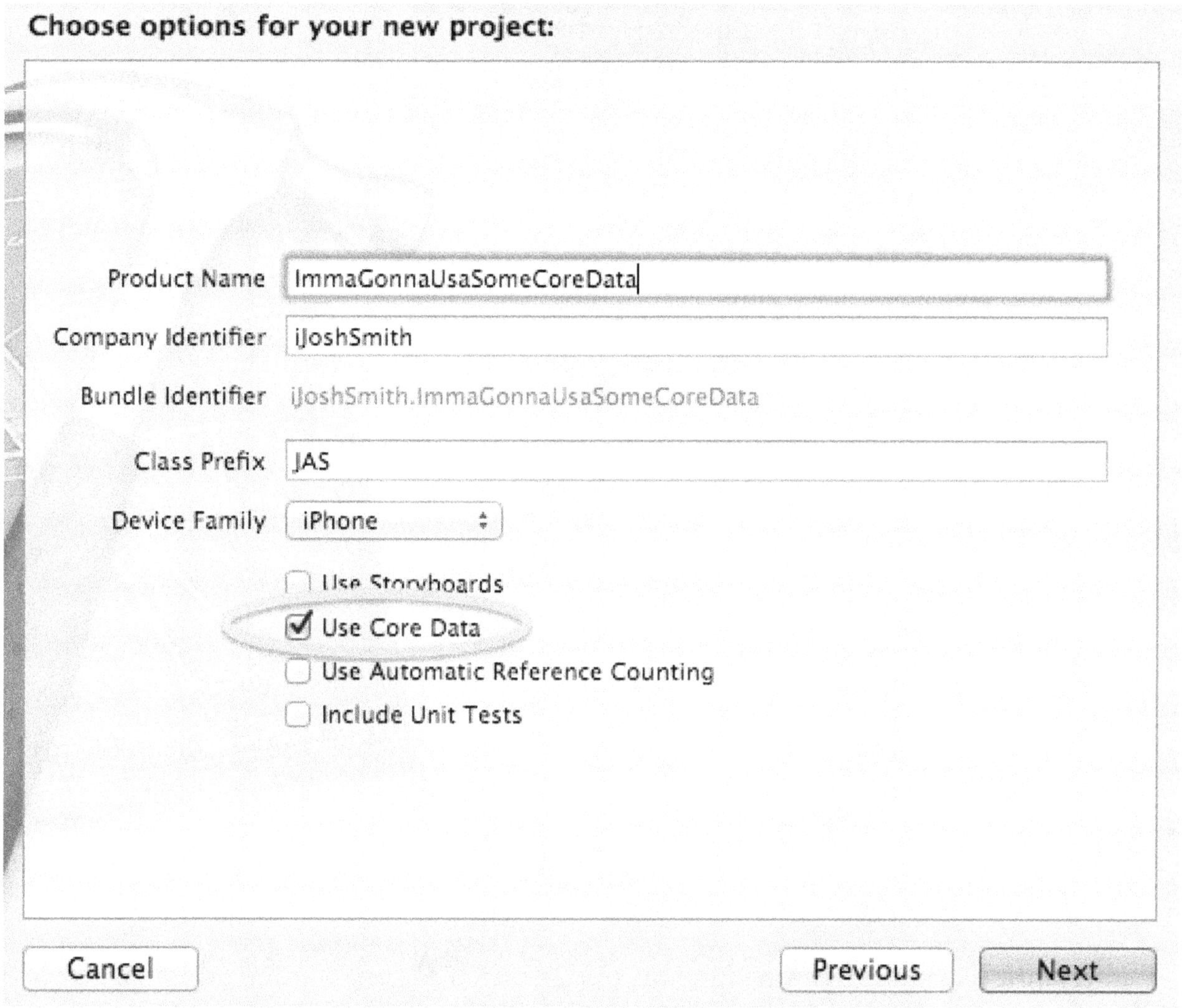

Choose options for your new project:

Product Name	ImmaGonnaUsaSomeCoreData
Company Identifier	iJoshSmith
Bundle Identifier	iJoshSmith.ImmaGonnaUsaSomeCoreData
Class Prefix	JAS
Device Family	iPhone ⟳

☐ Use Storyboards
☑ Use Core Data
☐ Use Automatic Reference Counting
☐ Include Unit Tests

Cancel   Previous   Next

Figure 2 - Including Core Data in a new project

Not all the iOS project templates provide this checkbox, which is a quirk in Xcode that makes no sense. As of Xcode 4.3.3 the only project templates for which Core Data boilerplate code can be included are:

- Master-Detail Application

- Utility Application

- Empty Application

Adding support for Core Data to an existing project can be accomplished by following these steps:

1. Click on the project item in Project navigator to view its settings page

2. Select the item under *Targets* that represents your application

3. In the "Linked Frameworks and Libraries" group add a link to *CoreData.framework*

4. In Project navigator open the *Supporting Files* group, click on the file whose extension is *.pch* (which stands for "precompiled headers")

5. In the PCH file type `#include <CoreData/CoreData.h>` at the end of the section that begins with `#ifdef __OBJC__`

6. Add a new data model file to the project by pressing Command+N and selecting the *Data Model* file template from the *Core Data* section

7. Create a new project with the *Use Core Data* option enabled

8. Copy the Core Data boilerplate code added to the new project's AppDelegate files and paste it into your project's AppDelegate files

9. Adjust the boilerplate code to use file names that make sense for your project, such as the name of the Data Model file added in step 6

10. Delete the new project from your file system

Later in this chapter I introduce an open-source library named Magical Record that allows you to remove Core Data boilerplate code from an AppDelegate, making the framework easier to use for all objects in an application.

Designing a managed object model

Core Data requires a detailed description of an application's data model, known as a *managed object model*, to properly function. A managed object model is defined using the Core Data model editor in Xcode. Technically, this can be defined in code, but it would be a very impractical thing to do. As mentioned in the previous section, an instance of NSManagedObject adheres to an entity description loaded by an NSManagedObjectModel. This class represents a managed object model defined in the Core Data model editor. It stores a collection of entity descriptions, each of which is analogous to a class declaration. An entity description contains attribute and relationship descriptions, analogous to relational database columns and foreign key constraints. **Figure 3** demonstrates how a managed object model is represented by Core Data.

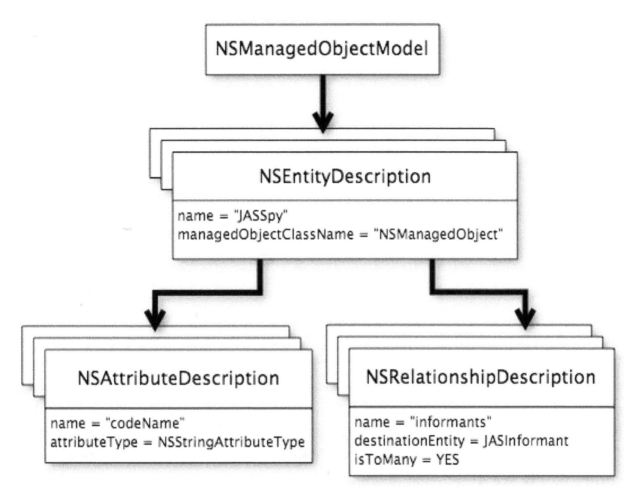

Figure 3 - Managed object model

The Core Data model editor is a graphical tool in Xcode that makes it easy to define a managed object model. It is opened from Project navigator by clicking on a Data Model file, which has the extension *.xcdatamodeld*. On the left side of the editor is the top-level components area which lists entities, fetch requests, and configurations. Next to the top-level components is the detail area, which shows attributes, relationships, and fetched properties of the selected top-level item(s). Configurations and fetched properties are advanced topics not reviewed in this book. Refer to **Figure 4** to see this editor in action.

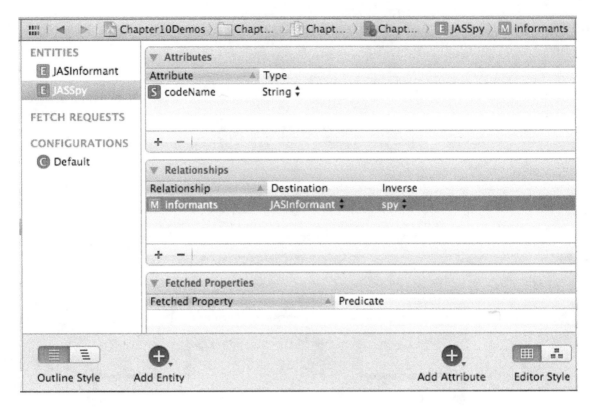

Figure 4 - The Core Data model editor in table mode

The detail area has two available modes with which to display a managed object model. The *table* mode, as seen in the previous screenshot, uses a tabular arrangement that is convenient when focusing on the details of a particular entity. Clicking on the righthand button of the *Editor Style* segmented control (bottom-right corner of **Figure 4**) puts the detail area into *graph* mode. This mode is useful for seeing the relationships between multiple entities. Refer to **Figure 5** to see what a managed object model looks like as a graph.

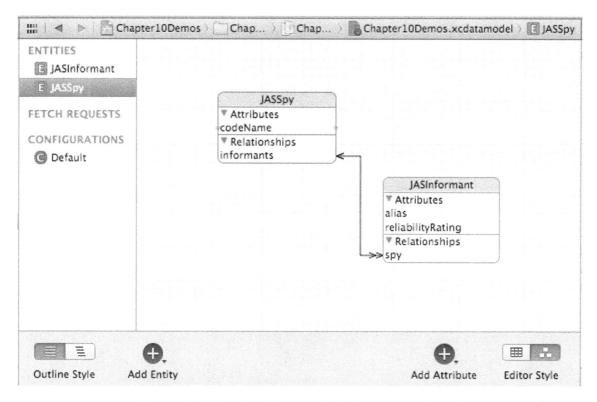

Figure 5 - The Core Data model editor in graph mode

Information about the selected item(s) in the Core Data model editor can be viewed and edited in the Inspector area, on the righthand side of the Xcode workspace window. Click on the rightmost toolbar icon in the Inspector area to open the Data Model inspector. **Figure 6** shows what the inspector displays when the JASSpy 'informants' relationship is selected in the detail area.

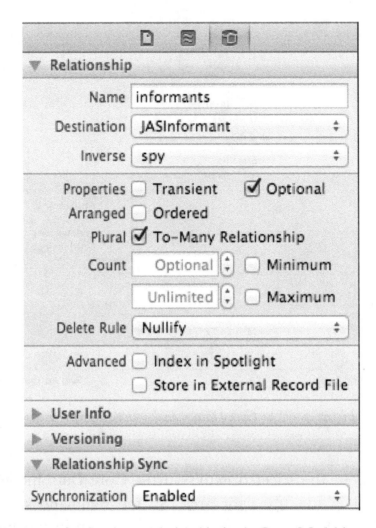

Figure 6 - Configuring a relationship in the Data Model inspector

One of the most commonly used fields in that inspector is the *To-Many Relationship* checkbox, which determines if a relationship is one-to-many or one-to-one. Relationships are one-to-one by default. Also note that this relationship has an *Inverse* value named 'spy'. This represents an inverse relationship that points from an informant back to a spy. Apple strongly suggests that all relationships between Core Data entities be given an inverse relationship, thus making them bi-directional. This is important because Core Data relies on inverse relationships to ensure the consistency of an object graph when changes are made.

Working with NSManagedObject

Using entities defined in a managed object model involves working with instances of NSManagedObject. Since all managed objects must exist in exactly one MOC, creating a new managed object requires specifying the MOC into which it will be inserted. This is accomplished by sending the conveniently named **insertNewObjectForEntityForName:inManagedObjectContext:** message to the NSEntityDescription class, as seen in **Figure 7**.

```objc
// Create a new spy with the code-name of Foxtrot.
NSManagedObjectContext *moc = self.managedObjectContext;
NSManagedObject *spy = [NSEntityDescription
            insertNewObjectForEntityForName:@"JASSpy"
                       inManagedObjectContext:moc];
[spy setValue:@"Foxtrot" forKey:@"codeName"];

// Try to save Foxtrot to the persistent store.
NSError *error = nil;
if (![moc save:&error])
    NSLog(@"Fail! %@", [error localizedDescription]);
```

Figure 7 - Working with NSManagedObject

NSManagedObject has no knowledge of an entity's attributes or relationships. This is why the code in **Figure 7** uses **setValue:forKey:**, part of the Key-Value Coding API, to set the **codeName** attribute. NSManagedObject overrides this method to store the assigned attribute value, which eventually gets saved to a persistent store.

This example uses hard-coded strings to identify parts of the managed object model. The entity name "JASSpy" is passed when creating the managed object, and "codeName" is passed when assigning the **codeName** attribute. It would be much safer and easier if the compiler verified that none of the hard-coded entity or attribute names are misspelled, and that the app does not accidentally assign a value of the wrong type to an attribute. In other words, it would be better if there was a strongly typed Objective-C class for each entity in a managed object model. Would you care to guess what the next section is about?

Working with generated entity classes

Xcode can create an Objective-C class that has the same name and schema as an entity defined in a managed object model. There is also a popular open-source tool called mogenerator, available on GitHub, that does a great job of generating developer-friendly entity classes. This chapter shows how to use the functionality built into Xcode.

With the Core Data model editor open, select the entities for which classes should be generated. In Xcode's menu select *Editor | Create NSManagedObject Subclass...* and then click the *Create* button, as seen in **Figure 8**. Generated class files are automatically added to your project.

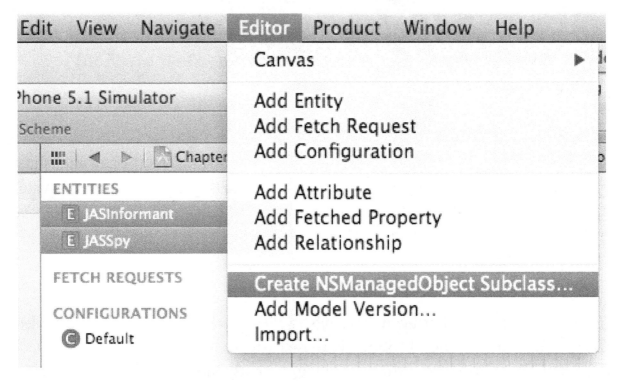

Figure 8 - Creating entity classes in Xcode

The class interface in **Figure 9** is based on the JASSpy entity. Notice that its attribute and relationship are both represented as properties. The **informants** property, which represents a one-to-many relationship with JASInformant, points to an NSSet. That type of collection is unordered, meaning that the objects in the relationship are not sorted by default.

```
@interface JASSpy : NSManagedObject

@property (nonatomic, retain) NSString * codeName;
@property (nonatomic, retain) NSSet *informants;
@end

@interface JASSpy (CoreDataGeneratedAccessors)

- (void)addInformantsObject:(NSManagedObject *)value;
- (void)removeInformantsObject:(NSManagedObject *)value;
- (void)addInformants:(NSSet *)values;
- (void)removeInformants:(NSSet *)values;

@end
```

Figure 9 - Class interface generated for the JASSpy entity

The CoreDataGeneratedAccessors category on JASSpy contains methods that can optionally be used to add and remove related managed objects. These methods are defined and added to the JASSpy class at run-time by Core Data. **Figure 10** shows the generated implementation file for the JASSpy entity, which only contains @dynamic property definitions. Core Data also defines and adds these properties at run-time.

```
#import "JASSpy.h"

@implementation JASSpy

@dynamic codeName;
@dynamic informants;

@end
```

Figure 10 - Class implementation generated for the JASSpy entity

Working with Core Data is much safer and easier when using generated entity classes. Unlike working directly with NSManagedObject instances, which requires hard-coded strings, the code in **Figure 11** is completely verifiable by the Objective-C compiler.

```
// Create a spy with the code-name of Foxtrot.
NSManagedObjectContext *moc = self.managedObjectContext;
NSString *className = NSStringFromClass([JASSpy class]);
JASSpy *spy = [NSEntityDescription
                insertNewObjectForEntityForName:className
                             inManagedObjectContext:moc];
spy.codeName = @"Foxtrot";

// Create an informant who leaks intel to Foxtrot.
className = NSStringFromClass([JASInformant class]);
JASInformant *inf = [NSEntityDescription
                insertNewObjectForEntityForName:className
                             inManagedObjectContext:moc];
inf.spy = spy;
inf.alias = @"Arthur Dent";
inf.reliabilityRating = [NSNumber numberWithDouble:42];

// Try to save Foxtrot and his informant to the store.
NSError *error = nil;
if (![moc save:&error])
    NSLog(@"Fail! %@", [error localizedDescription]);
```

Figure 11 - Working with generated entity classes

Setting an informant's **spy** property to a JASSpy object causes it to be added to the spy's set of informants, which is managed by JASSpy's **informants** relationship. When the MOC is saved and both of those objects are persisted, the relationship between them is persisted by Core Data.

When working with a generated class, which might need to be generated again later, it is not a good idea to add additional methods to the generated class file. Instead, add any additional methods to a category on that class. As explained in

Chapter 4, categories are similar to partial classes in .NET programming. They are not affected when the generated class file is replaced.

Browsing an app's SQLite database

Even though a persistent store managed by Core Data should be considered an implementation detail, it is often useful to inspect objects in a SQLite database when developing and troubleshooting an app. One way to query a SQLite database is to use the sqlite3 command line tool already installed on your Mac. If you prefer working with a graphical tool, I highly recommend the MesaSQLite app for OS X by Desert Sand Software.

Inspecting a SQLite database first requires access to the file that stores its data. How you find this file depends on whether it was created by running an app in the iOS Simulator or on an iOS device. This section shows how to find the file in both scenarios.

The iOS Simulator is an OS X app that stores iOS apps, and their data files, in the computer's file system. Finding the SQLite database file created by an app running in the simulator can be accomplished by using the **find . -name *.sqlite** command in a Terminal window, or by logging the absolute path of an app's Documents directory in Xcode. **Figure 12** shows code that logs where a SQLite database file is kept on the file system when using Xcode's boilerplate Core Data setup code.

```
// Print the file system path to the database file created
// when running the application in the iOS Simulator.
NSString *documents =
  [NSSearchPathForDirectoriesInDomains(NSDocumentDirectory,
                                       NSUserDomainMask,
                                       YES) lastObject];

NSLog(@"%@", documents);
```

Figure 12 - Printing out where the SQLite file is kept

When that code executes in your app, it prints out a path to the Console window in Xcode. Copy this path to the pasteboard (a.k.a. the clipboard) and then open a Finder window. After pressing Command+Shift+G the *Go to the folder* prompt opens and allows a path to be pasted into it, as seen in **Figure 13**.

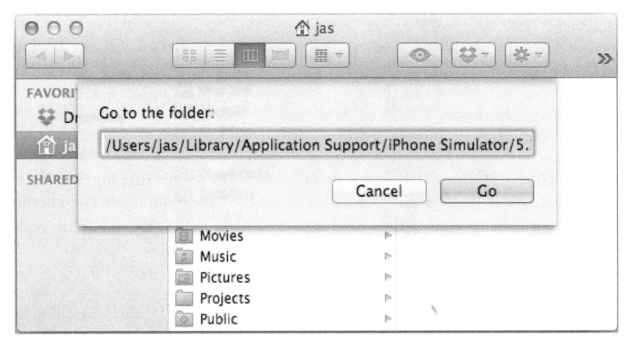

Figure 13 - Navigating to a SQLite file with Finder

Press Enter, or click the *Go* button, and Finder navigates to the directory in which your app's SQLite database file is kept, as seen in **Figure 14**.

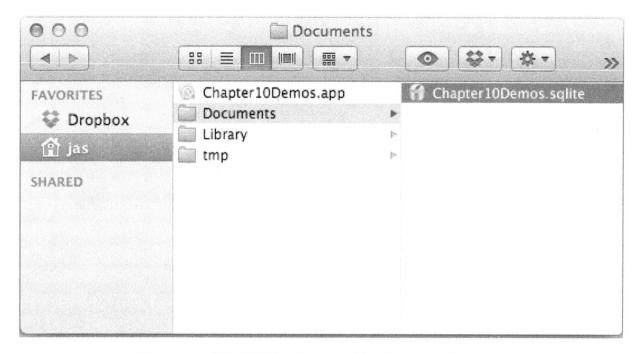

Figure 14 - The SQLite file created by Core Data for an app

When running an app on an iOS device it is necessary to download that app from the device to your development machine. First, plug the device into your computer so that Xcode can access it. In Xcode's Organizer window select the *Devices* tab, then click the *Applications* item shown for the device on which the database file exists. As seen in **Figure 15**, a list of all apps installed on the device created with your Apple developer profile is shown.

Figure 15 - Using Organizer to copy an app from an iDevice to the desktop

Simply drag and drop the item that represents the app with a SQLite database file from Organizer to the OS X desktop. If you prefer saving it to another folder, click the *Download* button on the bottom of the Organizer window. Once the *.xcappdata* file is on your development machine, right-click it and select *Show Package Contents* from the context menu, as seen in **Figure 16**. This opens a Finder window that shows directories and files of the downloaded app. The database file is in the Documents subdirectory, or whatever directory is specified in code when Core Data creates the persistent store.

Figure 16 - Accessing the downloaded app with Finder

Once the SQLite database file is available simply open it in MesaSQLite, or your tool of choice. A screenshot of MesaSQLite, in **Figure 17**, shows the table created by Core Data to store instances of JASInformant, an entity defined previously in this chapter.

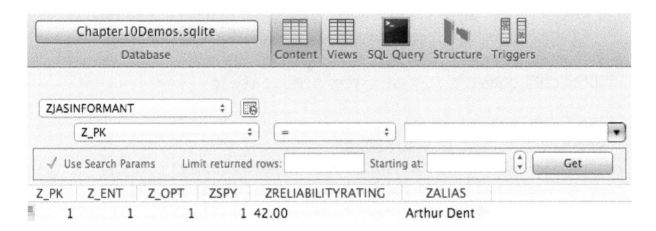

Figure 17 - Using MesaSQLite to browse the database file

Database tables and columns created by Core Data have uppercase names that start with Z. Every table also includes a few columns, such as Z_PK, used internally by Core Data. It is not a good idea to rely on the schema of a database managed by Core Data because it is subject to change in a future release.

Executing a fetch request

Retrieving managed objects from a persistent store is simply a matter of telling an NSManagedObjectContext to execute an NSFetchRequest. The request object stores information about what kind of data to retrieve, how to filter it, how to sort it, the maximum number of objects to retrieve, and more. As seen in **Figure 18**, the **executeFetchRequest:error:** method returns fetched objects in an NSArray. Those objects are put into the MOC that executes a fetch request.

```objc
// Create a request that fetches JASSpy objects.
NSString *name = NSStringFromClass([JASSpy class]);
NSFetchRequest *fetchRequest =
  [NSFetchRequest fetchRequestWithEntityName:name];

// Retrieve spies whose code-names start with F.
NSPredicate *predicate =
  [NSPredicate predicateWithFormat:
  @"codeName BEGINSWITH %@", @"F"];
[fetchRequest setPredicate:predicate];

// Sort the spies by their code-names.
NSSortDescriptor *sortDesc =
  [NSSortDescriptor sortDescriptorWithKey:@"codeName"
                                ascending:YES];

NSArray *sortDescs =
  [NSArray arrayWithObjects:sortDesc, nil];
[fetchRequest setSortDescriptors:sortDescs];

// Retrieve and iterate over the list of spies.
NSError *error = nil;
NSArray *spies = [aManagedObjectContext
                    executeFetchRequest:fetchRequest
                                  error:&error];
if (spies)
    for (JASSpy *spy in spies)
        NSLog(@"%@", spy.codeName);
```

Figure 18 - Fetching managed objects from a persistent store

In the previous code, the use of NSPredicate looks similar to an SQL statement. NSPredicate is part of the Foundation framework, but is commonly used in Core Data programming. It provides a small, yet convenient, set of operators, such as **BEGINSWITH**, that can be chained together with logical operators, such as **AND**. When Core Data uses a predicate to query SQLite, it converts those operators into the equivalent SQL statements for querying a database.

Magical Record makes life easier

Using the Core Data API involves writing a lot of code. Most of the code is simple and repetitive. It begs to be refactored into helper methods. Once you are comfortable using the Core Data API, include Magical Record in your project and Core Data will go from being tedious to terrific. Magical Record is an open-source library on GitHub that has many features, some of which are experimental. The core functionality is exposed as categories on Core Data classes, making them much easier to use. Refer to **Figure 19** to see just a few of the incredibly useful methods in Magical Record.

```
// This sets up Core Data so that it can work
// with updated versions of the schema over time.
[MagicalRecord setupAutoMigratingCoreDataStack];

// Easily create a spy with one line of code.
JASSpy *spy = [JASSpy createEntity];
spy.codeName = @"Foxtrot";

// Use the +defaultContext category method on
// NSManagedObject to access the main thread's MOC.
[[NSManagedObjectContext defaultContext] save];

// Fetch a spy whose code-name is Foxtrot using the
// +findFirstByAttribute:withValue: category method.
spy = [JASSpy findFirstByAttribute:@"codeName"
                          withValue:@"Foxtrot"];
```

Figure 19 - Using Core Data is much easier with Magical Record

Just the first line of code in **Figure 19** makes Magical Record worth using. It replaces the boilerplate code that Xcode adds to a new project's AppDelegate class which creates and configures Core Data infrastructure, such as the primary MOC. By not storing these objects in an AppDelegate, but instead exposing them via category methods, they become easier to access throughout an application's codebase. The next section in this chapter discusses this first line of code in more detail.

The **createEntity** message sent to the JASSpy class enables a managed object to be created in one line of code, without the need to pass an entity name or a MOC. This method makes creating a managed object more intuitive because it provides a factory method for all NSManagedObject subclasses, instead of sending the **insertNewObjectForEntityForName:inManagedObjectContext:** message to NSEntityDescription.

Magical Record adds a category on NSManagedObjectContext that includes a class method named **defaultContext**. This method returns the MOC designated as the "default" for an app, which is the main thread's primary MOC unless you specify otherwise. There are other methods that make it easy to access other MOCs, such as **contextForCurrentThread** which is useful in scenarios where managed objects are used on background threads. Working with Core Data from multiple threads is a complicated topic that falls outside the scope of this introduction to the framework.

Another way that Magical Record makes it easier to use Core Data is by offering a set of convenience methods for fetching objects. These methods, too, are exposed by a category on NSManagedObject, like the **createEntity** method reviewed earlier. The **findFirstByAttribute:withValue:** method in **Figure 19** creates and executes an NSFetchRequest and returns the result.

Instructions for adding Magical Record to a project, as well as API documentation, are available on the project's GitHub page.

Versioning a managed object model

For software to remain valuable, it must be adapted to the changing world in which it is used. Adaptation requires accommodating new data types and modifications to the schema of existing data types. A significant aspect of supporting changes to existing data types is migrating a user's data from an old schema to a new one. Fortunately, Core Data formalizes the process of changing a managed object model (which I refer to as a *schema*) and migrating data so that it can be implemented in a prescribed and systematic manner.

An entire chapter could be written about data migrations using Core Data, which, thankfully, is unnecessary. Apple has already thoroughly documented the topic in the Core Data Model Versioning and Data Migration Programming Guide. It is necessary to briefly review the topic, however, before I explain something crucial for any iOS developer working with Core Data. At a very high level, there are two kinds of data migration: *lightweight* and *ordinary*. A lightweight migration does not require you to write any code because Core Data infers the changes between two versions of a schema and makes necessary adjustments to persistent stores and the data in them. This is only possible if none of the changes made to a schema introduce ambiguity.

For example, Core Data knows how to add a column to a SQLite database table to accommodate a new attribute added to an entity. It cannot, however, figure out what to do if an attribute that used to be optional has been changed to non-optional and its default value has not been specified. How would Core Data know what to do for existing objects that were never given a value for that attribute? In situations where schema changes introduce ambiguity, it is the application developer's responsibility to write code that resolves the ambiguity at run-time. This is referred to as an "ordinary" migration in Apple's documentation, though one would hope that data migrations needed for an app are ordinarily lightweight. Obviously, lightweight migrations are preferable because they require no effort on behalf of the application developer.

Well, that's almost true. In order for a lightweight data migration to work, two things must be done.

1. The first time an app sets up the Core Data stack it must indicate that its persistent store supports lightweight migrations. This was demonstrated in **Figure 19** by sending the **setupAutoMigratingCoreDataStack** message to the MagicalRecord class. This helper method takes care of the configuration work involved with supporting lightweight migrations. If you choose to not use Magical Record, refer to Apple's documentation to learn how this can be implemented using their API.

2. An app's managed object model must be handled with caution throughout the development process. After each release of an app, be sure to create a new

version of its managed object model and set it as the current version. All changes made to an app's schema during development of the next release must be made only to the new version. Failing to do this will cause your app's users to lose access to their data when they install the next release, because Core Data won't know how to work with the user's persistent store(s). This can lead to unpleasant things such as hate mail and law suits.

For example, suppose I run version 1.0 of an app on my iPhone, causing Core Data to create a SQLite database whose schema is based on the app's managed object model. While developing version 1.1 of the app I add a new attribute to an entity, but I make the change in the original version of the schema. When v1.1 is run on that iPhone a rather unhelpful error message, similar to the one seen in **Figure 20,** will be logged.

```
All Output ⬍                                    Clear  ▢  ▢  ▢
2012-06-20 17:41:17.439 Chapter10Demos[1182:fb03] /Users/jas/Library/
Application Support/iPhone Simulator/5.1/Applications/
AC7E8BFB-2251-40E2-AA1F-4368574F7F84/Documents
2012-06-20 17:41:17.481 Chapter10Demos[1182:fb03] +
[MagicalRecord(ErrorHandling) defaultErrorHandler:](0x1bfc0) Error:
file://localhost/Users/jas/Library/Application%20Support/iPhone
%20Simulator/5.1/Applications/AC7E8BFB-2251-40E2-AA1F-4368574F7F84/
Library/Application%20Support/Chapter10Demos/Chapter10Demos.sqlite
2012-06-20 17:41:17.482 Chapter10Demos[1182:fb03] +
[MagicalRecord(ErrorHandling) defaultErrorHandler:](0x1bfc0) Error: {
    NSPersistenceFrameworkVersion = 386;
    NSStoreModelVersionHashes =     {
        JASInformant = <ce7c527d b5d56ccd b0dba67d 1eadc0e2 c61243f9
3c91a8d4 2d22e708 746690e9>;
        JASSpy = <fef51b10 fbfd8a9a 476a8172 84dd73f0 fd42d93e c6ee9776
d8f7deb2 000d908e>;
    };
    NSStoreModelVersionHashesVersion = 3;
    NSStoreModelVersionIdentifiers =     (
        ""
    );
    NSStoreType = SQLite;
    NSStoreUUID = "F25529DA-7E02-40D3-9FD2-7B59EC7F03F3";
    "_NSAutoVacuumLevel" = 2;
}
2012-06-20 17:41:17.483 Chapter10Demos[1182:fb03] +
[MagicalRecord(ErrorHandling) defaultErrorHandler:](0x1bfc0) Error:
Can't find model for source store
```

Figure 20 - Core Data reporting an invalid managed object model

The "Can't find model for source store" error message is Core Data's way of letting you know that there's a problem with the app's managed object model. The problem, of course, is that the original version was modified, instead of a new version. Core Data cannot infer changes between two versions of a schema if only one version exists. The solution to this problem is to give Core Data what it needs to do its job, and create a new version of the app's schema that contains the necessary modifications for the v1.1 release.

After reverting the schema file back to how it was for the v1.0 release, open it in Xcode by clicking on the *.xcdatamodeld* file in Project navigator. As seen in **Figure 21**, a new version of the managed object model can be added via the *Editor | Add Model Version...* menu item.

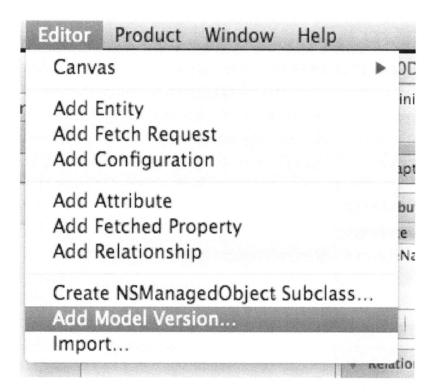

Figure 21 - Adding a new schema version before making changes

The next step, which is easy to forget, is to make the newly created schema version the *current* version. This can be done by selecting an *.xcdatamodeld* file in

Project navigator and viewing it's metadata in the File inspector. Use the *Current* selector to pick the new schema version, as seen in **Figure 22**.

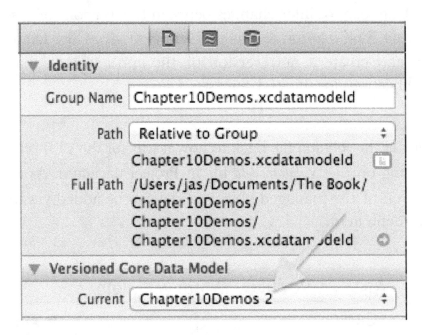

Figure 22 - Setting the current schema version

Once the current version is updated, edits made to the *.xcdatamodeld* file in the Core Data model editor will modify the new schema version. You can verify which schema version is current by expanding the *.xcdatamodeld* item in Project navigator. The current schema version displays a green checkmark icon, seen in **Figure 23**.

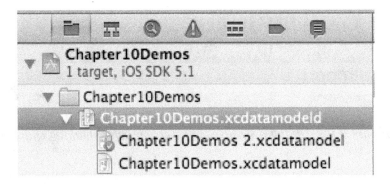

Figure 23 - Verifying the current schema version is active

I suggest not expanding this item, unless you just need to quickly check what the current schema version is. If a previous version of the schema is selected in Project navigator, it will be displayed in the Core Data model editor and is liable to be changed by accident. Changes made to previous versions of a schema are likely to confuse Core Data and lead to data migration problems.

Summary

Core Data performs the heavy lifting involved with saving and loading an application's object graphs. It was designed to use an arbitrary backing store for persisting data, but a SQLite database is usually the best choice because of its speed, and the fact that it does not need to load the entire database into memory. The Core Data framework should be used for apps that need to manage complex data and large data sets. This chapter has only scratched the surface of an immense subject. To learn more about Core Data, read Apple's Core Data Tutorial for iOS, the Core Data Programming Guide, and the Core Data Model Versioning and Data Migration Programming Guide. Another great resource is the book Pro Core Data for iOS by Michael Privat and Robert Warner.

Chapter 11: Debugging Techniques

Writing software is easy. Writing software that works properly is not, which is why most programming platforms include APIs and programs designed to assist developers with troubleshooting their code. This chapter examines the debugging tools provided by Apple. Developers accustomed to working in Visual Studio might initially find the support in Xcode for debugging limited and inconvenient. While Xcode certainly does not have the same rich visual debugging aides available in VS, it does provide a powerful set of tools that can be used to quickly track down bugs. This chapter also introduces Instruments, a tool that collects information about a running application which can be visually analyzed to identify the cause of performance problems.

Logging to the console

The most basic and limited form of debugging is writing text to the Console in Xcode. This can be done by calling the **NSLog** function. It logs an NSString, which can be a format string that includes the values of other variables, as seen in **Figure 1**. The format string syntax used by **NSLog** is the same used by NSString methods, such as **stringByAppendingFormat:**.

```
NSString *wisdom = @"DON'T PANIC";
int answer = 42;

// Use %@ for an object placeholder
// Use %d for an integer placeholder
NSLog(@"%@ the answer is %d!", wisdom, answer);
// Prints: DON'T PANIC the answer is 42!
```

Figure 1 - Logging with NSLog

Refer to **Figure 2** to see the text shown in the Console after calling **NSLog**.

Figure 2 - Viewing logged output in the Console

A downside of using **NSLog** is its effect on application performance. It can slow down an app, especially if used frequently, such as once per iteration of a rapidly iterating loop. Many developers have devised ways of sidestepping the overhead of **NSLog** by adding preprocessor directives that eliminate all calls to it. For example, the code in **Figure 3** redefines **NSLog** to be a no-op if the DEBUG symbol is not defined (i.e. in a Release build).

```
// This is in the project's .PCH file

#ifdef __OBJC__
    #import <UIKit/UIKit.h>
    #import <Foundation/Foundation.h>
#endif

// Redefine NSLog for Release builds.
#ifndef DEBUG
#define NSLog(...) {}
#endif
```

Figure 3 - Removing NSLog from a Release build

A notable side effect of this approach is that the line of code which logs information to the Console is removed from Release builds. A line of conditionally-compiled code should not modify the state of a program, such as incrementing an integer variable via the ++ operator, because the app will behave differently based on the active build configuration.

Another approach to removing **NSLog** from Release builds involves creating a macro with a custom name, such as **JASLog**, that is defined differently based on the active build configuration. In a Debug build the macro inserts a call to **NSLog**, but in a Release build it is a no-op. Code in an application should use this custom macro instead of directly calling **NSLog**.

Production software often needs more comprehensive support for logging than simply writing text to the Console. It can be useful to have multiple logging levels, such as Error, Warning, and Verbose. It is also useful when an app makes it easy for a user to email their log files to a development team if a problem occurs. In situations where logging is important, consider using the Lumberjack open-source library on GitHub. It has all the features mentioned above, and more.

Assertions

Throughout this book I have used the **NSAssert** macro to show that some condition is true. It is just like the Debug.Assert() method in .NET programming. If the expression passed to it evaluates to false, the application comes to a grinding halt and the error message passed to the assertion method is logged to the Console. Similar to the Debug.Assert() method, the **NSAssert** macro is disabled in Release builds (that is configurable, though).

Figure 4 shows another form of assertion commonly used in iOS programming.

```
- (int)divideX:(int)x
          byY:(int)y
{
    NSParameterAssert(y != 0);
    return x / y;
}
```

Figure 4 - Verifying a parameter is valid

The **NSParameterAssert** macro causes the app to crash if the expression passed to it is false. **Figure 5** shows that it logs a helpful message to the Console, including the asserted expression.

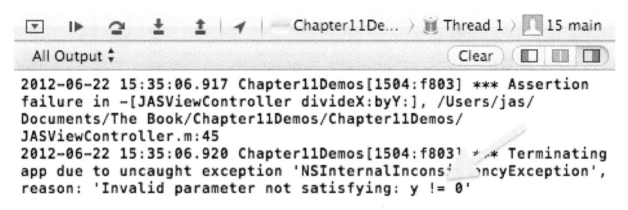

Figure 5 - Failed assertions appear in the Console

Asserting assumptions is a good practice because it encourages defensive programming. However, all calls to assertion macros are removed from Release builds. Lines of code that use assertion macros should not modify program state, to avoid discrepancies between builds created with different build configurations.

Breakpoints

Xcode's support for breakpoints is very similar to what .NET developers are accustomed to using in VS. Clicking in the area to the left of a line of code adds a breakpoint for that line. Another way to add and remove a breakpoint is to use the Command+\ keyboard shortcut. When running a Debug build of an app, executing a line of code that has a breakpoint causes the debugger to halt execution so that a developer can examine the state of the app. This is demonstrated in **Figure 6**.

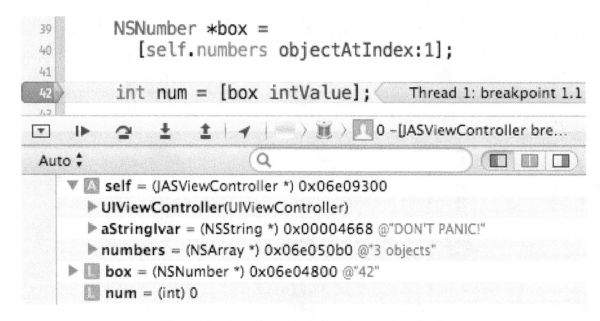

Figure 6 - Stepping through code at a breakpoint

When program execution stops at a breakpoint, the debugger enables a developer to step through the code line by line to inspect what the application is doing. The screenshot in **Figure 7** shows buttons in the toolbar of the Debug area used to step through code. The screenshot is annotated with the function of each button, and keyboard shortcuts to perform a few of them.

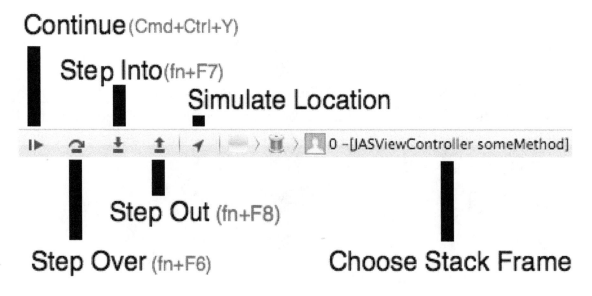

Figure 7 - Commands used while debugging

The first four buttons on the toolbar should be familiar to most .NET developers, since VS has the same navigation commands. The "Continue" button tells the debugger to let the application continue execution. "Step Over" executes the current line of code and moves to the next line. "Step In" instructs the debugger to execute the current line of code and, if it calls a routine, navigate to the first line of code in that routine. "Step Out" causes the debugger to finish executing the current routine and return to the routine from which it was invoked.

The "Simulate Location" button in **Figure 7** is useful when running an application for iOS 5.0 or later that uses the Core Location framework. It can be used to choose a geographical location where the application "pretends" to be running.

On the righthand side of the Debug toolbar is a multilevel selector that can be used to navigate to any frame in the backtrace (a.k.a. call stack) for any thread in the process. This is a convenient feature that allows for quickly viewing methods and functions in a backtrace without the need to open Debug navigator.

Right-click a breakpoint to reveal its context menu, as seen in **Figure 8**.

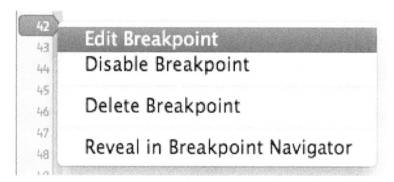

Figure 8 - Context menu shown for a breakpoint

This menu offers the ability to delete a breakpoint, which can also be done using the Command+\ shortcut mentioned earlier. The *Disable Breakpoint* menu item causes a breakpoint to be ignored by the debugger, but left in the code file for later use. Another way to disable a breakpoint is by clicking on it. Revealing a breakpoint in Breakpoint navigator, via the last menu item, selects it in the Navigator area on the lefthand side of the Xcode workspace window. The first option in the context menu opens a breakpoint editor, seen in **Figure 9**.

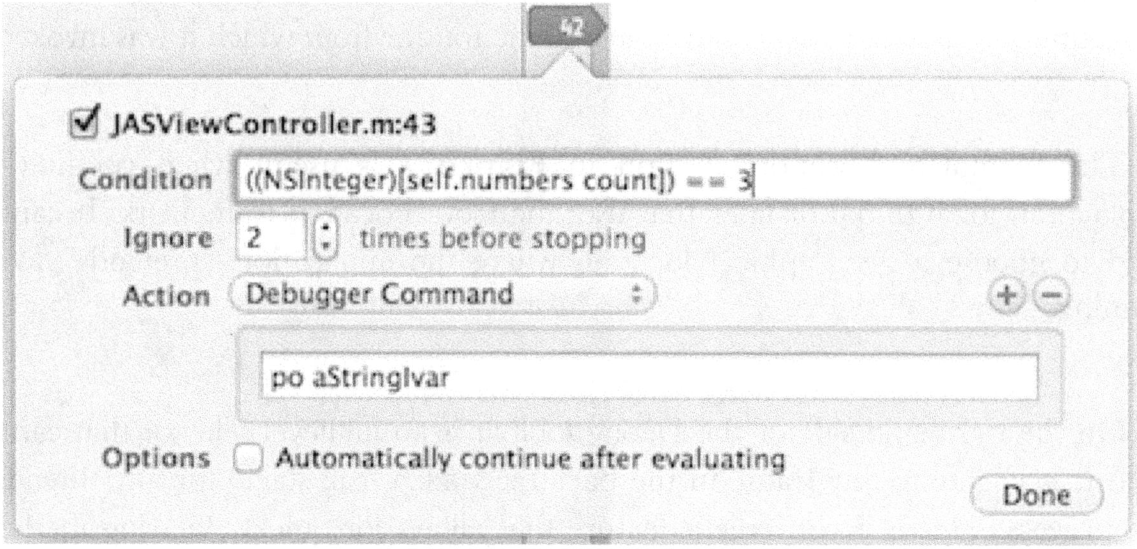

Figure 9 - Editing a breakpoint

Editing a breakpoint enables the debugger to be more selective about when to pause program execution. This is similar to the "conditional breakpoints" feature in VS. The breakpoint editor also supports adding custom actions that are executed when a breakpoint is hit. It is even possible to have the debugger execute custom actions without stopping at the breakpoint, which is useful for adding custom diagnostics to a running app, such as using a debugger command to log the value of some variable every time a certain line of code executes. Debugger commands are reviewed later in this chapter.

Exception breakpoints

Occasionally an exception is thrown that crashes an app and Xcode is unable to provide much in the way of details. The Console may only display a cryptic error message and Debug navigator may not show a backtrace. In a situation like this, it is helpful to use an *exception breakpoint* to find where the error is occurring. When an exception breakpoint exists, Xcode will bring up the line of code that causes any exception to occur. This is the same feature as the "Break on All Exceptions" option in VS.

Add an exception breakpoint by opening up Breakpoint navigator and clicking the add (+) button in the bottom left corner, as seen in **Figure 10**.

Figure 10 - Adding an exception breakpoint

After adding the exception breakpoint, a small breakpoint editor appears, allowing the breakpoint to be adjusted. Click the Done button to add a new exception breakpoint to the application. To have all of your Xcode workspaces include the exception breakpoint, right-click on it and open the *Move Breakpoint To* menu item, as seen in **Figure 11**.

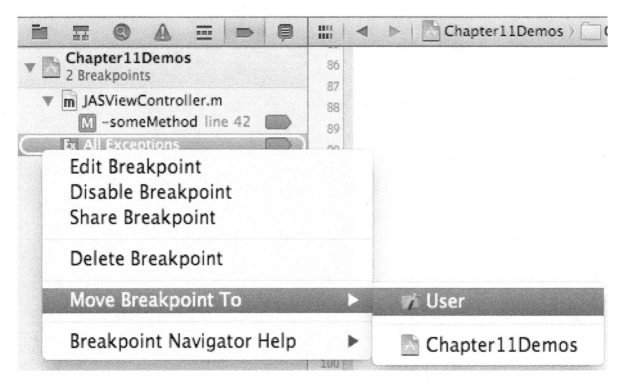

Figure 11 - Making the exception breakpoint appear in all workspaces

After clicking *User* in the submenu, the exception breakpoint is added to a group of breakpoints labeled "User" in Breakpoint navigator, as seen in **Figure 12**. It is automatically included in the list of breakpoints for all of your other Xcode workspaces.

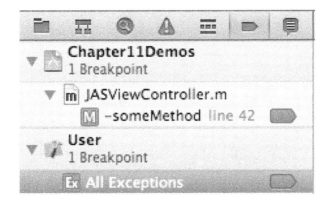

Figure 12 - An exception breakpoint that appears for all workspaces

The benefit of using an exception breakpoint is obvious. The downside, however, is that it can get annoying after a while. Some exceptions are expected to occur, and are handled appropriately. There is usually no reason to have the debugger pause an application for an exception that is going to be handled and dealt with appropriately. I leave an exception breakpoint defined but disabled, so that it is easily put to use when the need arises.

Variables View

When the debugger halts an application because a breakpoint was hit, the Variables View displays local variables for the current execution context. This serves the same purpose as the Autos and Locals windows in VS. As seen in **Figure 13**, the Variables View displays a variable's name, type, memory address, and, for certain types of objects, a description of its value.

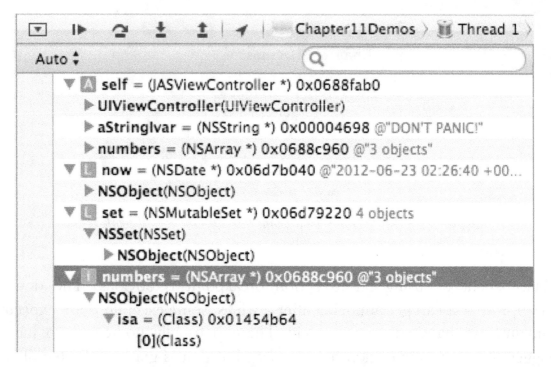

Figure 13 - Inspecting data in the Variables View

The Variables View contains a search box that filters the list based on any text displayed for a variable. This is useful, for example, when searching for an NSString object that contains a certain word. To the left of the search box is a selector that can be used to switch between "Autos," "Local Variables," and "All Variables, Registers, Globals and Statics." The default setting is "Autos" because it shows only the objects in which an application developer is most likely interested. The "Local Variables" setting includes all available local variables, including things like the _cmd argument implicitly passed into Objective-C instance methods. The last option shows information such as global variables and the values currently stored by various processor registers. For an iOS developer working with object-oriented code this setting is very rarely needed.

It is possible to add an expression to the Variables View, a feature similar to the Watch window in VS. This allows a developer to add an item to the list of variables and observe its value. If the expression happens to assign a variable, the value of the variable will be updated. Adding an expression begins by right-clicking the Variables View to summon its context menu, as seen in **Figure 14**.

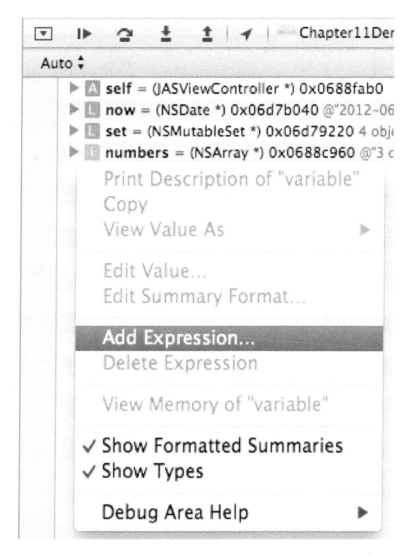

Figure 14 - Adding an expression to the Variables View

After clicking the *Add Expression...* menu item, the expression editor seen in **Figure 15** is displayed.

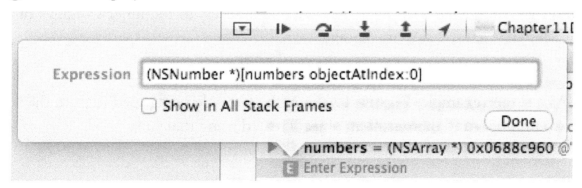

Figure 15 - Editing an expression in the Variables View

When finished typing an Objective-C expression into the expression editor, press the Enter key or click the Done button to dismiss it. The expression is added as an item in the Variables View and immediately evaluated by the debugger. The example in **Figure 16** uses an expression to view the first item in an array by sending it the **objectAtIndex:** message.

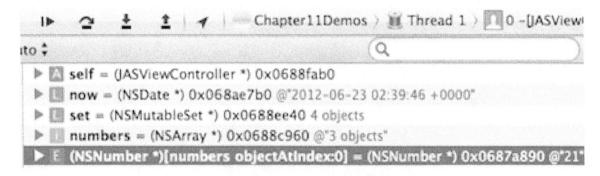

Figure 16 - Viewing the value of an expression

Note that the expression typecasts the object returned by the array. When working with the debugger it is often necessary to be very explicit and typecast variables, otherwise the debugger complains that it does not have enough information to do its job.

Using debugger commands

The Variables View is convenient for surface-level exploration of an app's data. When it is necessary to go deeper, a more powerful technique is available. Similar to the Immediate window in VS, the Console can be used to interact with the debugger by using built-in commands. This turns debugging into an interactive coding session, giving you practically unlimited access to the inner-workings of an app while it is paused at a breakpoint.

As a simple example, **Figure 17** shows the Console being used to print the sum of two numbers and then print an object created using that sum.

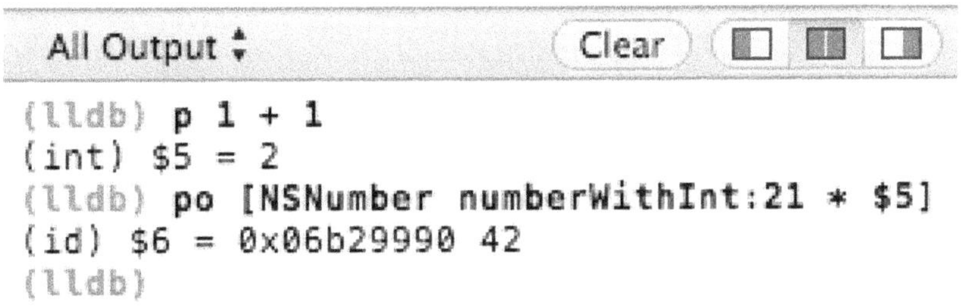

Figure 17 - Simple debugger commands in the Console

The **p** command prints the value of a non-object variable, such as an integer, to the Console. The result of that expression is stored in a variable by the debugger, in this example the variable is named **$5**. The next command is **po**, which prints a description of an object to the Console. This is implemented by sending the object a **debugDescription** message, which is defined by NSObject to return the result of the object's **description** method. Application developers can override **debugDescription** in their classes to provide useful information for debugging purposes, without modifying an object's **description** method, whose return value is commonly used for other purposes. This would be like if System.Object had **ToString**() and **ToDebugString**() and, by default, the latter returned the result of the former.

A more advanced use of debugger commands can be seen in **Figure 18**. This example assumes the existence of a variable named 'set' which points to an NSMutableSet object.

```
All Output ⊕
(lldb) po set
(NSMutableSet *) $5 = 0x06e2f230 {(
    <null>,
    21,
    42,
    84
)}
(lldb) expr (void)[set addObject:@"Bach"]
<no result>
(lldb) expression
Enter expressions, then terminate with an empty line to evaluate:
NSArray *objects = (NSArray *)[set allObjects];
for (int i = 0; i < (int)[objects count]; ++i)
{
  NSObject *obj = (NSObject *)[objects objectAtIndex:i];
  (void)NSLog(@"%@ -> %u", obj, (NSUInteger)[obj hash]);
}

<no result>
2012-07-04 13:44:26.201 Chapter11Demos[1179:f803] <null> -> 21363944
2012-07-04 13:44:26.203 Chapter11Demos[1179:f803] 21 -> 4203543429
2012-07-04 13:44:26.203 Chapter11Demos[1179:f803] Bach -> 2270217106
2012-07-04 13:44:26.204 Chapter11Demos[1179:f803] 42 -> 4112119562
2012-07-04 13:44:26.204 Chapter11Demos[1179:f803] 84 -> 3929271828
(lldb) |
```

Figure 18 - Interacting with an app using the LLDB commands

The **expr** command, short for **expression**, is used in this example to add a string to an NSMutableSet. To write multiple lines of code for the debugger to execute, the **expression** command is used without any parameters. Once a complete code snippet has been written into the Console, pressing the Enter key on an empty line causes the debugger to execute the code. As mentioned earlier, when typing Objective-C code into the debugger it is necessary to typecast pretty much everything, even the return value of **NSLog** to void.

In the past, Xcode shipped with a debugger named GDB. Starting with Xcode 4 the default debugger for iOS projects changed to the more modern LLDB, which has a different set of commands than GDB. When reading debugger command documentation, be sure that you're reading about the correct debugger. The easiest way to learn more about LLDB debugger commands is to type **help** into the Console and press Enter.

Checking for problems with static analysis

One way to locate the source of bugs is to have a tool find them for you. Xcode includes a static analyzer that can be used to find potential issues in the source code of an application. This is similar to the code analysis capabilities of VS, only it looks for issues common in Objective-C programs. The analyzer can be run via *Product | Analyze* in Xcode's menu, or by pressing Command+Shift+B. **Figure 19** shows an analyzer warning that correctly points out a memory leak in an application that doesn't use ARC.

```
37    // Note: This code does not use ARC.
38    - (void)someMethod
39    {
40        // The property retains the array, so
41        // it should be released after assignment.
42        self.numbers = [[NSArray alloc] init];
43    }                          ▶ Potential leak of an object allocated on line 42
```

Figure 19 - Detecting potential defects with the code analyzer

Device logs in Organizer

Apps running on an iOS device generate a log file that may contain useful information for troubleshooting a crash. The easiest way to get a log file from a device is by using the *Devices* tab in Xcode's Organizer window, seen in **Figure 20**.

Figure 20 - Selecting Device Logs in Organizer to view a crash report

If Xcode is unavailable when an app crashes, it is possible to access the log file through other means, such as by synching the device with iTunes. This is useful when working with beta testers who may be willing to jump through some hoops to send you a log file. Information about how to get a log file from an iOS device is thoroughly documented online.

Introduction to Instruments

Mobile software can exhibit a broad range of problems; such as simple logic errors, running out of memory, or quickly draining the device's battery. Certain kinds of problems are best solved by setting a breakpoint, stepping through source code line by line, and inspecting the state of data objects. So far this chapter has focused on the tools in Xcode which facilitate that type of debugging. Fortunately, Apple also provides a tool named Instruments that can be used to investigate problems not easily detected by stepping through lines of code with a debugger. Instruments is an OS X application that is included when Xcode is installed. It can be used without opening Xcode. However, Xcode makes it easy to launch Instruments for an application via its *Product | Profile* menu item, or by pressing Command+I.

The Instruments app contains a collection of tools, each known as an *instrument*, that collect data about a process running on an iOS device. One or more instruments can be added to a *trace document*, which defines a context in which an application is profiled and analyzed. A trace document can be saved to disk, enabling it to be loaded by Instruments later to compare multiple runs of the same application.

A major benefit of using Instruments is that each instrument in a trace document provides a different perspective of an application while it runs. The information gathered by each instrument can be correlated to find relationships between various run-time characteristics of an application. Suppose, for example, a trace document contains an instrument that monitors network activity and another that profiles memory allocations. After exercising an app while those instruments are profiling it, you might see that the total amount of allocated memory permanently increases every time a network call is made. Such information might indicate that network connections are not being closed properly, thus preventing their memory from being deallocated.

Instruments comes with a set of predefined *trace templates* designed to leverage this strength of the tool. A trace template contains multiple instruments that are commonly used together to identify a certain type of problem, such as how the "Leaks" template creates a trace document that includes the Allocations instrument and the Leaks instrument. This makes it possible to correlate memory allocations with leaked memory. Profiling an app for memory leaks is reviewed in the next section. Custom trace templates can be used to avoid setting up a trace document the same way every time an app is profiled. Custom templates can even be shared with other Xcode users to establish a standard profiling configuration for a development team.

An entire book could be written about Instruments. This chapter provides only a brief overview and a walkthrough example of using it to identify one kind of software defect. To learn more about what Instruments is capable of, and how it can be used, be sure to read Apple's Instruments User Guide.

Using Instruments to find a memory leak

Instruments can be used to uncover places where an app does not properly deallocate memory. Apple differentiates between two types of memory mismanagement, which is reflected in the way Instruments can be used to troubleshoot memory issues.

Abandoned memory refers to allocated memory that contains data objects accessible to, but unused by, an app. For example, suppose that every time a UIViewController subclass is pushed onto the navigation stack it adds a data object to a mutable array exposed by some singleton object. If the Controller accidentally does not remove that data object from the array when the user navigates back to a previous screen, the object's memory is considered "abandoned" because it is storing an unnecessary object. Abandoned memory can be detected by using the Allocations trace template in Instruments.

Leaked memory refers to allocated memory that is no longer accessible to an app. In other words, memory is leaked if it contains an object you created but your code no longer has a valid pointer to that object's memory address. Leaks are most often created because of *retain cycles*, which are a set of objects that retain themselves, typically through intermediary objects (ex. object A retains, and is retained by, object B). When application code releases an object it should assume that the object's memory is immediately deallocated, thus invalidating the pointer to which the **release** message was sent. If the object is part of a retain cycle, however, it will never be deallocated. Once all of an application's pointers to objects in a retain cycle are invalid (except for pointers that constitute the retain cycle), those objects are inaccessible to the rest of the application, making it impossible to free the memory they consume. This is not only a concern for applications where memory is manually managed. ARC cannot prevent you from creating retain cycles. It is very important to understand how to use the Leaks trace template in Instruments to find and "plug" memory leaks.

When Instruments is opened, it displays a list of available trace templates, seen in **Figure 21**. Select the "Leaks" template by double-clicking it.

Blank   Allocations   Leaks   Activity Monitor

Zombies   Time Profiler   System Trace   Automation

Figure 21 - Trace templates for iOS apps

Instruments attaches itself to the app for which it was launched in Xcode, and immediately begins collecting information about the app. In order for Instruments to collect useful information it is usually necessary for you to use the app and cause it to execute code that might have a problem. **Figure 22** shows the Allocations and Leaks instruments after briefly running an app. The pale orange bar in the Leaks track marks where a memory leak was created.

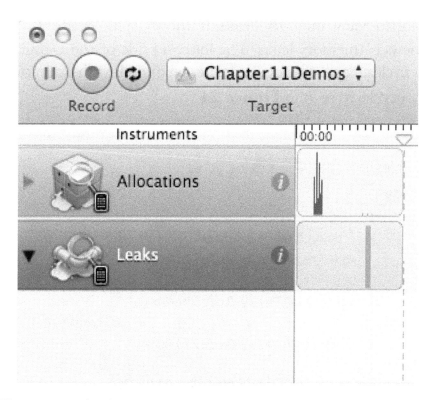

Figure 22 - Two instruments showing data collected from a running app

The lower area of the Instruments window contains the Detail pane. When the Leaks instrument is selected, the Detail pane offers several modes with which to view information about memory leaks recorded by the instrument. The default "Leaks" mode, selected in the top-left corner of the Detail pane in **Figure 23**, allows you to see which method or function (generically referred to as a *frame*) introduced a memory leak.

Leaks ⬍	Leaks by Backtrace		
Leaked Object	#	Size	Responsible Frame
JASFreakyLeaky	1	16 Bytes	–[JASViewController createMemoryLeak]
JASFreakyLeaky	1	16 Bytes	–[JASViewController createMemoryLeak]

Figure 23 - Two leaked objects detected by the Leaks instrument

Another way to view memory leaks is the "Cycles & Roots" mode, which provides two views of memory leaks. The lefthand side of the Detail pane contains a list of retain cycles, each of which can be expanded to show information about every object in a cycle, as seen in **Figure 24**.

Cycles & Roots ⬍	Leak Cycles	
#	Type	Details
	Cycles (1)	
1	▼JASFreakyLeaky – 2 nodes	Simple Cycle
	<JASFreakyLeaky 0xde72190>	
	bestFriend	JASFreakyLeaky*
	<JASFreakyLeaky 0xde5bef0>	
	bestFriend	JASFreakyLeaky*
	<JASFreakyLeaky 0xde72190>	

Figure 24 - Objects in a retain cycle

When viewing leaks caused by retain cycles, the righthand side of the Detail pane shows a graph of the objects in the selected cycle. The graph seen in **Figure 25** shows two JASFreakyLeaky objects that form a retain cycle because they each reference the other via the **bestFriend** property, which is declared to retain the object assigned to it.

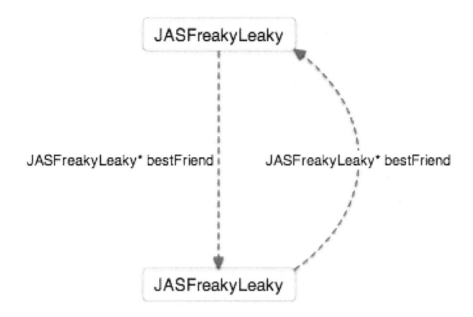

Figure 25 - Visualizing a retain cycle in a graph

Another useful mode the Detail pane offers for investigating memory leaks is named "Call Tree." This makes it possible to view the backtrace (call stack) that lead to a leak being created. When using this mode, I prefer to check every checkbox in the "Call Tree" group on the lefthand side of the Instruments window, as seen in **Figure 26**. Doing this makes it easy to view only the methods that I normally am interested in, and ignore a lot of information that does not help me plug a leak.

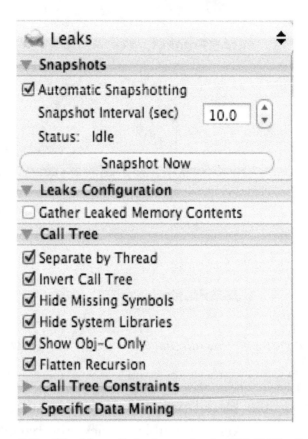

Figure 26 - Checking all the boxes in the "Call Tree" group

Once the Call Tree mode is configured to your liking, it can be used to see where memory leaks are created. **Figure 27** shows the Call Tree pointing out where a cycle of JASFreakyLeaky objects was created. Unfortunately, in most applications the methods that create a memory leak are not conveniently named **createMemoryLeak**!

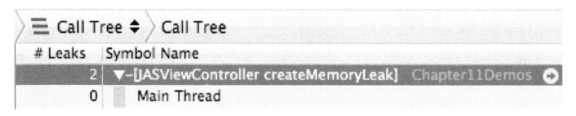

Figure 27 - The method that caused a memory leak

Double-clicking on a symbol name, such as a method in one of your classes, navigates to a read-only view of the code that created leaked objects. Refer to

Figure 28 to see this in action. To edit the code highlighted in Instruments, click the small Xcode icon in the Detail pane's toolbar, which opens that code file in an Xcode window.

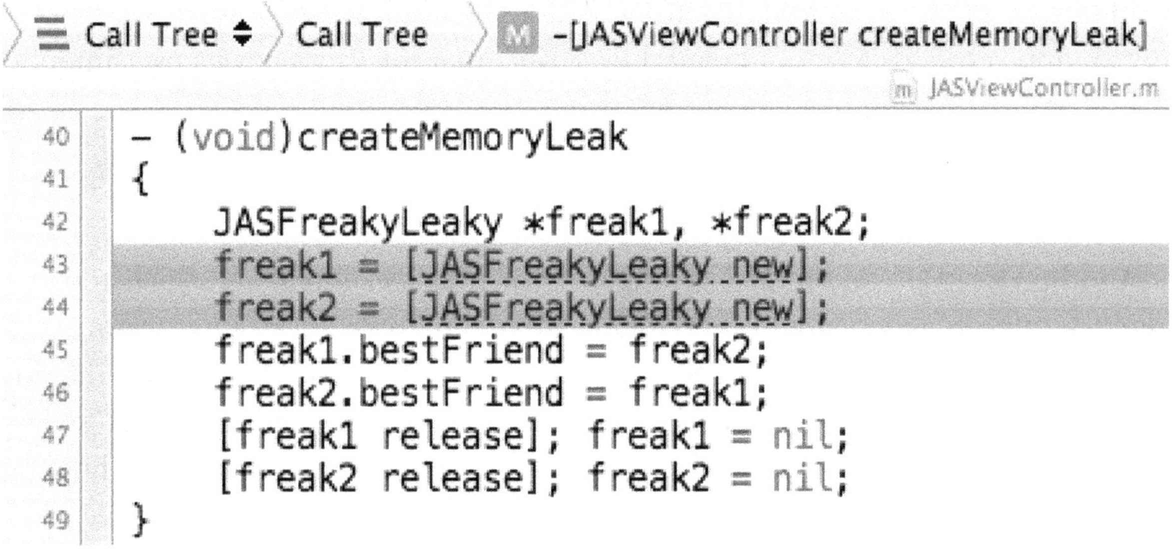

Figure 28 - Instruments highlighting leaked objects

Instruments does not suggest how to plug a memory leak, but it does provide enough information so that a developer proficient with memory management can quickly figure it out.

Summary

Like any worthwhile skill, debugging is hard-earned and acquired in the trenches. Learning how to fix iOS software becomes easier when you are aware of, and familiar with, Apple's debugging tools. These tools range from simple additions to the API, such as **NSLog** and **NSAssert**, to a full-blown software profiler known as Instruments. Be sure to learn and use the LLDB debugger commands, as they are often essential for productive debugging sessions. Debugger commands and Instruments are topics worth studying on their own.

Chapter 12: Unit Testing

Many developers write programs that test other programs. Having a computer verify the correctness of a program is generally referred to as *automated testing*. There are different kinds of automated tests. Automated UI testing involves evaluating how an app responds to input created by scripts that interact with its user interface. This form of testing can be done using the Automation instrument of the Instruments program. Automated UI testing is not covered in this book.

Another form of automated testing is known as *unit testing*, in which test code exercises a small, independent functional unit of an application. Unit testing is not only used for automated testing. Some developers write unit tests before the code that passes those tests, to keep their classes focused and simple. This style of programming is called *Test-Driven Development* (TDD). This chapter shows how unit tests are created in Xcode, whether for TDD or automated testing purposes.

OCUnit and SenTestingKit

Like much of Apple's development platform, support for unit testing iOS apps is based on an open-source project. The project is OCUnit, which includes a testing framework named SenTestingKit. It is not uncommon to see the terms OCUnit and SenTest used interchangeably. I use the term OCUnit when referring to the overall support in Xcode for creating and running unit tests, and SenTest when referring to the API available for creating tests (because the API members are prefixed with ST).

Mocking objects with OCMock

It is often important to remove objects from a unit test that are not the subject of the test. This helps to isolate the functionality being tested. In these cases, it is useful to create *mock objects* that are used by the object under test. A mock object pretends to be another object, records which of its methods are called, and returns pre-canned values from methods invoked by the object under test. Writing mock objects by hand can be tedious and error-prone, which is why developers create tools that automate making mock objects. A popular open-source implementation for mocking Objective-C objects is called OCMock. This book does not explain OCMock, but it is straightforward to use and well documented on the Web.

Logic tests and application tests

Apple draws a distinction between two styles of unit testing. *Logic tests* are what .NET developers typically think of as unit tests. They are methods executed by running a test runner application, not the application whose units are being tested. Every test's result is recorded by the testing framework and displayed in a user interface. Logic tests can only be executed in the iOS Simulator, not on an iOS device. Beware, Xcode will allow you to run a project's unit tests when an iOS device is the selected execution target, and will report that all tests passed without having actually run them. In the testing world, this is known as a false positive!

Xcode also supports *application tests*. This is a form of unit test where the test code runs inside of the application being tested. These tests can be used to verify things that are not easily tested by traditional unit tests, such as ensuring that all of a Controller's outlets are assigned a View when loaded from a NIB file and displayed on the screen.

This chapter focuses on logic tests, not application tests. When most developers refer to unit tests, they mean logic tests.

Creating a unit test target

The code in a project can be exercised by unit tests if that project has a *testing target*. Projects and targets are reviewed in detail in Chapter 3. The easiest way to add a testing target is to check the *Include Unit Tests* checkbox when creating the project, as seen in **Figure 1**.

Product Name	Chapter12Demos
Company Identifier	iJoshSmith
Bundle Identifier	iJoshSmith.Chapter12Demos
Class Prefix	JAS
Device Family	iPhone ⌄

☐ Use Storyboards
☐ Use Automatic Reference Counting
☑ Include Unit Tests

Figure 1 - Including a unit test target in a new project

A project created with a testing target includes additional files and a separate target whose name ends with "Tests" as seen in **Figure 2**.

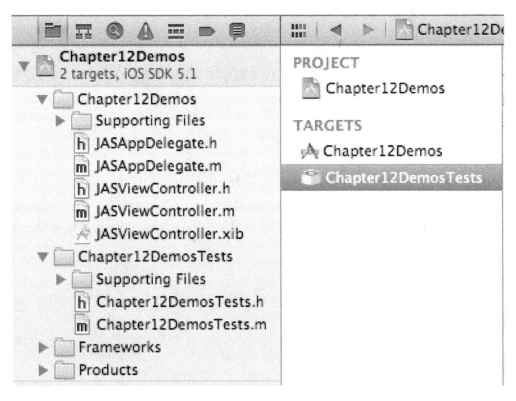

Figure 2 - A new project with a unit test target

Adding a testing target to an existing project involves a few extra steps. A step-by-step walkthrough of adding support for testing to an existing project is thoroughly documented by Apple. Refer to the "Setting Up Unit-Testing in a Project" section of the <u>Xcode Unit Testing Guide</u> document available online.

Adding a class to the test target

Unit test methods can only create and test a class in your project if its implementation file (*.m*) is added to the testing target. This is easily accomplished when adding a new class to a project by checking the testing target's checkbox in the *Targets* group of the new file dialog. This is demonstrated in **Figure 3**.

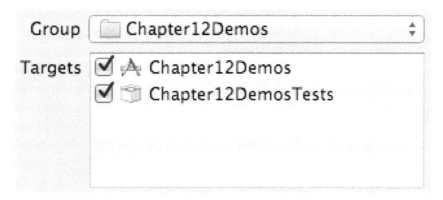

Figure 3 - Including a new class in the testing target

Existing class files can be added to, or removed from, a testing target by using File inspector on the righthand side of the Xcode workspace window. As seen in **Figure 4**, the "Target Membership" group includes a list of checkboxes that control which targets include the selected file. Remember, it is only necessary to add implementation files to a testing target, not header files.

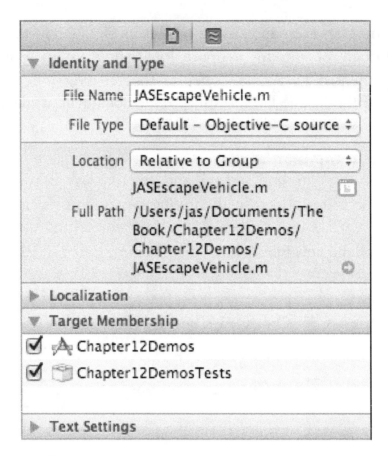

Figure 4 - Viewing which targets include an implementation file

Writing a test method

When Xcode includes a testing target for a new project, it generates a class in which test methods can be written. A testing target can have many classes that contain test methods, all of which must derive from the SenTestCase base class. Xcode includes a file template named "Objective-C Test Case Class" that should be used to create the boilerplate code needed for a test class. **Figure 5** shows the header file of a test class.

```
#import <SenTestingKit/SenTestingKit.h>

@interface Chapter12DemosTests : SenTestCase

@end
```

Figure 5 - A class in which test methods are written

Figure 6 shows the implementation file for a simple test class. It includes two infrastructure methods and one test method.

```
@implementation Chapter12DemosTests {
    JASEscapeVehicle *theVehicle;
}
- (void)setUp {
    [super setUp];
    theVehicle = [[JASEscapeVehicle alloc]
      initWithVehicleType:JASVehicleTypeSpacecraft];
}
- (void)tearDown {
    [theVehicle release];
    [super tearDown];
}
- (void)testPropolsionSystem {
    STAssertEquals([theVehicle propulsionSystem],
                   JASPropolsionSystemNuclearReactor,
                   @"Invalid propolsion system.");
}
@end
```

Figure 6 - Setting up, testing, and tearing down

setUp and **tearDown** are scaffolding methods declared in the SenTestingKit framework. The **setUp** method can execute multiple times for a single test case object; once for each test method before it runs. It provides a well-known place to initialize objects used by a test method. It is paired with the **tearDown** method, which executes immediately after a test method completes. As its name suggests, this method is used to dispose of the objects created by **setUp**.

The method in **Figure 6** that performs a test is named **testPropolsionSystem**. This method is run by the testing framework because it:

- Is defined in a SenTestCase subclass

- Is prefixed with "test"

- Accepts no parameters

- Returns void

There is no need to declare test methods in the header file of a test class. Test methods are detected at run-time based on the criteria listed above.

Running a test suite

The most convenient way to run a suite of unit tests in Xcode is the Command +U keyboard shortcut. This is available through Xcode's menu under *Product | Test*. The result of running tests is shown in Log navigator, as seen in **Figure 7**.

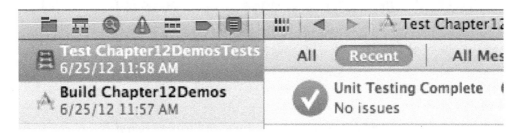

Figure 7 - Viewing test results in Log navigator

The previous screenshot shows what it looks like when all tests pass. If one or more tests fail, Xcode treats it as a build error and shows descriptions of the failed test(s) in Issue navigator, as seen in **Figure 8**. Clicking on an item that represents a failed unit test navigates to the line of code that caused the test to fail.

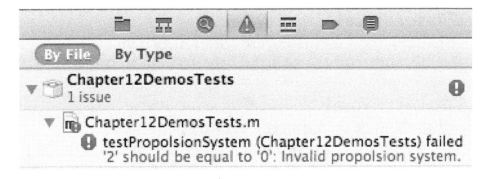

Figure 8 - Failed tests are reported as build errors

Unfortunately, Xcode does not provide a quick and easy way to run a single test method, or run only the methods in a certain category. Later in this chapter I review a way to implement support for the latter use case.

Forcing a test to fail

When developing a set of test methods it is sometimes helpful to intentionally make a test fail. This technique is used for ensuring that unimplemented test methods do not accidentally pass and create a false positive. As seen in **Figure 9**, the SenTest API includes the **STFail** macro for this purpose.

```objc
- (void)testNotYetImplemented
{
    STFail(@"This test is incomplete");
}
```

Figure 9 - Intentionally failing a test

Asserting a Boolean value

Unit tests verify that something is either true or false by *asserting* a condition. The most basic form of assertion is checking a Boolean value. These are known as Boolean assertions, and are supported by SenTest via the **STAssertTrue** and **STAssertFalse** macros, seen in **Figure 10**.

```
STAssertTrue(
  [theVehicle firesHeatSeekingMissiles],
  @"Spacecrafts should be fully armed.");

STAssertFalse(
  [theVehicle hasKickstand],
  @"Spacecrafts do not have a kickstand.");
```

Figure 10 - Testing a Boolean value

Asserting for equality

A commonly asserted condition is that two data items are equal to each other. SenTest provides support for asserting the equality of two scalar values, such as two integers, with the **STAssertEquals** macro. Checking for the equality of two Objective-C objects is accomplished by using the **STAssertEqualObjects** macro, as seen in **Figure 11**.

```
// Compare two scalar values.
int x = 42, y = 42;
STAssertEquals(x, y, @"x should equal y");

// Compare two objects.
NSNumber *numX, *numY;
numX = [NSNumber numberWithInt:x];
numY = [NSNumber numberWithInt:y];
STAssertEqualObjects(numX, numY, nil);

// Check if the difference between two
// numbers is within an accuracy range.
double accuracyRange = 1.5;
STAssertEqualsWithAccuracy(
   0.42, 1.0, accuracyRange,
   @"Did not fall within range of 1.5");
```

Figure 11 - Testing for equality of variables

The **STAssertEqualsWithAccuracy** macro is useful when checking whether numeric values fall within a certain range of values.

Asserting for nil

SenTest includes convenient macros, named **STAssertNil** and **STAssertNotNil**, that check if a pointer is nil or not. These macros are seen in the **Figure 12**.

```
STAssertNotNil(
    [theVehicle transdimensionalHyperdrive],
    @"Spacecrafts can restructure space-time");

STAssertNil(
    [theVehicle wheels],
    @"Spacecrafts don't use caveman technology");
```

Figure 12 - Testing if a pointer is nil

Asserting for exceptions

When working with methods that throw exceptions it is important to verify that they are thrown at the correct times. Unlike in many .NET unit testing frameworks, there is no need to decorate a test method with anything that indicates what kind of exception should be thrown. Because the SenTest API is based on preprocessor macros, which are expanded into large chunks of code during the build process, all the exception handling code needed to detect and process exceptions is automatically inserted into test methods. There are quite a few macros in SenTest dedicated for testing exceptions, which is ironic since Objective-C code typically does not use exceptions to communicate failure. **Figure 13** shows three of SenTest's macros used when testing for exceptions.

```
STAssertNoThrow(
    [theVehicle ejectAccomplice],
    @"Ejecting an accomplice once is allowed.");

STAssertThrows(
    [theVehicle ejectAccomplice],
    @"Should not be allowed to eject twice.");

STAssertThrowsSpecific(
    [theVehicle ejectAccomplice],
    JASVehicleException,
    @"Should throw custom exception object.");
```

Figure 13 - Testing if a method throws an exception

Grouping and running tests by category

As mentioned earlier in this chapter, Xcode's support for running unit tests is not very flexible. Unlike many other unit testing frameworks, there is no built-in support for running only one test, or only the tests in a user-defined category. Xcode's scheme editor, opened by the Command+Option+R shortcut, makes it possible to select which tests to run, but this is very inconvenient because multiple changes cannot be applied as a named group/configuration. For example, after opening the scheme editor, select the *Test* item in the list of build actions, seen in **Figure 14**.

Figure 14 - Selecting the Test build action in the scheme editor

Once the Test build action is selected, the scheme editor displays information about it, including a list of test methods that can be executed when running the project's unit tests, shown in **Figure 15**. Selecting which test methods to run involves opening this editor and updating many checkboxes.

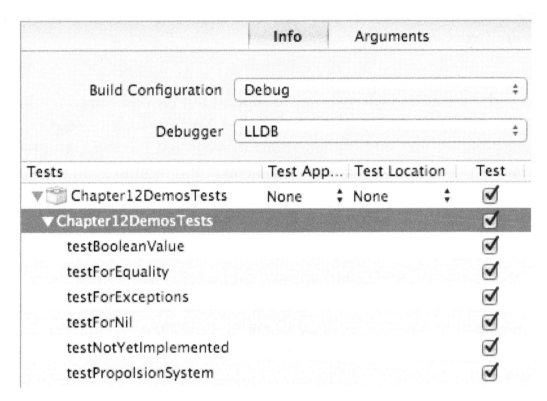

Figure 15 - Selecting which tests to run in the scheme editor

This is an unfortunate limitation in the current version of Xcode. Many software projects include hundreds or even thousands of unit tests. Managing that many test methods with the limited functionality in Xcode is asking for a headache. One of the most conspicuously missing features is the ability to categorize test methods, and only execute methods in one or more category. There are many reasons to do this, such as excluding test methods that take a long time to complete. By keeping the duration of running a test suite short, it encourages developers to run tests more often. Long-running test methods might only need to be run once per day, or on a build server after a developer commits changes to a source control repository.

There are several ways to implement grouping and running test methods by category. The simplest is to use `#if` directives to conditionally compile test methods based on the presence of preprocessor macros that represent a test method category. However, this approach requires a developer to edit preprocessor macros in source code files and/or build settings to specify which test method categories to run. Configuration changes that require manually editing multiple settings are error prone.

I devised a simple and effective way to support test method categories that does not require editing code files or build settings. My approach leverages Xcode's convenient support for build configurations to select test method categories. The remainder of this section shows how to implement this technique. In the following example, test methods are split between two categories: slow and fast. Slow test methods take a long time to complete, fast methods complete quickly.

The first step is to add a build configuration for every test method category, and another configuration that includes all the categories. Creating custom build configurations is reviewed in detail by Chapters 3 and 9. As a reminder, to access the list of build configurations, select the project item in Project navigator, as seen in **Figure 16**.

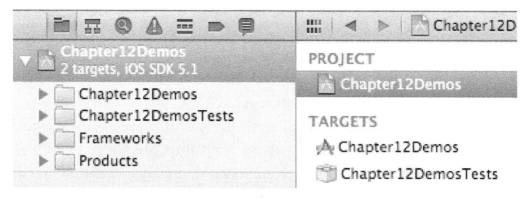

Figure 16 - Selecting the project to add build configurations

Locate the "Configurations" group and duplicate the Debug configuration once for each new build configuration. Rename the new build configurations to indicate which test method categories they represent. Refer to **Figure 17** for an example.

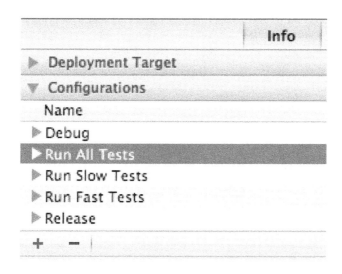

Figure 17 - Three duplicates of the Debug configuration

Next to the *Info* tab is the *Build Settings* tab, which has a search box that filters the huge list of build settings. Search for "preprocessor" to locate the "Apple LLVM compiler 3.1 - Preprocessing" group, seen in **Figure 18**. Select one of the new build configurations, press the Enter key to put it into edit mode, and type an identifier that will be used later to determine which test methods to execute when that build configuration is active.

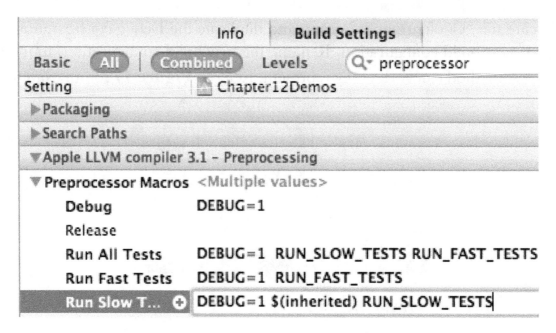

Figure 18 - Editing each configuration's preprocessor macros

Ignore the **$(inherited)** symbol seen in **Figure 18**, it is included in the build settings automatically. Note that the "Run All Tests" build configuration includes both category identifiers: **RUN_SLOW_TESTS** and **RUN_FAST_TESTS**. The completed list of preprocessor macros is shown in **Figure 19**.

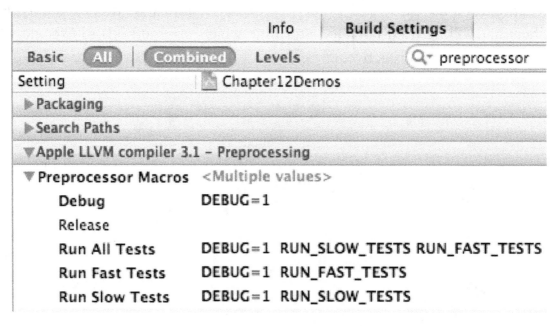

Figure 19 - All three testing configurations properly configured

Now that there is a build configuration for each category of unit test methods, and one that includes all of them, it's time to make one of these configurations active for the Test build action. This can be done with the scheme editor, as seen in **Figure 20**.

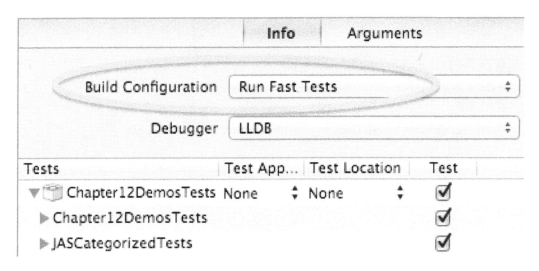

Figure 20 - Selecting a configuration for the Test build action

So far I have created build configurations that represent one or more test method categories. I defined preprocessor symbols (known as *macros*), such as **RUN_FAST_TESTS**, for each of the build configurations. Lastly, I selected one of the build configurations for the Test build action, so that its macros are available during the build process. The next step is to make use of the active build configuration's macros to affect which test methods are run by the test runner.

This part of the solution involves another form of preprocessor symbol known as a *function-like macro*. Like all macros, function-like macros are just a fancy way of replacing text before the Objective-C compiler processes a source code file. A function-like macro can accept arguments, as seen in the SenTest API for asserting conditions. The macros defined in **Figure 21** conditionally modify the name of a test method, which is passed as an argument named '__TEST'.

```
// UnitTestMacros.h

#ifdef  RUN_FAST_TESTS
#define JAS_FAST(__TEST) -(void) __TEST
#else
#define JAS_FAST(__TEST) -(void) skip_##__TEST
#endif

#ifdef  RUN_SLOW_TESTS
#define JAS_SLOW(__TEST) -(void) __TEST
#else
#define JAS_SLOW(__TEST) -(void) skip_##__TEST
#endif
```

Figure 21 - Macros that conditionally modify test method names

If a test method definition includes the **JAS_FAST()** macro, and the **RUN_FAST_TESTS** symbol is defined, that test method's name is unchanged and it will be run by the test runner (assuming the method's name begins with "test", which is a requirement for all test methods run by OCUnit). If that symbol is not defined, such as when the "Run Slow Tests" build configuration is active, the test method's name is modified so that it starts with "skip_". This ensures the method will not be run because its name does not start with "test". For example, a method named **testFoo** would be renamed to **skip_testFoo**, which means that the test runner would ignore that method. In case you're curious, the ## operator in those macros is used to concatenate two pieces of text together, which is how it prepends "skip_" to the method name.

Finally, an example of creating categorized test methods is shown in **Figure 22**. These methods are conditionally executed based on the active build configuration of the Test build action, as seen earlier.

```
#import "JASCategorizedTests.h"
#import "UnitTestMacros.h"

@implementation JASCategorizedTests

JAS_FAST(testTheSpeedOfLight) {
    // Perform a quick test.
}
JAS_SLOW(testAnIceAge) {
    // Perform a long-running test.
}
JAS_SLOW(testPaintDrying) {
    // Perform a long-running test.
}
@end
```

Figure 22 - Defining conditionally executed test methods

Summary

Automated tests can save development teams a lot of time, if properly implemented. Xcode supports the creation and execution of unit tests, which is code that tests independent pieces of application functionality. Classes in a project can be exercised by test methods added to that project's testing target. The SenTest API provides macros that assert conditions in test methods, such as if two objects are equal or if a pointer is nil. These test methods can be put into categories and executed as a group, by leveraging the flexibility of preprocessor macros.

Hello, World!

Welcome to the world of iOS programming. I hope you no longer consider it *terra incognita*. This guided tour covered a large and diverse set of essential topics for iOS developers. Although it's time for this book to come to an end, it's really just the beginning. There are many fascinating and important things still to be discovered, much of which I pointed out along the way. Refer to the Appendix for a list of documentation, books, and blogs I suggest you read next. If you would like to catch up with me, stop by iJoshSmith.com or drop me a line at iOSArtisan@gmail.com

Thank you for reading my book!

Appendix

This contains further reading material, grouped by chapter. I include URLs for all resources except books.

Chapter 1: Greetings, Earthling!

- AppCode
  - http://www.jetbrains.com/objc
- iOS Developer Center
  - https://developer.apple.com/devcenter/ios
- iOS Developer Program
  - https://developer.apple.com/programs/ios
- MonoTouch
  - http://xamarin.com/monotouch
- PhoneGap
  - http://phonegap.com
- Sencha Touch
  - http://www.sencha.com/products/touch
- Using iOS Simulator
  - http://tinyurl.com/8a64snz

Chapter 2: From Windows to OS X

- Mac OS X Keyboard Shortcuts
  - http://support.apple.com/kb/HT1343

Chapter 3: From Visual Studio to Xcode

- Cornerstone 2
  - http://www.zennaware.com/cornerstone
- SvnBridge
  - http://svnbridge.codeplex.com
- Versions
  - http://versionsapp.com
- Xcode 4 by Wentk (book)
- Xcode 4 User Guide
  - http://tinyurl.com/7x6dpew

Chapter 4: From C# to Objective-C

- Objective-C Programming: The Big Nerd Ranch Guide by Hillegass (book)
- The C Programming Language by Kernighan and Ritchie (book)
- The Objective-C Programming Language
  - http://tinyurl.com/6pet977

Chapter 5: From Garbage Collection to ARC

- How I Manage Memory by Brent Simmons
  - http://inessential.com/2010/06/28/how_i_manage_memory
- Advanced Memory Management Programming Guide
  - http://tinyurl.com/7byk6qr

Chapter 6: From System. to NS**

- Date and Time Programming Guide
  - http://tinyurl.com/7nazycq
- <u>iOS 5 Programming - Pushing the Limits</u> by Napier and Kumar (book)
- Key-Value Coding Programming Guide
  - http://tinyurl.com/84k4vbj
- Key-Value Observing Programming Guide
  - http://tinyurl.com/6rm7ukh
- NSBlog by Mike Ash
  - http://www.mikeash.com/pyblog

Chapter 7: From XAML to UIKit

- <u>Beginning iOS 5 Development</u> by Mark, Nutting, and LaMarche (book)
- Concurrency Programming Guide
  - http://tinyurl.com/8xfnne7
- Event Handling Guide for iOS
  - http://tinyurl.com/7ckrmlk
- iOS App Programming Guide
  - http://tinyurl.com/d59ty62
- iOS Human Interface Guidelines
  - http://tinyurl.com/4o8pdwq
- <u>iOS Programming: The Big Nerd Ranch Guide</u> by Conway and Hillegass (book)
- Table View Programming Guide for iOS
  - http://tinyurl.com/7dzpuem

- Threading Programming Guide
  - http://tinyurl.com/7dqfdf8
- View Programming Guide for iOS
  - http://tinyurl.com/7w62f3w

Chapter 8: Building UIs with Interface Builder

- Designing User Interfaces in Xcode 4
  - http://tinyurl.com/3wjy8rj

Chapter 9: Calling Web Services

- AFNetworking
  - https://github.com/AFNetworking/AFNetworking
- ASIHTTPRequest (unsupported project)
  - http://allseeing-i.com/ASIHTTPRequest
- Charles Web Debugging Proxy
  - http://www.charlesproxy.com
- GDataXML
  - http://code.google.com/p/gdata-objectivec-client
- iPhone HTTP Connection Debugging (setting up Charles)
  - http://blog.mediarain.com/2009/08/iphone-http-connection-debugging
- JSONKit
  - https://github.com/johnezang/JSONKit
- KissXML
  - https://github.com/robbiehanson/KissXML
- Reachability
  - http://tinyurl.com/42mxger

- SBJson
  - http://stig.github.com/json-framework
- WSDL2ObjC
  - http://code.google.com/p/wsdl2objc

Chapter 10: Overview of Core Data

- Core Data Model Versioning and Data Migration Programming Guide
  - http://tinyurl.com/7j6453l
- Core Data Programming Guide
  - http://tinyurl.com/8yc47r6
- Core Data Tutorial for iOS
  - http://tinyurl.com/5r47vo5
- Getting Started with Mogenerator
  - http://raptureinvenice.com/getting-started-with-mogenerator
- Magical Record
  - https://github.com/magicalpanda/MagicalRecord
- Pro Core Data for iOS by Privat and Warner (book)
- SQLite
  - http://www.sqlite.org

Chapter 11: Debugging Techniques

- Debug Your App (Xcode 4 User Guide)
  - http://tinyurl.com/7xvcj9j
- Instruments User Guide
  - http://tinyurl.com/3pcsw8p

- LLDB Tutorial
  - http://lldb.llvm.org/tutorial.html
- Lumberjack
  - https://github.com/robbiehanson/CocoaLumberjack

Chapter 12: Unit Testing

- OCMock
  - http://ocmock.org
- UI Automation Reference Collection
  - http://tinyurl.com/7qnxhf9
- Xcode Unit Testing Guide
  - http://tinyurl.com/87nmx8t